Guernsey
An Island Community of the Atlantic Iron Age

Bob Burns, Barry Cunliffe & Heather Sebire

with contributions from
Mike Allen, Ann Burns, Esther Cameron, Jennifer Coy,
Philip de Jersey, Brian Gilmour, Brian Hartley,
Julian Henderson, Mike Hill, Alan Howell, Ian Kinnes,
Chris Salter, David Williams, Mark Wood and Jessica Winder

Oxford University Committee for Archaeology Monograph No. 43

Guernsey Museum Monograph No. 6

*To the memory of Frederick Corbin Lukis
(1788–1871) in whose footsteps we all tread*

All rights reserved. No part of this publication may be reproduced, stored in a retrieval system, or transmitted, in any form or by any means, electronic, mechanical, photocopying, recording or otherwise, without the prior permission of the authors.

This book is sold subject to the condition that it shall not, by way of trade or otherwise, be lent, re-sold, hired or otherwise circulated without the publisher's prior consent in any form of binding or cover other than that in which it is published and without a similar condition, including this condition, being imposed on the subsequent purchaser.

Copyright © Oxford University Committee for Archaeology
and individual authors 1996

Published with the aid of a generous grant from the Kali Le Page Fund

Published by the Oxford University Committee for Archaeology
Institute of Archaeology
36 Beaumont Street
Oxford

ISBN 0-947816-44-5
Designed and produced by Production Line, Oxford
Printed in Great Britain by Redwood Books, Trowbridge

Contents

LIST OF ILLUSTRATIONS v

INTRODUCTION
by Barry Cunliffe 1

    Acknowledgements 2

EXCAVATIONS AT KING'S ROAD, ST. PETER PORT 1980-3
by Bob Burns, Heather Sebire and Ann Burns 3

    Introduction 3
        The circumstances of the excavation 3
        The situation 4
        Previous archaeological activity 5

    The Excavations 6
        Introduction 6
        Summary 7
        Site 1 8
            Introduction 8
            The settlement features 9
            Index of features and finds from Site 1 12
        Sites 2 and 3 15
            Introduction 15
            The initial trial trenches 16
            Site 2 16
            Index of features and finds from Site 2 20
            Site 3 22
            Index of features and finds from Site 3 24
        Site 4 26
            Introduction 26
            The settlement features 26
            Index of features and finds from Site 4 31

    The Pottery 45
        Introduction 45
        The Bronze Age pottery 46
        The Early-Middle Iron Age pottery 46
            Fabric 1 46
            Fabric 2 46
            Fabric LPC 3 46
            Fabric LPC 4 46
            Fabric LPC 5 47
            Fabric LPC 6 47
            Haematite-coated ware 47
        Late La Tène pottery 47
            Imported pottery 47
                Rilled wares 47
                Black cordoned wares 47
                Graphite-coated wares 47
            Local fabrics 48
                Fabric 1 48
                Fabric 2 48
                Fabric 3 48
                Fabric 4 49
                Fabric 5 49
                Fabric 6 49
            Quantification 49
        Gallo-Roman wares 49
            Roman amphorae by David Williams 49
            Terra Sigillata dish by Brian Hartley 52
            North Gaulish grey ware by Mark Wood 52
            Terra-Nigra type ware by Mark Wood 53
            Romano-British ware by Mark Wood 54
            Coarse grey ware by Mark Wood 54
        Medieval pottery 55
        Catalogue of illustrated pottery 55
            Bronze Age pottery from Sites 1 and 4 56

   Late La Tène imported wares from Sites 1 and 4 56
   Late La Tène local wares from Sites 1 and 4 56
   Early-Middle Iron Age pottery from Sites 2 and 3 67
   Gallo-Roman pottery from Sites 1 and 4 68
   Medieval pottery from Site 4 71

 Small finds 71
   Copper alloy objects 71
   Iron objects 71
   Objects of shale 71
   Ceramic spindle whorls 71
   Utilized stone objects (stone identifications by Alan Howell) 72
   The flintwork by Ian Kinnes 75
   Catalogue of antiquarian finds (stone identifications by Alan Howell) 77

 Specialist Reports 79
   Slag by Chris Salter 79
   Animal bones by Jennifer Coy 80
   Molluscs by Jessica Winder and Mike Allen 81

 Discussion 81

THE IRON AGE BURIALS OF GUERNSEY
by Barry Cunliffe 83

 Introduction 83

 Descriptions of the principal burials 83
   The cemetery at King's Road, St. Peter Port 83
   The cists at Le Catioroc, St. Saviour's 92
   The cist at La Hougue au Comte, Castel 99
   The cist at Les Issues, St. Saviour's 104
   The cist burials at Richmond, St. Saviour's 106
   The cist burial found at Les Adams, St. Peter-in-the-Wood 112

 Note on the technology of the swords based on a radiographic study by Brian Gilmour 112

 Note on the technology of the glass beads by J. Henderson 113

 Discussion 114
   Burial rite 114
   Location 114
   Cultural implications 114
   Historical context 116

GAZETTEER OF IRON AGE SITES AND FINDS IN GUERNSEY, HERM AND SARK
by R.B. Burns, Barry Cunliffe, Philip de Jersey and Mike G. Hill 117

GUERNSEY AND THE CHANNEL ISLANDS IN THE IRON AGE
by Barry Cunliffe 125

BIBLIOGRAPHY 128

List of Illustrations

1	The location of Guernsey	1
2	Sites mentioned in the text	2
3	The King's Road area in 1787	3
4	St. Peter Port in the Iron Age and Roman period	4
5	The King's Road excavations 1980-3	6
6	Summary of Iron Age features	7
7	Summary of Gallo-Roman and medieval features	7
8	King's Road: Site 1	8
9	Key to drawn sections	9
10	King's Road: grave pit F21	10
11	King's Road: Site 1, sections	12
12	King's Road: sections	14
13	King's Road: Site 2	17
14	King's Road: Site 2, sections	18
15	King's Road: Site 2, grave 1 plan	19
16	King's Road: Site 2, grave 1 during excavation	20
17	King's Road: Site 2, grave 1 after excavation	21
18	King's Road: Site 2, grave 2 during excavation	21
19	King's Road: Site 3	23
20	King's Road: Site 3, grave 3 during excavation	24
21	King's Road: Sites 2 and 3, plans of the cists	25
22	King's Road: Site 4	27
23	King's Road: Site 4, general view of east end of excavation	28
24	King's Road: Site 4, general view of west end of excavation	29
25	King's Road: Site 4, sections along north bank	30
26	King's Road: Site 4, sections along east and west banks	32
27	King's Road: Site 4, sections of features comprising the circular and rectangular structures	34
28	King's Road: Site 4, sections of pits and post-holes	36
29	King's Road: Site 4, post-hole, F10	37
30	King's Road: Site 4, sections of main ditch, F17	38
31	King's Road: Site 4, sections of main ditch	39
32	King's Road: Site 4, plans of Gallo-Roman working area	40
33	King's Road: Site 4, the anvil stone, F29	41
34	King's Road: Site 4, medieval gully, F28, and spade marks	42
35	King's Road: Site 4, Gallo-Roman working area, F31 and F37	43
36	King's Road: Site 4, timber structure, F80-F110	44
37	Pottery quantification	50
38	Amphorae from King's Road	51
39	Terra Sigillata dish from King's Road	52
40	Late Bronze Age pottery from King's Road, Sites 1 and 4	55
41	Late La Tène imported wares from King's Road, Sites 1 and 4	55
42-6	Late La Tène local wares from King's Road, Sites 1 and 4	57-64
47-8	Early to Middle Iron Age wares from King's Road, Sites 2 and 3	66-69
49	Gallo-Roman and medieval pottery from King's Road, Sites 1 and 4	70
50	Objects of copper alloy from King's Road	71
51	Objects of iron from King's Road	72
52	Objects of shale from King's Road	73
53	Objects of baked clay from King's Road	73
54	Utilized stone objects from King's Road	74
55	Flintwork from King's Road	76
56	Stone implements from the King's Road area	78
57	Sword from King's Road	86
58	Sword from King's Road	87
59	Shield boss from King's Road	89
60	Shears, knife and spear from King's Road	90
61	Brooch, iron fittings, bronze ring and amber bead from King's Road	91
62	Sword from Le Catioroc, cist 1	93
63	Sword from Le Catioroc, cist 1?	95
64	Sword, spears and shield boss from Le Catioroc	96
65	Shield boss from Le Catioroc	97
66	Miscellaneous finds from Le Catioroc	98
67	Pottery from Le Catioroc	99
68	Sword from La Hougue au Comte	101
69	Miscellaneous objects of iron from La Hougue au Comte	102
70	Miscellaneous objects of copper alloy, glass, amber and jet from La Hougue au Comte	103
71	Pottery from La Hougue au Comte	104
72	Sword from Les Issues	105

73	Iron weapon and pot from Les Issues	107
74	Sword and spear from Richmond	108
75	Details of the sword from Richmond	110-11
76	Radiograph of sword from Le Catioroc	113
77	Cliffside earthworks	118
78	Pottery from Jerbourg Point	119
79	The Tranquesous from the air	120
80	The Tranquesous: plan of features	121
81	Copper alloy objects from The Doyle	122
82	Kimmeridge shale rough-outs from St. Peter Port Harbour and Herm	123
83	Pottery from Herm	123

Introduction

by Barry Cunliffe

The island of Guernsey is a triangular slab of igneous rock some 63 sq km [25 sq miles] in extent lying 50 km west of the Cotentin peninsula of Normandy (Fig. 1). Its position, well clear of coastal reefs, sets it apart from its larger neighbour, Jersey, which lies in shallower water, its approaches flanked by treacherous semi-submerged shelves – the Iles Chausey and Les Minquiers to the south and the Ecrehous and Dirouilles to the north. For sailors travelling between the north coast of Armorica and the south coasts of Britain, Guernsey was the obvious haven conveniently sited 90 km from Armorica and 120 km from the western approaches to the Solent.

Figure 1 *The location of Guernsey.*

The surface of the island tilts from south to north, at the south rising to over 100 m OD (Fig. 2). For this reason the southern shore presents a formidable face of cliffs and promontories, while the long north-west-facing shore is fringed with shelving rocks and sandy bays. The east-facing shore, protected to some extent by the islands of Herm and more distant Sark, changes along its length from the rocky headland of Jerbourg in the south to the bays and reefs of St. Sampson's to the north. Midway along this shore, where St. Peter Port has grown up, the conditions are ideal for a protected landfall. The situation is well summed up by Heylin writing in 1629 in *A Survey of Guernsey* when he describes St. Peter Port as 'The principal honour and glory of the island'. The 'large capaciousness of the harbour ... is able to contain the greatest navy that ever sailed the ocean fenced from the fury of the winds by the islands of Guernsey, Serk and Erme.'

Until twenty years ago little was known of the Iron Age occupation of the island apart from the 11 cist burials, representing five cemeteries, which had been discovered between 1818 and 1905. The burials from Le Catioroc, Les Issues and Les Adams were described with characteristic thoroughness by F.C. Lukis in 1848 whilst those from La Hougue au Comte and Richmond were noted by others (Derrick 1906 and Anon 1901). The entire ensemble was briefly discussed by de Guérin (1918) and more thoroughly treated by Kendrick in his masterly review of the island's archaeology (1928). It was clear from these discoveries that the rite of inhumation in cists was widespread in the island at the end of the first millennium BC and that the male élite were buried with sets of warrior gear. This was in marked contrast to Jersey where no comparable burials have been discovered.

In summing up the Iron Age occupation of Guernsey in 1928 Kendrick had little else to add apart from a few occurrences of undated briquetage from salt-working on the west coast and the then-undated earthworks of Jerbourg.

A new era began in 1976 with the work of Bob Burns and members of La Société Guernesiaise. In that year, during the long dry summer, the buried ditch of a settlement appeared on an air photograph at the Tranquesous, St. Saviour's. Trial excavations which followed showed that occupation spanned the first century BC and early first century AD (Burns 1978). Thereafter Iron Age material appeared with some rapidity. In 1979 a research excavation began on the main defence of Jerbourg and was to last until 1981 (Burns 1988). In the same year, 1979, building work brought to light the extensive settlement and cemetery at King's Road which was excavated between 1980 and 1983 and is reported in detail in this volume.

Meanwhile, in 1980, in a research excavation on the medieval fortification of Vale Castle, traces of an Early Iron Age defensive circuit were identified (Barton 1984). The renewed interest in promontory fortifications inspired by the Jerbourg excavation led to a programme of systematic survey by Mike Hill between 1981 and 1983, as the result of which hitherto unknown defences were identified at Jerbourg Point, Pointe de la Moye and La Corbière, all on the south coast (this volume, pp. 117-19).

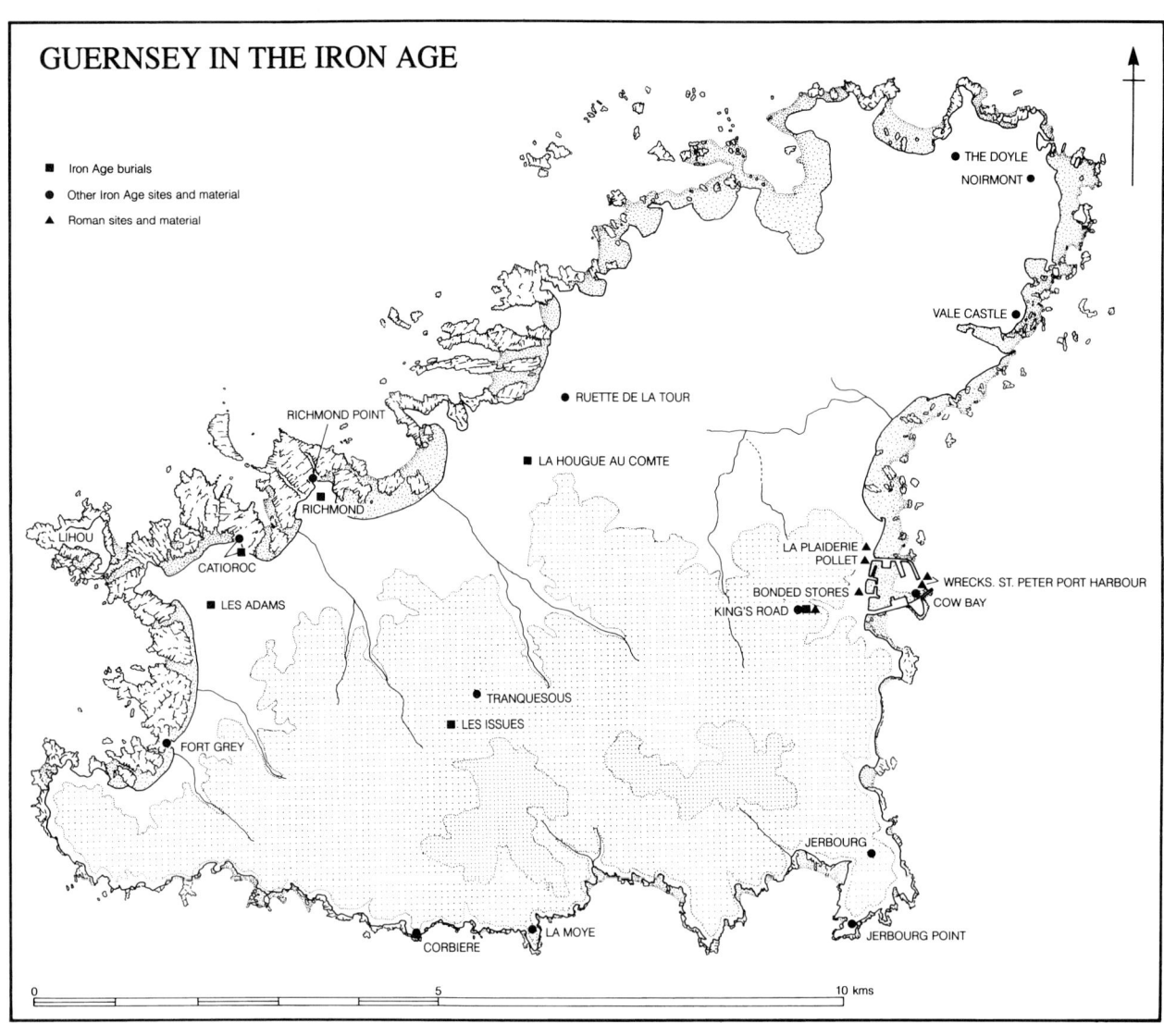

Figure 2 *Guernsey: sites mentioned in the text.*

Thus, in the brief period 1976-83, our knowledge of the Iron Age of Guernsey was suddenly transformed.

In parallel with this period of discovery the present writer, in conjunction with the Guernsey Museum, began a systematic study of the material derived from the cist burials, much of which was in urgent need of conservation. Items were taken to Oxford and cleaned and conserved in the Conservation Laboratory of the Institute of Archaeology, where they were drawn, photographed and recorded in detail. The discovery and excavation of a new cemetery at King's Road added a welcome new dimension to the work. The results of this programme are presented in this volume (pp. 6-82).

From all this activity – excavation, fieldwork and museum studies – a great deal has been learned of the island community in the Iron Age. The present volume attempts to bring the evidence together and to present it in detail as a contribution to the continuing debate. In the concluding essay the significance of the island in the broader Atlantic Iron Age system is tentatively explored.

Acknowledgements

This volume, like so much archaeological work these days, is the result of the work of many people. The names of those who have contributed their specialist knowledge are recorded on the title page and their individual contributions are attributed to them in the text. The line illustrations have been produced at the Institute of Archaeology, Oxford. Alison Wilkins prepared the drawings of the King's Road site based on originals provided by Bob and Ann Burns and drew the Jerbourg sherds from the original material. The finds from the cist burials were drawn from the original objects by Christina Unwin and Simon Pressey. The photographs of the King's Road excavations are the work of Bill Tipping while those of the cist burial finds were prepared by Bob Wilkins, head of the photographic department at the Institute of Archaeology, Oxford. The text has been prepared for publication by Lynda Smithson, editorial assistant at the Institute, with her usual meticulous attention to detail. To all those named here and to the unnamed volunteer diggers the authors extend their most grateful thanks.

Excavations at King's Road, St. Peter Port 1980-3

by Bob Burns, Heather Sebire and Ann Burns

Introduction

The circumstances of the excavation

King's Road is a thoroughfare some 400 metres long which runs approximately north to south and is situated on what is today the western edge of the busy town of St. Peter Port, the island of Guernsey's main urban centre.

The road was originally named La Grande Marche and was a 'chemin le roi' or king's highway, leading out of the town. Until the early part of the nineteenth century it ran through an area of largely agricultural land with scattered farms and orchards. The survey carried out by William Gardner for the Duke of Richmond in 1787 shows the area to be occupied by a single dwelling at its northern extremity (Fig. 3). During the last century or two it has slowly changed its pastoral identity to that of a desirable residential area close to, but not actually in, the town itself. Villas, large houses and even the odd mansion or two were built here by those wealthy enough to escape the growing urban pressures generated by the island's increasingly successful ventures into various maritime and commercial enterprises. The most recent changes have witnessed the gradual infilling of part of the remaining open space with small private housing estates. The overall impression gained today is one of quiet and desirable suburbia.

The present report results from one of these recent changes. Elizabeth College, founded in 1563 by Royal

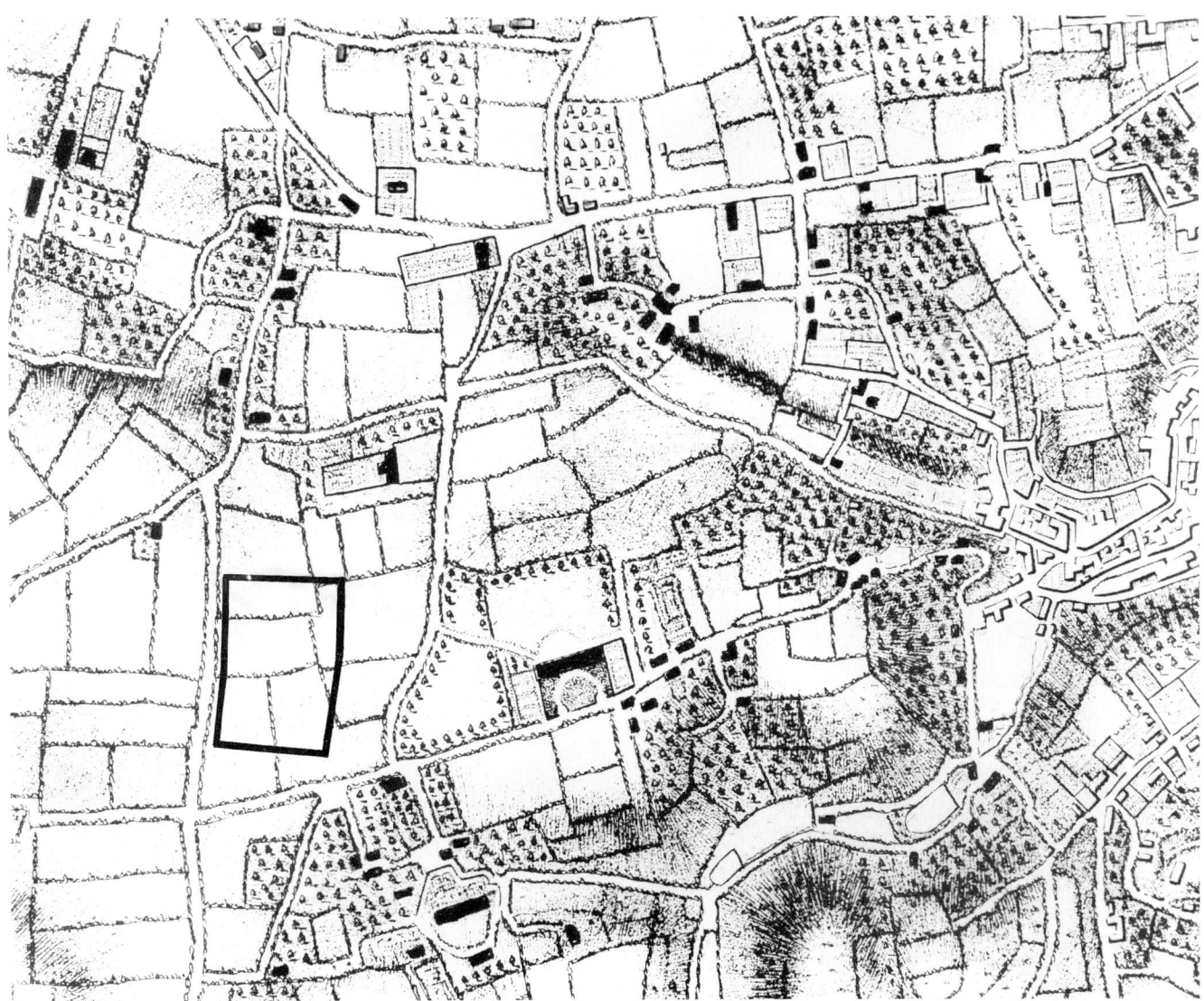

Figure 3 *The King's Road area in 1787: the site is outlined in black. From the Duke of Richmond Survey.*

Charter, is the island's public school for boys. The main school occupies a prime site further east toward St. Peter Port. The Lower School, Beechwood, which is for junior pupils, lies on an extensive area fronting onto Queen's Road which parallels King's Road, running some 200 metres to its east. In the spring of 1980 initial work commenced upon the construction of a new college boarding house, on land lying between these two roads and fronting onto King's Road. This work revealed that the basic geology of the site, composed of a gritty decayed granitic rock, had been cut into and disturbed by a variety of irregular pits and linear features. The authors of this report were asked by the builders to undertake an investigation of these unexpected anomalies and to assess whether they had any archaeological significance. The builders had in fact partially dug into one of the largest of these features with a mechanical excavator. Our initial examination resulted in the discovery of several sherds of Late Iron Age wheel-turned pottery and other domestic refuse, including well-preserved animal bone. Permission was then sought and willingly given for a short-term rescue excavation to take place upon what was to be the first of the four areas to be ultimately examined (Site 1, Fig. 5).

This preliminary exercise was followed by the excavation of a series of small trenches situated some 80 m to the south of Site 1. This investigation was considered necessary in advance of the construction of a small estate of private houses to be erected on the area. Once again the limited time available proscribed large-scale and detailed excavation, but nevertheless revealed the presence of a cemetery of some size, which appeared to be contemporary with Site 1. Four trenches were opened up in this area; two revealed little of archaeological significance, the others contained a series of stone-lined graves. These latter sites are designated Sites 2 and 3.

The results and implications arising from these hurried, and therefore less than perfect, archaeological exercises, made investigation of the area in a more thorough manner absolutely imperative. In 1983 the Governors of Elizabeth College gave permission for an area of land situated between Site 1 and Sites 2 and 3 to be examined. The area involved comprised a strip of land immediately adjoining Site 1 and some 50 m north of Sites 2 and 3. It was perfectly situated to examine the relationships in the nature, usage and relative chronologies of all four sites. In the event, the results gained from the excavation of this last site, Site 4, were to prove essential to our understanding of the settlement and its surrounding ditches.

The series of excavations was, for those who took part, an exciting, exhausting, fulfilling and sometimes frustrating experience. It does, however, illustrate what can be achieved by a small local community, given the right set of circumstances. In the case of the King's Road excavations we would like to thank the builders, M.G. Flouquet, and the architects, Lovell, Ozanne and Partners, as well as the many individuals, organizations, commercial enterprises and local authorities who also played essential and invaluable roles. Their contributions are gratefully acknowledged by us in this introduction and in proper detail in the relevant sections of this report.

The situation (Fig. 4)

The King's Road settlement and the associated cemetery are situated on a plateau which is approximately 75 m above sea-level. The settlement does not lie exactly on the highest part of the plateau which is some 250 m to the north-east. There is, however, a discernible rise in height in that portion of the site assumed to be the approximate centre of the settlement.

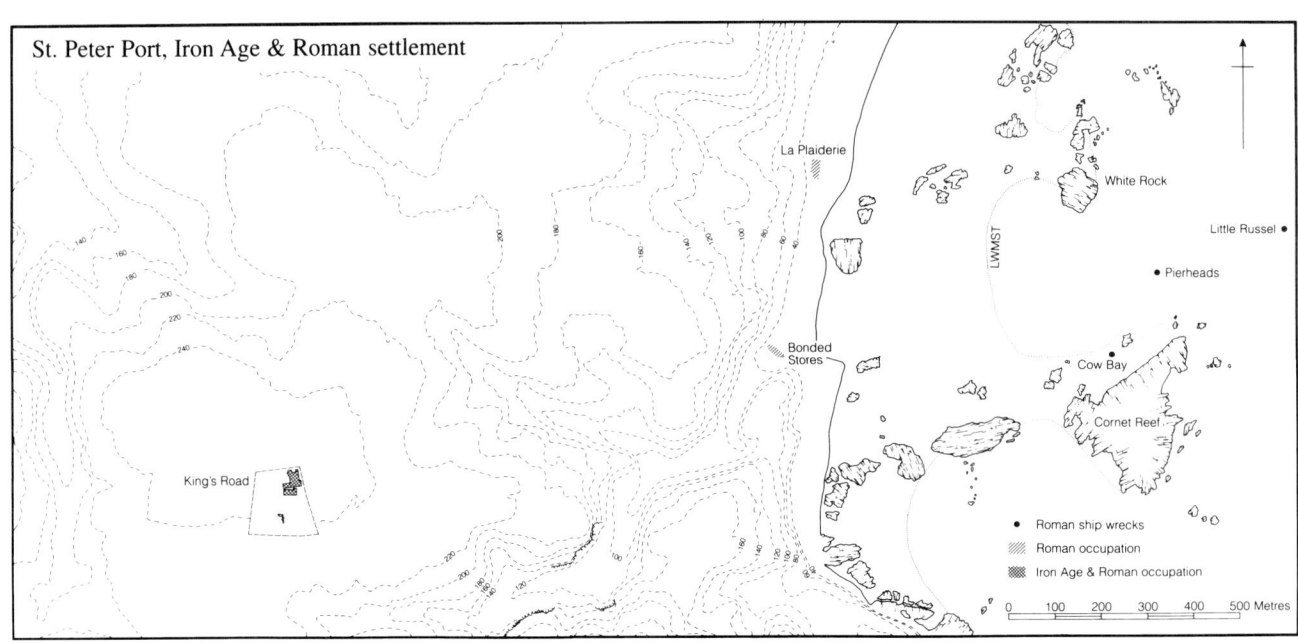

Figure 4 *The King's Road site in relation to St. Peter Port Harbour.*

The site would have had a commanding viewpoint to the sea and what is now St. Peter Port Harbour, dependent of course upon the tree-cover and vegetation prevalent during the various phases of its occupation. Although no ceramic evidence of the Late La Tène period has yet been gathered from the harbour, the recent discovery of a Kimmeridge shale bracelet rough-out from the sea-bed is, perhaps, an indication that the harbour may have been frequented during the life-time of the site. Abundant discoveries of both material and wrecks dating from the second to fourth centuries AD show that the harbour was intensively used during the later period of occupation represented at the site. The surrounding land also slopes gradually away to both the east and the west of the site, providing the security of near all-round visibility. The Late Iron Age site at the Tranquesous (Burns 1977) is similarly sited.

The site at King's Road, in common with that at the Tranquesous, has as its natural bedrock a decaying, gravelly granitic soil, easy for the digging of ditches or pits and with the ability to retain its excavated form with the minimum of erosion damage. The 'pea-gravel' consistency of this natural rock also provides a matrix which quickly drains and dries after rain, perhaps another desirable benefit for those who settled upon it. Whilst no traces of springs or watercourses were discovered during the excavations, there are several springs situated in a small valley some 400 m to the west of the site and others undoubtedly existed closer to the settlement proper. The adjoining property is named Springfield, the small estate at the end of the site is named after a field entitled Le Courtil des Fontaines and there are two nineteenth-century houses close to the site which include the word Fontaine in their name.

Much of the land to the west of King's Road is still open and composed of parkland and pasture, having been preserved from the general trend toward urban accretion for a variety of reasons. The large sports fields belonging to Elizabeth College lie immediately to the west of King's Road and the extensive parkland of Havilland Hall, together with the farmland and pasturage of Hill Farm have all, so far, proved immune to the inexorable growth of the town. Adjoining the site to the east is the large garden of Springfield House. The 1900 Ordnance Survey shows that all of the sites excavated in the exercise under discussion once lay beneath the extensive grounds of this property, a fortunate circumstance which further protected the archaeological deposits from major disturbance. Adjoining Springfield House to the north are the playing fields of the college lower school, Beechwood.

The excavation indicated that much of the ditched settlement lies, presumably relatively intact, beneath the surface of the latter properties. On the immediate southern edge of the site lie several houses with sizeable gardens and the newly built clos with its dwelling houses. The excavations at Sites 2 and 3 indicated that the construction of these new houses will have disturbed the relatively shallow deposits in the cemetery to a serious extent, but it is to be hoped that a major part of this site will be preserved beneath the gardens and other open spaces on the clos.

Indications for usage of the area, other than for small-scale allotment-type gardening, are sparse after the medieval period.

The building boom brought about by the prosperity of the late eighteenth and nineteenth centuries is evidenced by pottery and other artefacts of the period, these presumably emanating from the properties, then newly built, at Mount Row and at King's Road. There is little representing use of the area during the later nineteenth and twentieth centuries. Sites 2 and 3 were covered, in part, by small greenhouses belonging to the Springfield estate, the concrete pads for their column bases cutting slightly into the archaeological horizons. Site 1 produced rows of fairly deeply dug features, which were probably 'French Beds' for the cultivation of asparagus or other deeply rooted crops. There was, surprisingly and fortunately, no indication of large-scale twentieth century disturbance, either in structural or artefactual form. The risks to the so far unexcavated portions of the site, which comprise by far the greater proportion of it seem, at present, to be small. It is to be hoped that this important area will be preserved for the attentions of future generations of researchers.

Previous archaeological activity

The assiduous collecting and recording of the Lukis family during the latter half of the nineteenth century has left the island with an invaluable corpus of artefacts and information, relating in the main to its archaeological past. There are, amongst these records and artefacts, several items from the immediate area of the site at King's Road (below, pp. 77-9). Two fine stone pick-axes, both found in a field named La Courtil de la Longue Pierre, a common name in the island for standing-stones, perhaps take pride of place. They belong to a group of seven such implements in the collections of the Guernsey Museum and display great skill and craftsmanship in their manufacture. Although these artefacts are called for convenience pick-axes, it is most unlikely that they served such a prosaic purpose. They are so similar in design that they could well have been produced by a single craftsman and perhaps served as a 'tomahawk-type' weapon or indeed as a symbol of rank. The area where they were discovered is now the site of the Elizabeth College playing fields. Other examples were found not far away on the parish boundary of St. Peter Port and St. Andrew's. Although none were found in an archaeological context, they are generally regarded as being of Late Neolithic or Early Bronze Age date (Kendrick 1928, 47-8). Kendrick also notes that in the Lukis MSS there is a record of megalithic remains which were found on Lukis' own property at La Grande Marche (King's Road). These comprised 'five or six' props, buried in a hedge. Enquiries made at the time (1843) revealed that many other stones had been removed from the area during the preceding decades. Lukis also illustrates a circle of stones in the Courtil Simon, which are very probably those stones referred to above (Lukis, *Coll. Ant.* IV, 89). De Guérin, in his paper on local place and field-names, records La Rocque à L'Or as a probable menhir or standing-stone. This also stood on, or close to, the College playing-fields (de Guérin 1921, 33). It should be noted that during the builder's clearance operations at Site 1, a very large isolated granite 'boulder' was removed from the site. Unfortunately this was not witnessed or recorded archaeologically and its possible significance must remain unclear. Several ground and polished stone axes have also been discovered at differing times in or around the same locality (Fig. 56).

These few, but significant place-names and the small corpus of finds are all that can be extracted from the surviving record.

The evidence, however, points to activity in the area during the later Neolithic and the Bronze Age, a possibility supported by the small amount of early prehistoric material discovered during the recent excavations.

The excavations (Fig. 5)

Introduction

Whilst the several excavations were stimulated by similar objectives, they were, of necessity, controlled and constrained by the varying time-scales available for their investigation. The excavations at Site 1 were carried out under typical rescue or salvage conditions, in fact parts of that exercise could be no more than a watching brief. Nevertheless, the co-operation of the architects and the builders enabled some features of the site to be excavated in a more detailed fashion. The main benefit thus gained was an insight into the possible site layout, which was to prove an invaluable aid during the excavation of Site 4, immediately to the south.

The trenches excavated on Sites 2 and 3 were originally designed as an exercise in determining the possible extent of the occupation area of Site 1. The discovery of the cemetery, and the realization that it was set into an earlier occupied landscape, added not only another dimension to the time-scale involved but also new

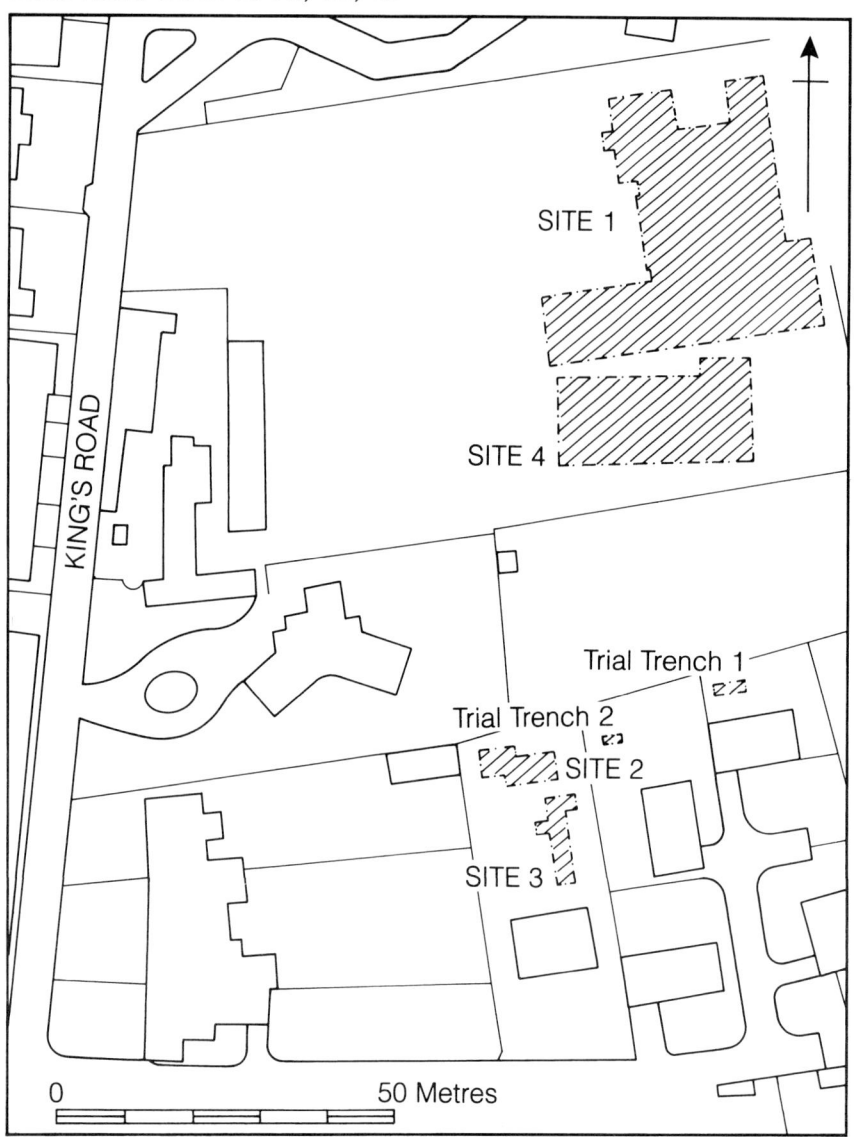

Figure 5

information of some significance to our comprehension of the ritual practices of these early peoples.

Site 4 was to receive a full and thorough investigation, made possible by an ample allowance of both time and resources from the relevant authorities and a skilled and enthusiastic work-force. Our thanks are here conveyed to the Elizabeth College Governors, Bursar, School House Warden and the then States of Guernsey Ancient Monuments Committee. Many other organizations and individuals helped during this last exercise and due thanks are conveyed to them in the acknowledgement section of this report.

Summary (Figs. 6 and 7)

The main phases of occupation revealed in the excavation may be summarized as follows:

Earlier prehistoric: scatter of pottery and flints of Neolithic and Bronze Age date but no structural evidence.

Earlier Iron Age: ditch, possibly once taking a palisade found on Site 2 (F5) containing pottery of Early to Mid Iron Age in date.

Late Iron Age: ditch system (F1 and F10 on Site 1 and F17 on Site 4) and associated occupation features. The associated pottery is mostly of local type but includes imports from Armorica and Roman Dressel 1 amphorae and probably dates to the early first century BC.

A cemetery represented by four cist burials, one furnished with warrior gear, lay to the south of the main occupied area.

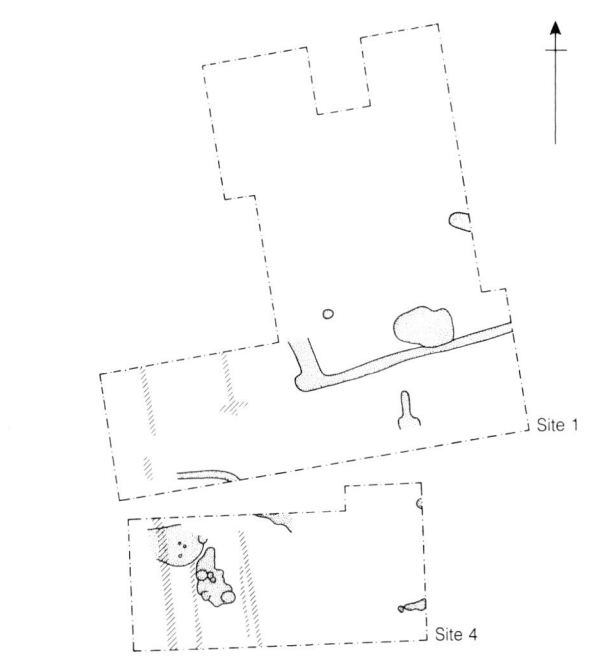

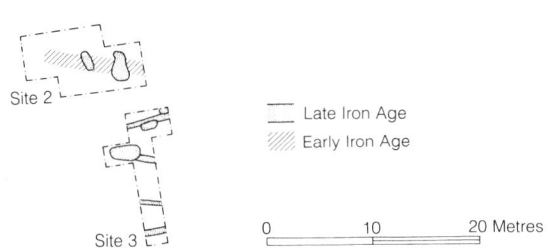

Figure 6 *King's Road: summary plans of Early and Late Iron Age features.*

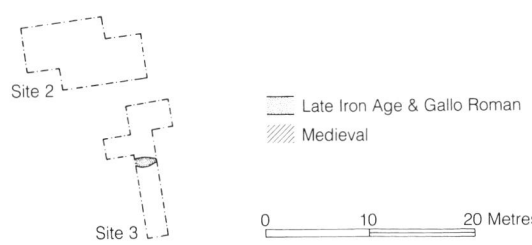

Figure 7 *King's Road: summary plans of Late Iron Age/Gallo-Roman and medieval features.*

KING'S ROAD 1980 SITE 1

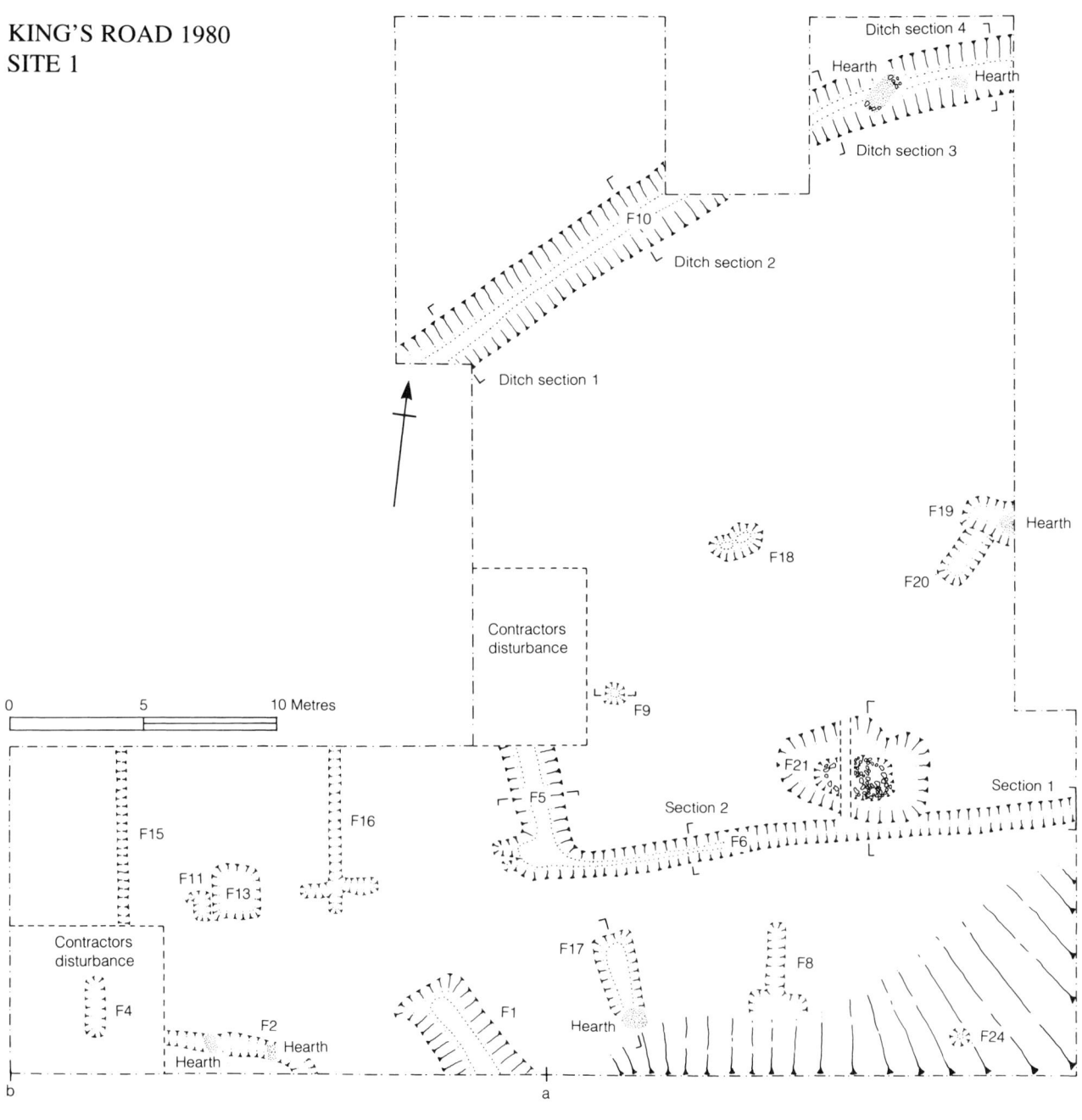

Figure 8

Gallo-Roman: gullies, working areas and at least one burial represented a phase of occupation which developed over the Late Iron Age settlement area. Associated pottery suggests a first and second century AD date.

Medieval: agricultural activity in the thirteenth and fourteenth centuries.

Site 1 (Fig. 8)

Introduction

The area mechanically stripped by the builders in preparation for the construction of the new boarding-house comprised some 1150 sq m. The upper horizons of the site had been totally removed to a depth of approximately 1.5 to 2 m. This stripping had truncated and, in an unknown number of cases, almost certainly totally removed shallower features such as pits and post-holes. As the excavation of Site 4 was to demonstrate, the western portion of Site 1 is likely to have contained much evidence of domestic activity, now unfortunately beyond recall. Two of the present authors (RB and HS) were asked by the vigilant foreman at the site to examine a deep pit (F1) cut into the natural decomposed granite and situated close to the southern edge of the builder's excavated area. This brief reconnaissance revealed several sherds of Late La Tène cordoned pottery and a small amount of limpet shell and animal bone. Permission was then sought, and immediately granted, for a rescue operation to be set into motion. These excavations were carried out alongside the ongoing building operations by a volunteer force comprising local archaeological volunteers and members of La Société Guernesiaise. The overall

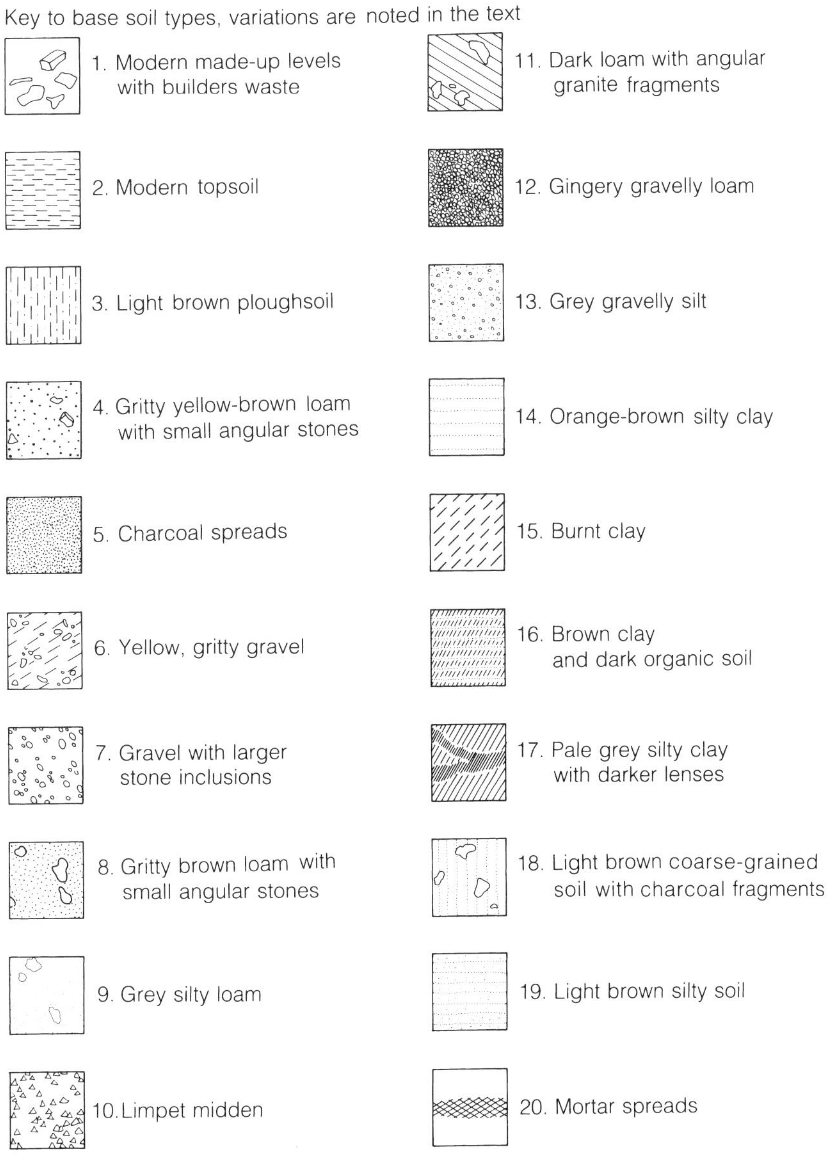

Key to base soil types, variations are noted in the text

1. Modern made-up levels with builders waste
2. Modern topsoil
3. Light brown ploughsoil
4. Gritty yellow-brown loam with small angular stones
5. Charcoal spreads
6. Yellow, gritty gravel
7. Gravel with larger stone inclusions
8. Gritty brown loam with small angular stones
9. Grey silty loam
10. Limpet midden
11. Dark loam with angular granite fragments
12. Gingery gravelly loam
13. Grey gravelly silt
14. Orange-brown silty clay
15. Burnt clay
16. Brown clay and dark organic soil
17. Pale grey silty clay with darker lenses
18. Light brown coarse-grained soil with charcoal fragments
19. Light brown silty soil
20. Mortar spreads

Figure 9 *Key for all sections.*

stratigraphy of the area excavated by the builders was difficult to establish. The baulks left at the edges of the excavated area indicated that there had been an uppermost layer of dark organic soil present over most, if not all, of the area. This soil lay upon an earlier ploughsoil, distinguished by its slightly paler colour and virtual absence of stony inclusions. This ploughsoil lay immediately above those features which could be seen in the builder's baulks. It seemed reasonably certain, therefore, that the area had been cultivated fairly intensively at some period after the Late Iron Age occupation of the area had ceased. Investigation of the severely truncated bases of several gullies running roughly north-south revealed a few sherds of late medieval pottery, giving some indication of the date of this agricultural activity.

The settlement features (Figs. 10-12)

In the account to follow a general description is given of the features recovered in relation to each other. Detailed descriptions of each feature will be found on pp. 12-15 together with a summary of the finds which each contained.

Those areas of the site which showed soil colours differing from the orange-brown gritty decomposed gravel of the natural undisturbed bedrock of the area, were thoroughly cleaned. This revealed the presence of a substantial curvilinear feature which was interpreted as forming an enclosure ditch. Feature 1, the first to be examined, was a terminal of this ditch and an irregular feature on its western side was, almost certainly, an indication of a large post-setting, perhaps part of a gate system. About 4 m north of Feature 1 another possible stretch of ditch (F5) terminated with what appeared to be two more post-settings. A smaller V-shaped gully running roughly east-west (F6) ran into Feature 5 at a right-angle. The longest stretch of the enclosure ditch (F10) ran in a gradual arc around the northern edge of the excavated area and the greater part of the time available on the site was spent excavating this stretch down to the natural decomposed granite. It was not possible to establish the relationship, if any, between

Features 5 and 10 since the area involved lay outside the contractor's excavation.

The area enclosed by the ditch rose slightly in height to what was assumed to be the centre of the settlement. This rise contributed to the machine removal of most of the shallower features in this area. Only a scatter of pits survived, some small and well-cut, some larger and ill-defined.

The underlying bedrock rose sharply to the southern edge of the excavated area, in places even outcropping through the surface to show as gravelly patches in the grass. It was in this area, close to the southern baulk, that the only convincing post-hole (F24), was discovered. This was a circular well-cut feature approximately 0.85 m in diameter which survived to a depth of 0.67 m from the present-day surface. No other post-settings appeared close to it but it did provide some hope for the survival of other such structural evidence in the undisturbed parts of the site, directly to the south of the contractor's trenches. Also cut into the bedrock in this area were two further features. F8 comprised a short length of shallow gully running into what remained of a sub-rectangular pit, which had been severely disturbed as a result of the building work. The second feature, F17, had survived in a much better state and it was possible to excavate and partially record it, before it too was swallowed up by construction. This feature, which was roughly oblong in shape, was aligned approximately north-south and was obviously of an industrial nature. It had been set against the sharply rising bedrock, which had been reddened by significant heating; areas of soot and charcoal, initially thought to be a hearth, lay upon its surface. The fill survived to a depth of approximately one metre and contained two distinct charcoal spreads lying directly upon a clay lining applied over the base of the feature. The clay lining had also been subjected to a high degree of heating and had fired to a deep reddish hue. No real indication as to the purpose of this feature could be ascertained either from its form or its content. All that could be concluded from the evidence was that it was perhaps some form of furnace, utilizing the natural updraught formed by the rising bedrock, as an aid to the heating process.

Close to the eastern side of the builder's excavated area were two sub-rectangular pits. The first, F20, had been drastically truncated and only 0.15 m of its deposits remained. F20 had been cut at a later date by F19, which contained La Tène pottery, amphorae sherds and fragments of daub and charcoal. Some of the sherds in this feature were very abraded, perhaps an indication of redeposition.

Figure 10 *King's Road, Site 1: F21, the grave-pit, under excavation.*

Toward the centre of the excavated area, a small clay-lined pit, F9, survived despite truncation of its upper portion; the clay lining was blue-grey in colour and the pit was observed, after rain, to hold water with no apparent leakage.

The small V-shaped gully, F6, which ran into the southern end of F5, was cut near the eastern edge of the site by a large irregular feature (F21) containing a darker fill (Fig. 10). An attempt was made to excavate this feature in advance of a builder's concrete footings trench being cut through it. This work had only been partially accomplished before the builders moved in and it was left to the sharp eyes of one of the contractors to spot and carefully collect all the fragments of a samian bowl, presumably intact when originally deposited. The excavation of the footing and the subsequent concreting removed a portion of the central part of the feature but enough remained for proper excavation. The upper fill consisted of a dark brown loam with small granitic fragments, which overlay a roughly oval setting of small granite stones. It was from this stone setting that the samian bowl was collected. Beneath these stones was a layer of grey, gravelly soil which lay in its turn upon a gingery gravel. At the base of the feature was a massive worn blue granite boulder approximately 1 m across. The boulder, and any deposits which might have existed beneath it, were left *in situ* as removal would have damaged the footing. The bowl was a complete example of samian form 31R and was the first complete vessel of this ware to be discovered in the Channel Islands. The specialist report indicates a date for its manufacture of post AD 160 (p. 52). Associated with the bowl were other sherds of Gallo-Roman pottery including the rim of a wide-mouthed redware amphora (Fig. 38, No. A1). This discovery, at first seen in isolation, was assumed to have been an isolated burial. It was only during post-excavation studies of the material hastily recovered from Site 1, confirmed by identifiable deposits on Site 4, that the later occupation of the site was to be fully appreciated.

F21 had cut on its southern edge the gully, F6, and obviously post-dated it. F6 contained two fills: the uppermost was a light-brown coarse-grained gravelly soil with many small fragments of charcoal; the basal fill was a grey silty loam with small fractured granitic fragments. This gully, in common with the other early linear features, ran east-west, as opposed to the north-south trend of the medieval cultivation gullies or trenches. Another significant difference between the Late Iron Age and medieval gullies was in their shape, the Iron Age gullies being V-shaped in comparison to the rounded or U-shaped profiles of the medieval variety.

The main enclosure ditch, F10, was perhaps the best preserved of the surviving features on the site. It ran in a gradual curve across the northern part of the area. Exactly what form or direction it took in the central portion, which lay outside the builder's excavated area, could not be established. Nevertheless our original assumption, that F1 was a terminal of the enclosure ditch, was borne out by the later excavations on Site 4. It cannot be stated with as much conviction that F5 formed the opposing terminal of the ditch, although it was certainly sited in the appropriate place, some four metres to the north of and level with F1. The stratigraphy of F5 differed from that seen in other sections of the main ditch, and finds, relatively abundant elsewhere in the ditch, were almost completely absent. As much of F10 as possible was excavated using trowelling techniques but toward the end of the operation faster work with pick and shovel was made necessary. The medieval ploughsoils had slumped partially into the top of the ditch and where they had not been disturbed by the machining it was reasonable to assume that the ditch contents were intact. In places however the machining had removed not only the ploughsoil but also the upper ditch fill and the ditch shoulders. The upper fill consisted, wherever excavated, of a gritty yellow-brown loam with small fragments of angular granite scattered throughout.

Several areas of burnt soil and charcoal lay on top of the slight hollow caused by the slumping and compression of the ditch fill. These were recorded as hearths, although only one of them possessed a stone setting; the others may have been more ephemeral, perhaps bonfires. Whatever their purpose, they were created when the enclosure ditch was fully silted up and probably represent activity during the second phase of the site's occupation. Beneath the gritty yellow-brown soil lay a deposit of a browner, more organic nature, also with a scatter of small angular stones; this lay on a grey silty loam which was virtually stone-free. At the base of the ditch lay a shallow deposit of decayed granitic material resembling pea-gravel, presumably derived from the sides of the ditch when first exposed. Although careful watch was made for traces of a palisade slot or timber-setting in the base of the ditch, none was observed, nor were there any indications of post-packing material.

The ditch terminal, F1, exhibited a more complex stratigraphy and appeared to have been partially recut on at least one occasion. On either side of the ditch, beneath the gritty yellow-brown loam, was a thick layer of yellow gravel which appeared to have been cut through, or was perhaps worn through, by water action. No other obvious recuts of the enclosure ditch were encountered either on Site 1 or on Site 4.

The ditch provided the majority of finds recovered from Site 1 and these are listed in the index of features and finds below.

It is of interest to note that the spindle whorls and the loom weight were found in close association and perhaps indicate a dedicated textile-working area on this part of the site.

KING'S ROAD 1980
SITE 1

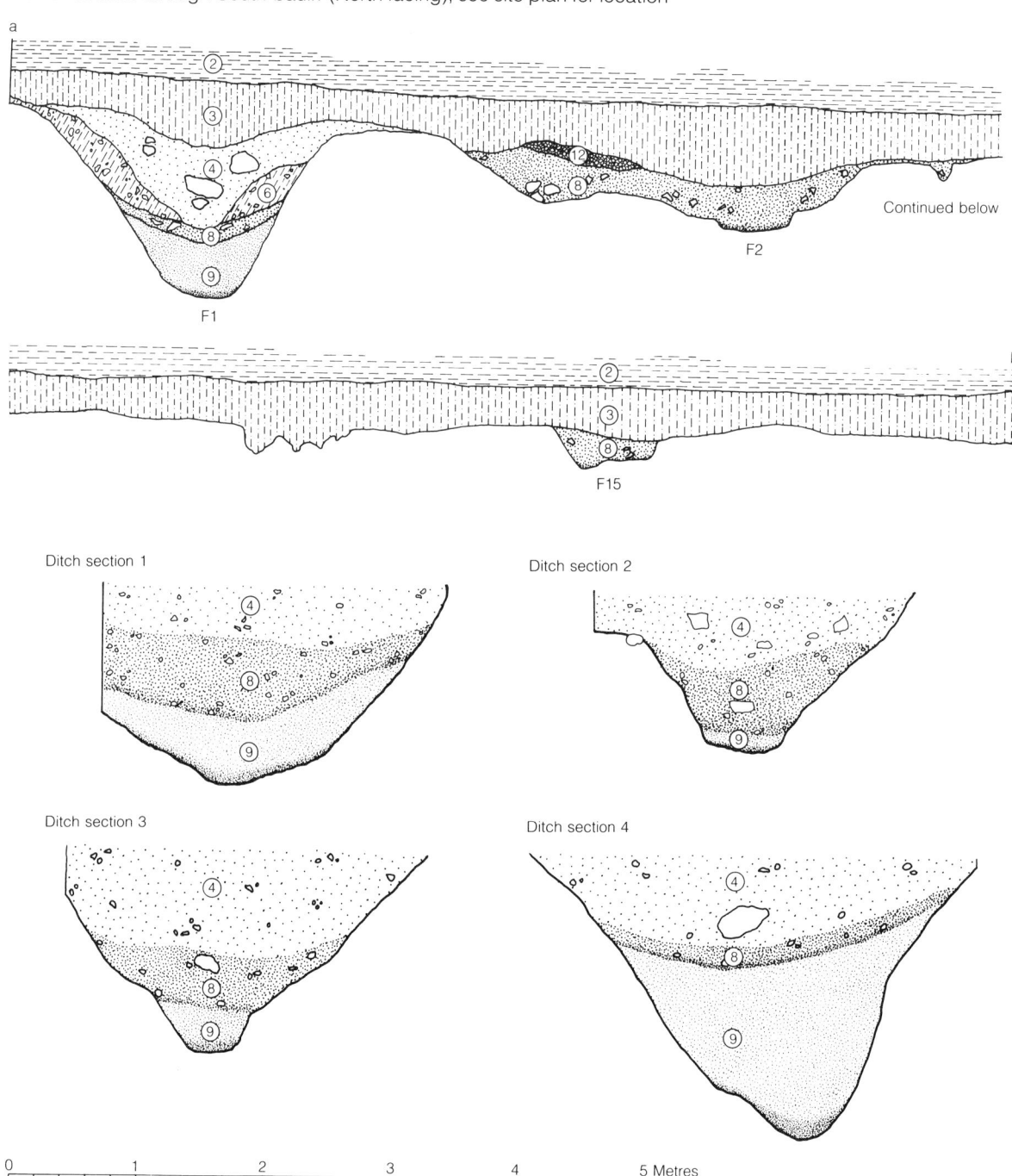

Figure 11 *King's Road, Site 1: sections.*

Index of features and finds from Site 1

A brief description of each feature shown on Fig. 8 is given together with a simple listing of the finds. For descriptions of the pottery types and fabrics see pp. 45-55; for the faunal remains see pp. 80-1; and for the other finds see pp. 71-9.

Feature 1 (Fig. 11) Late La Tène
A terminal of the main ditch, approximately 2.75 m wide and 1.6 m deep. A roughly circular bulge occurred at the north-western corner of this feature; there was not time to excavate it fully, but it appeared to be a large post-setting.

Contents:

Pre-Roman pottery	Rims	Bases	Bodysherds	Remarks
Fabric 1			7	
Fabric 2	1		2	
Fabric 3	3		10	1 with cordon
Fabric 4	2	1	8	2 decorated with cross-hatching
Fabric 5	1		1	
Fabric 6	1	1	12	
Amphorae			15	1 with handle stub
Flint			4	
Animal bone			48 fragments	

Feature 2 (Fig. 11) Gallo-Roman
A round-bottomed gully emerging from the southern baulk and describing a right-angled turn to the west. Badly truncated and removed completely at its western end by the building operations. The gully was approximately 1 m across and 7 m in length. The fill comprised a gritty brown loam with small angular stone inclusions. Where this feature emerged from the baulk it was overlaid by a large, c.4.5 m across, irregular shallow pit or scoop which had a very similar fill. This pit or scoop was capped in one small area with a lens of gingery, gravelly soil approximately 0.25 m deep.

Contents:

Tegulae   1 large sherd with micaceous inclusions

Feature 4 Dating uncertain, but possibly medieval
A short length of shallow gully, disturbed and virtually removed by the builders, but on the same axis as the medieval cultivation trenches.

Contents: Nil

Feature 5 (Fig. 12) Dating uncertain
The termination? of a linear? feature approximately 1.90 m wide by 1.45 m deep. The uppermost layer was a light-brown ploughsoil, beneath which was a paler brown soil flecked here and there with charcoal. This lay on a lens of gritty brown gravel which covered a grey silty loam. At the very base of this round-bottomed feature was a primary deposit of small angular granitic stones. The shape and fill of this feature mitigate against it being the northern terminal of the main ditch and the few finds contained in the fill do not greatly help with dating.

Contents:

Pre-Roman pottery	Rims	Bases	Bodysherds	Remarks
Fabric 1			4	Abraded
Daub				Several small fragments
Stone				Fragment of a rubbing stone

Feature 6 (Fig. 12) Late La Tène or Gallo-Roman
A V-shaped gully, 1.20 m wide and 0.90 m deep, which ran approximately east-west across the site for some 20 m before it met the east baulk. At its western end it terminated by joining Feature 5. The upper fill of this gully was a light-brown soil with scattered charcoal fragments. In both places sectioned, the upper fill was separated from the lower, primary fill by a lens of charcoal; beneath the charcoal was a grey silty loam. Slightly to the east of its central portion the gully was cut by the irregularly-shaped F21. It was not clear whether F5 and F6 were part of a single system or whether in fact they were chronologically separated. The fact that they met and ended in a right-angle at their south-western corner, does not necessarily indicate contemporaneity.

Contents:

Gallo-Roman pottery	Rims	Bases	Bodysherds	Remarks
Redware		1		
Gritty Ware		1		Not medieval
Slag			2	

Feature 8 Late La Tène or Gallo-Roman
A T-shaped feature measuring approximately 2.6 m by 2 m. It was almost completely truncated by the building activities, thus its possible nature and purpose were impossible to ascertain. The little fill which remained was some 0.04 m deep and comprised a dirty, dark-brown soil which contained pottery, flint, charcoal and daub.

Contents:

Pre-Roman pottery	Rims	Bases	Bodysherds	Remarks
Fabric 3	1			
Fabric 4			1	Cordoned
Tegulae				Fragment

Feature 9 (Fig. 12) Late La Tène or Gallo-Roman
A sub-rectangular pit measuring 0.85 m by 0.85 m and some 0.30 m in depth. Lined on its sides and base with a layer of blue-grey clay approximately 0.04 m thick.

Contents:

Pre-Roman pottery	Rims	Bases	Bodysherds	Remarks
Fabric 2			3	
Fabric 4			1	Cordoned
Tegulae			1	
Utilized stone			1	

Feature 10 (Fig. 11) Late La Tène with Gallo-Roman deposits overlying
A stretch of the main enclosure ditch averaging 2.50 m wide and between 1.50-1.75 m in depth. The ditch was traced over a distance of some 25 m. In places the base of the ditch had a deeper, flat-bottomed slot which might have possibly been a palisade slot, but no soil-markings, post-holes or stone settings, which might have confirmed this, were discovered. The ditch was sectioned in four places (Figs. 8 and 11) and three stratigraphic levels were present throughout. The uppermost was a gritty yellow gravel, beneath which was a gritty brown loam; the lowest layer was a grey silty loam, with a primary deposit of gravel along the base, derived from the initial erosion of the sides of the ditch. As noted previously, two areas of soot and charcoal were discovered on top of the uppermost fill. Much of the Gallo-Roman pottery was found at the interface between this upper layer and the traces of ploughsoil which once presumably overlaid the whole feature. This ploughsoil had mostly been removed by the machining of the site, but was visible in section at the places where the ditch met the builder's baulks. Throughout much of the length of ditch available for investigation, site clearance had removed varying amounts of the upper levels and in some cases had also cleaned away the ditch shoulders. This made any hard and fast decisions concerning the relationship between the La Tène and Gallo-Roman deposits difficult and to a certain extent unreliable. This problem was only resolved during the excavation of Site 4.

Contents:

Pre-Roman pottery	Rims	Bases	Bodysherds	Remarks
Neo-EBA		1	9	7 with hatched decoration
Fabric 1	3	8	179	
Fine Gritty fabric (variant of Fabric 1)			2	Rilled
Fabric 2	6	4	246	
Fabric 3	14	10	72	19 with cordons or grooves
Fabric 4	11	1	53	3 with burnished lines, 2 with cordons
Fabric 4 variant			15	3 with cordons, 3 with burnished lines
Fabric 5	3	7	63	1 cordoned
Fabric 6	6		52	
Graphite-coated	1			cordoned
Micaceous	4	1	11	
Daub				19 fragments
Gallo-Roman pottery				
Pink-buff flagon			1	
Colour-coated			2	
Greyware			3	
TN Type	2	1	7	
Fine pinkware			1	
Amphorae	1		9	
Imbrex				1 fragment
Spindle whorls, ceramic			3	
Loom weights, ceramic			2	
Shaped ceramic object			1	
Cu fragments			2	
Fe nails			7	
Utilized stone			1	
Flint			6	
Animal bone				3 fragments

Feature 11 Late La Tène
The base of a sub-rectangular pit, truncated by the contractors and measuring approximately 1 m by 0.50 m by 0.15 m deep.

KING'S ROAD 1980
SITE 1

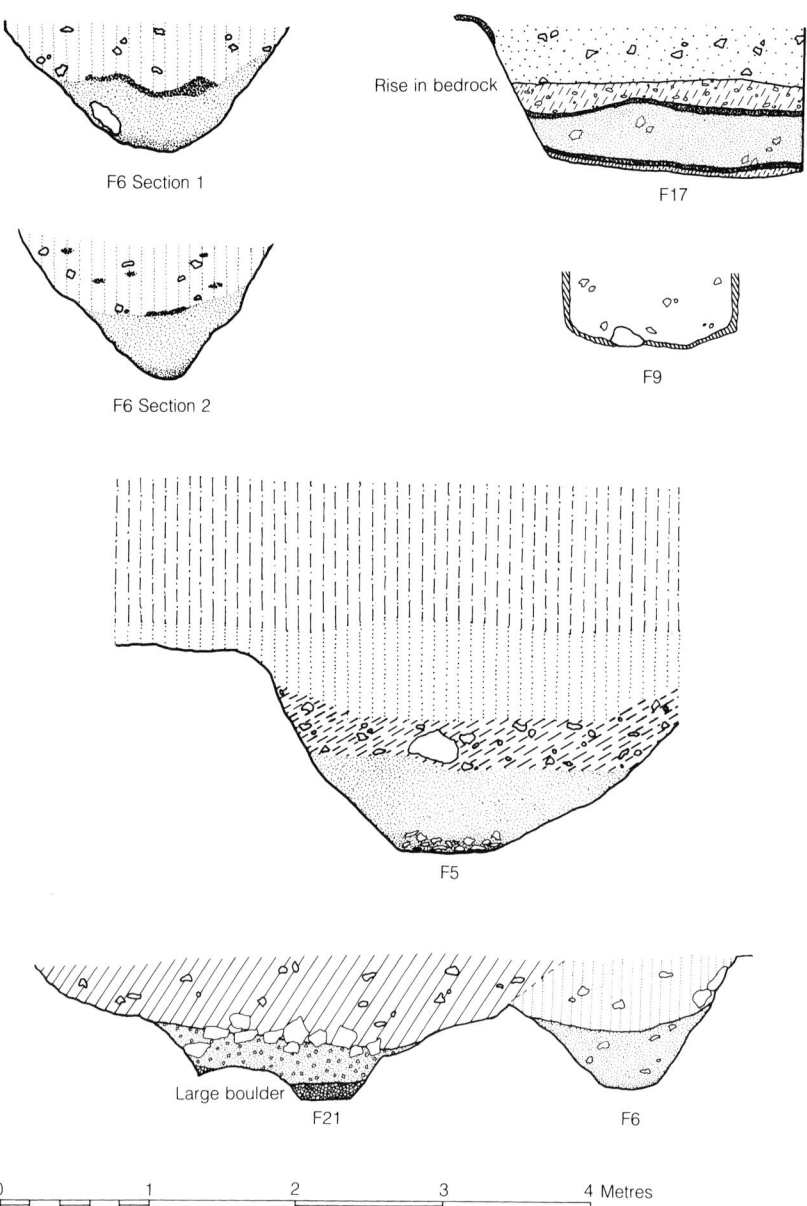

Figure 12 *King's Road, Site 1: sections.*

Contents:

Pre-Roman pottery	Rims	Bases	Bodysherds	Remarks
Fabric 3	1		1	
Utilized stone			1	rubber
Flint			2	

Feature 13 Late La Tène
The base of a sub-rectangular pit adjoining F11, severely truncated by building activity, only 0.04 m of the fill remaining.

Contents:

Pre-Roman pottery	Rims	Bases	Bodysherds	Remarks
Fabric 1			1	
Fabric 5			1	

Features 15 and 16 (Fig. 11) Medieval?
Narrow round-bottomed gullies or cultivation trenches running north-south. Although these features provided only two Gallo-Roman potsherds, they were almost certainly medieval in date and formed part of the cultivation system examined more fully during the excavation of Site 4.

Contents:

Gallo-Roman pottery	Rims	Bases	Bodysherds	Remarks
Greyware	1			
Flagon			1	Slip-coated

Feature 17 (Fig. 12) Late La Tène?
An industrial feature measuring approximately 3.5 m by 1.5 m. Its use involved a high degree of heat. Two distinct and separate layers of charcoal and soot averaging some 0.04 m in thickness were present. The base of the feature had been lined with clay some 0.03-4 m thick; this clay lining had been fired and had turned a deep brick-red colour due to heating.

Contents:

Pre-Roman pottery	Rims	Bases	Bodysherds	Remarks
Fabric 3			1	

Feature 18 Late La Tène?
An irregularly-shaped pit in the centre of the site, truncated by the builders.

Contents:

Pre-Roman pottery	Rims	Bases	Bodysherds	Remarks
Fabric 2			3	
Utilized stone				1 fragment rubbing stone

Feature 19 Gallo-Roman
A sub-rectangular pit bisected by the eastern baulk of the site, filled with a gritty yellow-brown soil. This feature had been cut into by F20.

Contents:

Pre-Roman pottery	Rims	Bases	Bodysherds	Remarks
Fabric 1			1	
Fabric 2			3	
Fabric 4			1	
Gallo-Roman pottery				
Redware			6	
Greyware			4	
Amphorae			1	
Hard-fired with spots of glaze			1	Not medieval
Daub				4 fragments
Fe objects			2	
Utilized stone			1	
Flint			3	

Feature 21 (Fig. 12) Gallo-Roman
A large irregular area of dark, discoloured loamy soil with angular granitic inclusions. This feature measured some 7 m by 5 m and partially cut into F6, the gully, which ran immediately to its south. It was situated in an area of the site subjected to much disturbance by the builders but fortunately escaped the worst of the damage. It lay immediately on top of F21a, which was to prove to be the grave pit.

Contents:

Pre-Roman pottery	Rims	Bases	Bodysherds	Remarks
Fabric 1			6	
Fabric 2			1	
Fabric 4			4	
Gallo-Roman pottery				
Greyware			3	
N. Gaulish greyware			1	
Samian			1	
Amphorae			3	
Utilized stone				1 worked fragment
Quern				1 fragment
Flint			1	

Feature 21a (Fig. 10) Gallo-Roman
The grave-pit in which the samian bowl by HONORATUS was discovered. The feature measured some 3 m by 1.50 m and was cut into the natural gravel of the site to a depth of approximately 0.95 m. If the dark loamy soil of F21 overlying it was part of the original backfilling for the burial, the total depth of the pit was 1.65 m. The pit was roughly oval, but was squarer cut at its eastern end. Stones were set roughly around its perimeter with two smaller, roughly circular stone settings inside the perimeter at the eastern end. The samian bowl and the associated pottery came from the level of the stone settings or just beneath them. As noted previously, the fragments of the bowl were retrieved by a building worker during the casting of a concrete footing through the area. Although this work obviously caused some disturbance, enough was left of the deposit for the remainder to be carefully excavated. No obvious signs of human remains could be discerned, the acidic nature of the gravel having done its worst, but in the grey, gravelly soil immediately to the east of the footings trench were two soil stains, associated with small air cavities in the soil. These were possibly traces of the lower legs and feet of the burial. If this deduction is correct, the burial was of extended form, lying east-west, with the head to the west.

Contents:

Pre-Roman pottery	Rims	Bases	Bodysherds	Remarks
Fabric 2			6	
Fabric 4	1			
Gallo-Roman pottery				
Redware	1			
Greyware	5		1	
N. Gaulish greyware			1	
Samian	1 complete bowl	1		

Feature 24 Probably Late La Tène
A well-cut circular post-hole situated in the higher part of the site at the south-western corner, it measured 0.85 m in diameter and was 0.35 m deep. The fill comprised a gritty gravel; no signs of a post-mould could be discerned.

Contents:

Pre-Roman pottery	Rims	Bases	Bodysherds	Remarks
Fabric 4			2	

Sites 2 and 3 (Fig. 5)

Introduction

In November 1981, some eighteen months after the initial excavation, one of the authors (HS) was informed that sections of several back gardens, situated significantly close to Site 1, were in the process of being sold for development as building plots. These back gardens belonged to houses on Mount Row, the road that runs between the southern ends of King's Road and Queen's Road. Mount Row is a wide road which is now a major thoroughfare running out of the town of St. Peter Port.

C.E.B. Brett, in his architectural survey of the buildings of St. Peter Port, describes Mount Row as 'a wide road with an excellent mixed bunch of two-storey and three-storey stucco houses of various dates, quite a lot retaining their original Georgian glazing pattern. Some rather shabby: if all the houses were painted as well as the best of them there would be a vast improvement in the appearance of a potentially very attractive road.' (Brett 1975, 76). The rear boundaries of these gardens lie approximately 80 metres to the south of Site 1. The first area to be examined was at the rear of the garden of No. 11 Mount Row, a large Victorian terraced house.

This garden backed onto the gardens of the bungalow adjoining Site 1. The good fortune of gaining access to an area of land threatened by such development and so close to the original excavation could not be ignored. As a result, an excavation was commenced; this was designed initially as an evaluation exercise, having two main aims, firstly to establish the possible extent of settlement on Site 1, and secondly, in the absence of any such settlement traces, to check for any other evidence of archaeological activity in the area.

The Gardner Survey of 1787 shows a single dwelling to the north of the area, surrounded by extensive gardens and orchards. The excavation of Sites 2 and 3 was to demonstrate that a continuing lack of significant development had protected the area from serious disturbance.

A small team, which consisted in the main of volunteers from La Société Guernesiaise, began to excavate a series of trial trenches in November 1981.

In contrast to the conditions encountered on Site 1, which had been stripped of its upper levels by mechanical excavator, the soil horizons on Sites 2 and 3 were essentially intact.

The initial trial trenches (Fig. 5)

A small trench, measuring 2 m by 5 m, designated Trench 1, was opened initially. The natural gravel or hoggin was located 1.15 m below the modern garden surface. This gravel was identical to that encountered on Site 1 but with dark staining in patches on its surface. There were no discernible indications of habitation. The natural gravel was overlaid by a yellow-brown clay 0.55 m in depth. This contained a few very small fragments of Iron Age pottery. Lenses of mortar on the surface of this clay and at a depth of 0.9 m below the present surface suggested building activity, probably of the eighteenth century.

The yellow-brown clay was overlaid by a much disturbed garden soil c.0.46 m deep. This layer contained a great deal of modern pottery, charcoal, glass, coal, slate and kitchen refuse. The only visible features were a small modern pit which was roughly circular, measuring approximately 0.30 m in diameter, and a Victorian brick-lined drain which cut the trench at right angles.

The soil horizons, while containing no features or finds of significance, were very similar in appearance and consistency to those of Site 1. The finds consisted of two very small fragments of Fabric 1 coarseware and a few sherds of post-medieval wares.

A second, smaller trial trench, measuring 3 m by 1 m, was opened in the neighbouring garden. The natural gravel or hoggin was overlaid by a similar orange-brown clay-rich soil, as in the previous trench. This soil was some 0.5-0.6 m deep and it contained a few very small sherds of Iron Age pottery of Fabric 1. Some very disturbed areas contained charcoal, glass, slate and other modern materials but no features were discovered. Above this layer, a fine black soil, some 0.6 m in depth, lay immediately beneath the modern ground surface. This layer was also very disturbed, and contained building rubble, slate, glass, coal and sherds of eighteenth and nineteenth century pottery.

Site 2 (Fig. 13)

As no significant Iron Age material was uncovered in the first two trial trenches, it was decided to open a third trench in a neighbouring property, situated to the west of the garden of 11 Mount Row. This garden had recently become available for investigation and had access through a property named La Petite Croute on King's Road. The whole area was now designated as a building site for the development of five properties, with access along a newly-constructed private road. This new site formed part of a commercial venture and permission was sought from the developer and architect for further excavation to take place. This permission was willingly granted, although the time available for archaeological work was strictly limited.

The trench initially measured 3 m by 3 m but was eventually enlarged to approximately 11 m by 6 m. The turf, modern topsoil and disturbed soils, which were approximately 0.7 m in depth, were removed. Beneath the disturbed soils the orange-brown, clay-rich soil encountered in the trial trenches appeared. At the north-eastern end of the trench the appearance of several large stones indicated possible archaeological activity. Further examination revealed a ditch running across the trench in an east-west direction. Excavation of the fill of the ditch revealed the presence of a large stone feature, which appeared to have been deliberately set into it. At this early stage in the excavation only a scattering of Iron Age potsherds in local fabric had been found. As it became apparent that the stone-lined feature was in fact a burial, a decision was made to extend the excavation and it was not until late April 1982 that it was possible to examine the grave in proper detail.

Speculation that in fact the site contained a cemetery was soon verified as an additional but smaller, stone-lined feature appeared.

Running diagonally across the site was a slightly curved linear feature (F5) aligned roughly east-west. The western end of this feature, identified as a ditch, was cut by another shallow ditch or gully (F10). As F5 was only examined over a length of approximately 9 metres it was difficult to define its function or to establish whether it was an enclosure ditch of the type encountered in Site 1. Determining the extent of this ditch and its possible direction were obviously beyond the scope of this small excavation. However, there was sufficient time to excavate thoroughly the portion available and so examine its fill in detail.

The ditch was 1.75 m wide at its eastern end, where it cut the eastern baulk at a slightly oblique angle. Under the turf-line a dark organic garden soil some 0.6-0.7 m in depth was present. This soil contained glass, iron, coal and modern pottery. Below this garden soil was a yellow-brown gritty soil containing small pieces of angular granitic stone scattered throughout, similar to the soils encountered in the uppermost level of the main enclosure ditch in Site 1. This layer averaged some 0.6 m deep and comprised the uppermost layer of the ditch fill, lying approximately level with its shoulders. On the surface of this layer, a small distance from the stone setting, lay a scattering of coarseware potsherds from large cooking pots. Beneath these sherds was an area of charcoal and burning on the surface of the underlying ditch fill, indicating some occupation activity on the silted up surface of the ditch.

The base of the ditch lay some 1.20 m below the garden soil and for the most part had an open U-shaped profile. Along part of the ditch base survived a well-cut slot, suggesting that there may once have been

KING'S ROAD 1982
SITE 2
(TRENCHES 3 & 4)

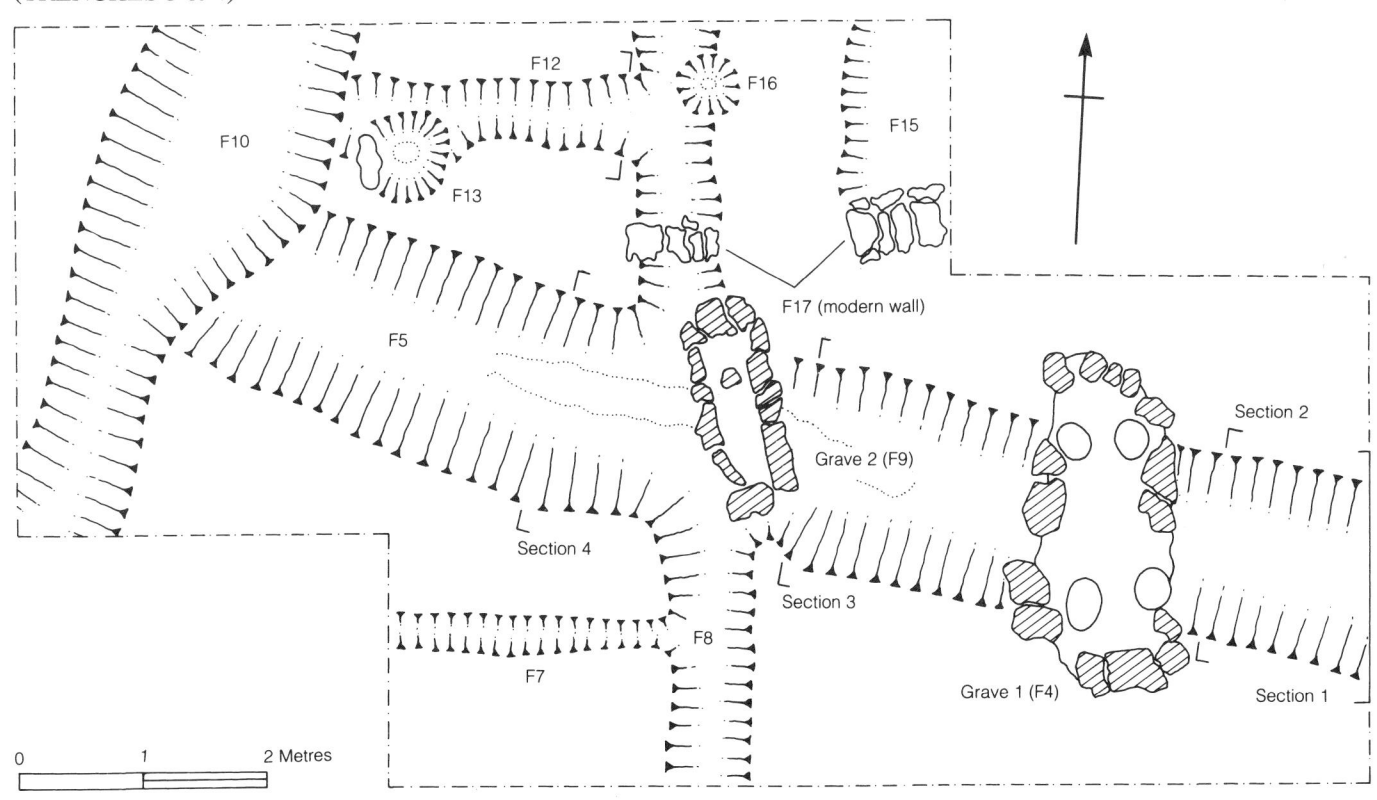

Figure 13 *King's Road, Site 2: plan.*

a palisade or fence present. This slot was only traced for 4 m, perhaps indicating that the palisade had been removed and the ditch used for other purposes, either as a boundary ditch or for drainage. The basal fill of the ditch consisted of an orange-brown gritty soil, finer in consistency than the soil which overlaid it. It is probable that, at the time of the burial, the silted up ditch may still have been visible, perhaps now on the periphery of the settlement, providing an ideal place for burials.

Towards its western end the ditch was shallower, measuring approximately 1 m in depth, and at this point a wide, shallow gully (F10), aligned north-south, cut across it. This feature was partly disturbed at its southern end by a modern pit, and due to this disturbance it was difficult to trace the edges of the gully. The fill was a lighter, sandier, orange-brown soil which was very similar to the sandy clay which lay above the natural gravel. As the land was rising slightly to the west, the upper layers of the ditch (F5) and of the gully (F10) had been subject to rather more modern disturbance, making their exact relationship more difficult to define. At the northern end of the trench, F10 measured approximately 2 m in width, narrowing to approximately 1 m at the southern end. The drainage in this area was very poor and there was a noticeable seepage of water into the trench, perhaps indicating the presence of a nearby spring. The finds included a few sherds of local coarsewares, flecks of charcoal, daub and a few sea-rolled beach pebbles. There was also a single bodysherd of Normandy Gritty Ware, suggesting that the feature may have been a later medieval gully.

A second, narrower gully (F8) running north-south cut through the main ditch toward the western end of the site. Its fill was an orange, sandy soil of fine consistency. As with F10 there were very few finds, but these included three sherds of Normandy Gritty Ware suggesting that this feature was also a part of a later medieval field system. The gully was 0.74 m wide and was approximately 0.33 m deep; it appeared to have only one fill.

Cut into the main ditch (F5) was a grave (designated F4) which contained weapons and personal accoutrements (Figs. 15-17). The first indication of the presence of this grave was a series of stones forming a rectangular surround, 2.6 m long and 1.9 m wide. This stone setting was located approximately 0.87 m below the modern ground surface and at this level a spear head was discovered. There was no stone capping or any other evidence of a covering to the grave. A detailed description of the grave and its contents are given below, pp. 83-92.

Approximately 1.10 m to the west of F4, a small cist burial was located. This feature (Grave 2, F9) was also cut into the filling of the ditch and was orientated on the same north-south axis as the larger burial (Fig. 18). The stone surround of this grave was well set into the top layer of the ditch, forming a rectangle measuring 1.68 m by 0.6 m. The stones averaged between 0.3-0.5 m in size and their internal faces were butted vertically forming a coffin-like surround to the burial. The small

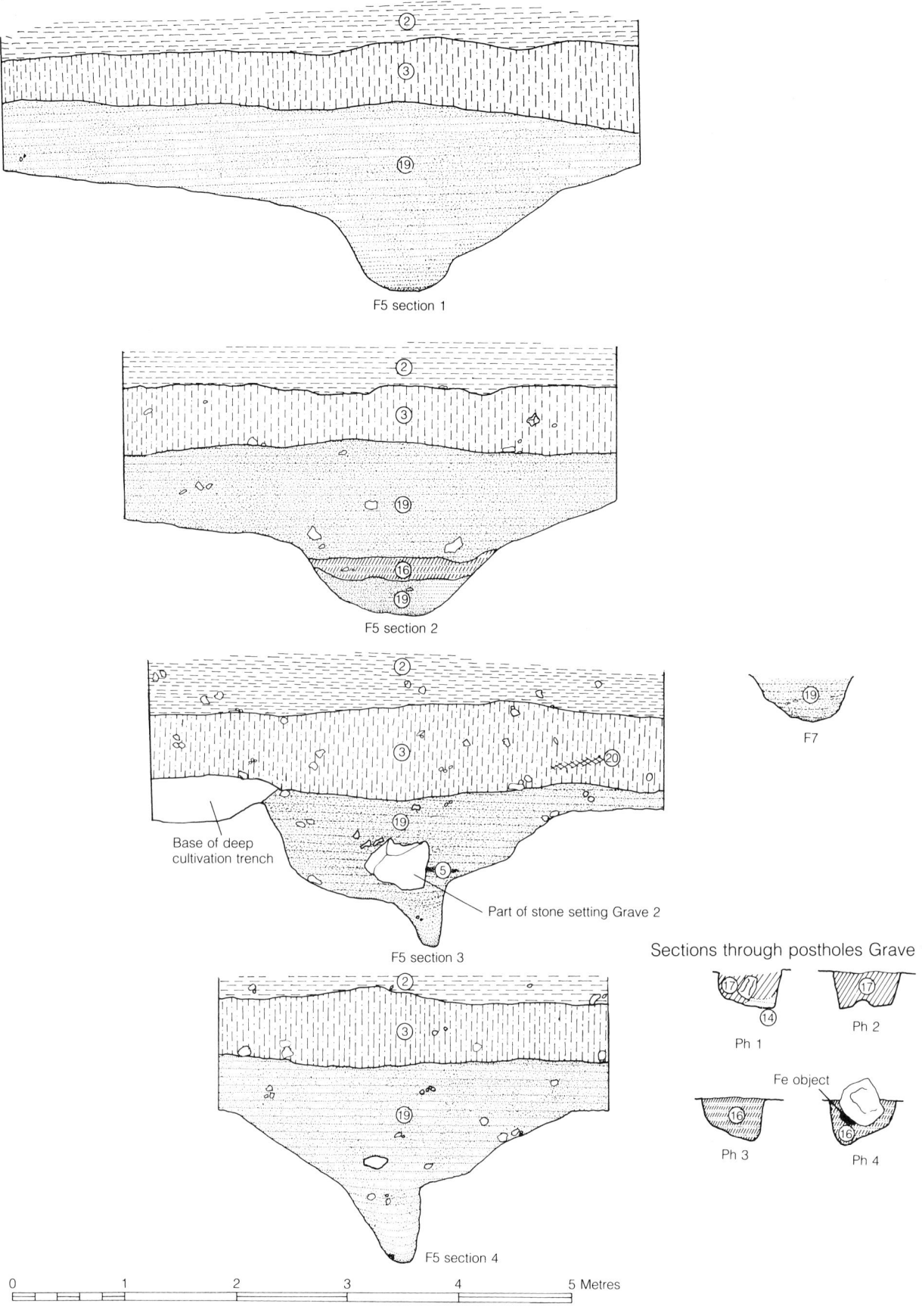

Figure 14 *King's Road, Site 2: sections.*

size of the stone surround suggests that the grave may have been for a child, since there was no evidence to indicate a cremation. A single upright stone was set into the central axis of the grave, approximately 0.45 m from its northern end and 0.1 m from each edge. It was difficult to establish whether in fact this stone had tumbled from the edge or was a marker stone. It was however well-set into the bottom of the grave fill. This fill was similar to that of the other burial (F4) and was composed of a light, orange, gritty, sandy soil flecked with charcoal. The fill contained noticeable air-spaces, indicating decayed bone. The finds consisted of one bodysherd of vesicular ware of Late La Tène date with burning evident on the internal surface and several sherds of local coarseware. Some pieces of daub and a few flint flakes were also recovered. After removal of the stone surround the underlying ditch (F5) was clearly visible. Although particular care was taken to check for the presence of timber posts in the area beneath the stones, none were discovered.

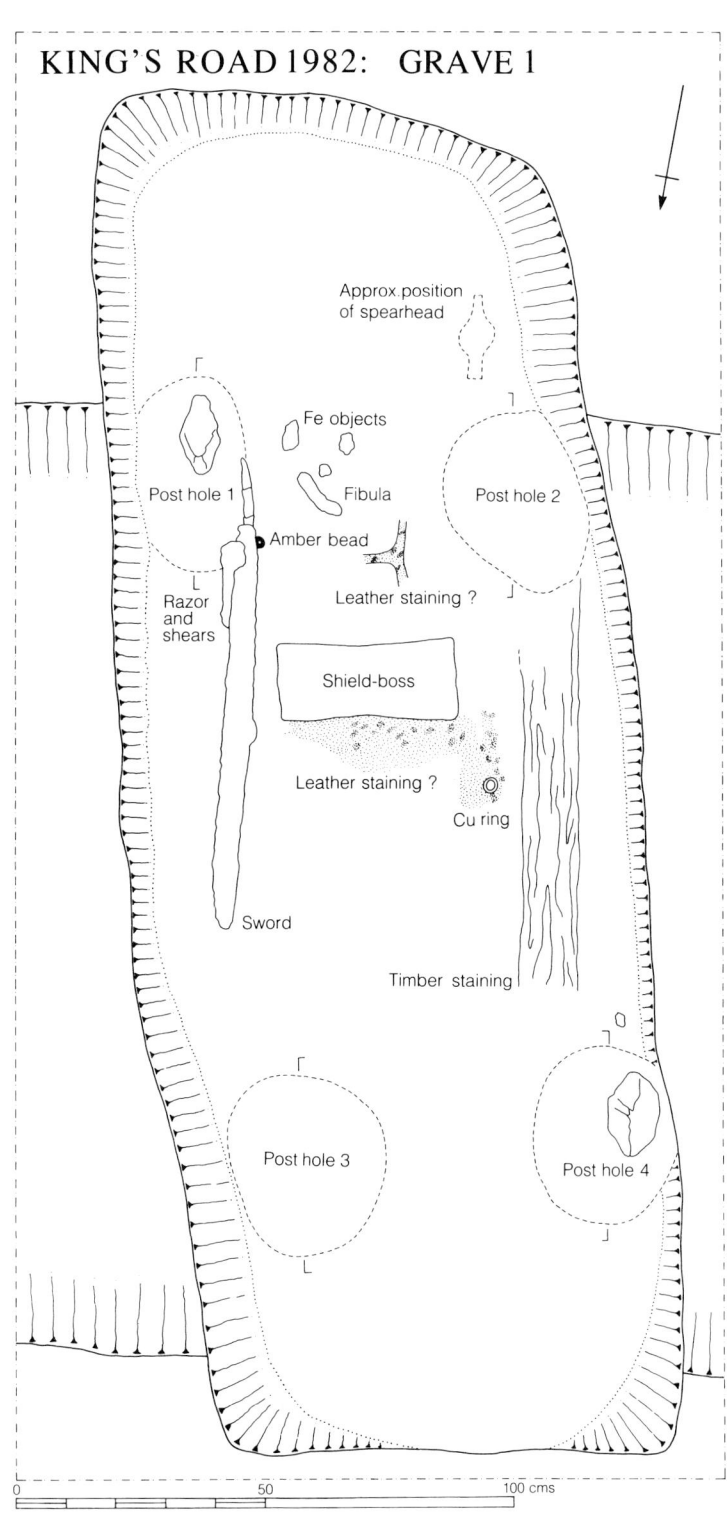

Figure 15 *King's Road, Site 2: plan of grave 1.*

Figure 16 *King's Road, Site 2: grave 1, showing sword, shield-boss and other objects.*

The gully (F8) described above had a further, smaller gully (F7) draining into it from the west, slightly to the south of the main ditch (F5). This small gully measured 0.43 m at its widest point and had a shallow U-shaped profile some 0.24 m deep. A single sherd of Iron Age coarseware was the only find. Although no medieval wares were found in its fill, its relationship to F8 indicates a medieval date.

The area of the excavation to the north of F5 was much disturbed by modern pits and a later wall running parallel with the ditch.

A short length of gully (F12), cut at either end by F10 and by F8, contained medieval pottery. This and its shallow round-bottomed form shows it to have been part of the medieval drainage system. The area to the north of F5 was disturbed by three modern pits (F13, F15 and F16).

Index of features and finds from Site 2

For detailed descriptions of pottery types and fabrics and of other finds and faunal remains, see the relevant specialist reports.

Feature 1 Modern
A small circular pit contaminated by nineteenth century disturbance.

Contents:

Pre-Roman pottery	Rims	Bases	Bodysherds	Remarks
Fabric 1			5	
Modern pottery				Transfer-printed wares

Feature 2 Modern
A small pit 0.9 m in diameter, at the eastern end of Site 2, containing nineteenth century builders' rubble.

Feature 3 Modern
A small pit running into the north-eastern baulk, contaminated by nineteenth century disturbance.

Feature 4: Grave 1 (Figs. 15-17 and 21) Late La Tène
Grave 1. A rectangular stone setting, measuring 2.6 m by 1.9 m, in the north-eastern corner of Site 2. For a detailed description of this feature see below, pp. 83-92.

Contents:

Pre-Roman pottery	Rims	Bases	Bodysherds	Remarks
Fabric 1	1		45	
Fabric 2	1		2	
Fabric LPC/4			3	1 with decoration
Gallo-Roman pottery				
Redware flagon			1	
Fe				2 Fe objects
Flint				3 flakes
Charcoal				small quantity

Figure 17 *King's Road, Site 2: grave 1, showing the post-holes.*

Figure 18 *King's Road, Site 2: grave 2.*

Feature 4: SE post-hole Late La Tène

Contents:

Pre-Roman pottery	Rims	Bases	Bodysherds	Remarks
Fabric 1			3	
Grave goods: see specialist report				

Feature 5 (Fig. 14) Iron Age
A curving ditch traced for approximately 9 metres across the site and measuring 1.7 m wide and 1.2 m deep. The ditch contained two fills. The uppermost was a yellow-brown gritty soil which contained large quantities of broken pots in Fabric 1. The basal fill was a finer brown gritty soil. Two graves were cut into the ditch and it was also cut at its western end by a wide shallow gully.

Contents:

Pre-Roman pottery	Rims	Bases	Bodysherds	Remarks
Fabric 1	7	6	497	
Fabric 2	4	2		
Fabric LPC/3	13	2	76	
Fabric LPC/4	21		38	
Fabric LPC/5	1		11	
Fabric LPC/6	1	4	9	
Haematite-coated			2	
Gallo-Roman pottery				
Gritty-buff			3	
Fe				1 Fe object
Flint			6	

Feature 7 (Fig. 14) Medieval?
A small gully running east-west across the site and draining into F8. The gully was U-shaped and measured 0.43 m wide by 0.24 m deep.

Contents:

Pre-Roman pottery	Rims	Bases	Bodysherds	Remarks
Fabric 1			1	

Feature 8 Medieval?
A narrow gully running north-south across the site. Its profile was of shallow U-shape and it measured 0.74 m wide by 0.33 m deep. The fill was an orange, sandy soil of fine consistency.

Contents:

Pre-Roman pottery	Rims	Bases	Bodysherds	Remarks
Fabric 1	2	1	31	
Fabric LPC/4			2	
Medieval pottery				
NGW			1	
Shale				3 bracelet fragments
Flint				1

Feature 9: Grave 2 (Figs. 18 and 21) Late La Tène
A small cist burial cut into the ditch (F5). Rectangular in plan, it measured 1.68 m by 0.6 m. The grave was bordered by granite stones averaging 0.3-0.5 m in size. The fill was a light orange gritty soil, flecked with charcoal.

Contents:

Pre-Roman pottery	Rims	Bases	Bodysherds	Remarks
Fabric 1			6	
Fabric 3			1	
Daub				1 lump

Feature 10 Medieval?
A wide shallow gully which cut the western end of the ditch (F5). At the southern baulk its width was approximately 1 m but it widened to twice that width over a distance of approximately 6 m. The fill was a light sandy, orange-brown soil.

Contents:

Pre-Roman pottery	Rims	Bases	Bodysherds	Remarks
Fabric 1			7	
Fabric 2			1	
Medieval pottery				
NGW			1	
Stone				1 beach pebble
Daub				1 piece
Charcoal				significant quantity

Feature 12 Medieval
A shallow round-bottomed gully approximately 0.7 m wide and 0.45 m deep which was cut on its western side by F10 and on its eastern side by F8. Traced for 2.5 m across the site.

Contents:

Pre-Roman Pottery	Rims	Bases	Bodysherds	Remarks
Fabric 1	2		21	
Medieval pottery				
NGW			8	
Flint				10 flakes

Features 13, 15, 16 Modern
A series of modern pits containing a few sherds of Late Iron Age pottery and large quantities of nineteenth century transfer-printed wares, glass, etc.

Site 3 (Fig. 19)

The time available for access on Site 2 was very limited but because of the significance of the finds a further trench, trench 5, was dug at right angles to that opened on Site 2, in an effort to determine the possible extent of the cemetery. The trench originally measured 2 m by 11.5 m but was later extended at its northern end to complete the excavation of several features in this area.

After the removal of approximately 0.65 m of topsoil, a cluster of stones appeared at the northern end of the trench. At a depth of 0.85 m it was apparent that these stones formed the setting of a third grave (Figs. 20 and 21). This grave, unlike the graves in Site 2, was aligned on an east-west axis. The burial was outlined by stones. Further stones, which at first appeared to form a covering to the grave, were found to have tumbled from the sides. The outer stones, which varied in size from 0.21 m by 0.14 m to 0.11 m by 0.03 m, formed a rectangle measuring 1.57 m by 0.8 m.

Grave 3 differed from Graves 1 and 2 in that the bordering stones were smaller than those of the first burial, Grave 1 (F4), and also that they were not set in an upright position as in Grave 2 (F9). In the centre of the grave there was a considerable amount of charcoal staining, with cavities and air-spaces in the soil, indicating traces of decayed organic material. After approximately 0.2 m of this fill had been removed a stony layer appeared. At this point the eastern end of the grave was deeper and wider than at the western end. The stones could have formed a crude basal lining to the burial, but could equally have been tumble from the sides.

The few finds within the grave consisted of several sherds of local coarsewares and a flint flake. There were also several ferrous objects, the distribution of which may have some significance. One small unidentifiable iron object was located in the north-eastern corner of the grave and another slightly larger iron object was found wedged under a stone in the south-western corner. This was later identified as an iron strip with traces of leather and textile surviving in its corrosion products. Just outside the grave, some 0.35 m to the north-east, lay a cluster of small metal objects consisting of a piece of slag and two iron strips, possibly the remains of strapping associated with a coffin or other container. Two sherds of Fabric 3, the vesicular ware, may indicate that the burial was contemporary with the first phase of occupation of Sites 1 and 4. This type of pottery was absent from the occupation horizons of Sites 2 and 3 into which the burials were inserted. At the western end of the grave, beneath the basal stones, an area of dark staining was particularly noticeable and a ridge of orange sandy clay indicated the negative impression of the grave-pit. Beneath the tumbled stones in the centre of the grave and toward its northern edge was a rectangular post-hole measuring 0.12 m by 0.12 m, filled with a noticeably darker soil.

The northern side of the grave was cut into a small gully. This gully (F11) formed part of a series of gullies, similar in nature, running in an east-west direction across the trench.

The largest of these gullies (F11) was aligned east-west and was cut on its southern edge by Grave 3. It measured 0.48 m wide and was 0.15-0.2 m deep. The feature was traced for 3.7 m across the site and its eastern end was cut by a large post-hole (F12). It was also cut at its western end by a modern greenhouse pillar foundation. The fill of this gully consisted of a gritty orange soil, and the only find was a single sherd of Fabric 1 pottery. The pit or post-hole (F12) was 1.03 m in diameter and contained an orange-brown gravel with a post-mould 0.63 m in diameter, indicated by the presence of a darker more organic soil. A layer of charcoal staining was clearly visible at the base of the feature. Finds were few in number and consisted of a few sherds of local coarsewares.

F2 was a small gully 0.88 m wide and 0.15-0.2 m deep running east-west across the site. This gully was cut by the fourth and largest grave on the site. One flint flake and several bodysherds of local Fabric 1 coarseware were the only finds present in this feature. Another gully, F3, was situated slightly to the south of F2. It narrowed from 0.68 m in width at its western end to 0.34 m at the eastern end and contained a small circular cluster of stones, but nothing of significance was found beneath them. Among the finds were two sherds of Gallo-Roman gritty-ware indicating that it belonged to a later phase of the site.

F4 and F5 were also shallow gullies situated toward the southern end of the trench, some 2 m from F3. The gullies had been truncated by later activity and were ill-defined. F4 contained a few flints and some sherds

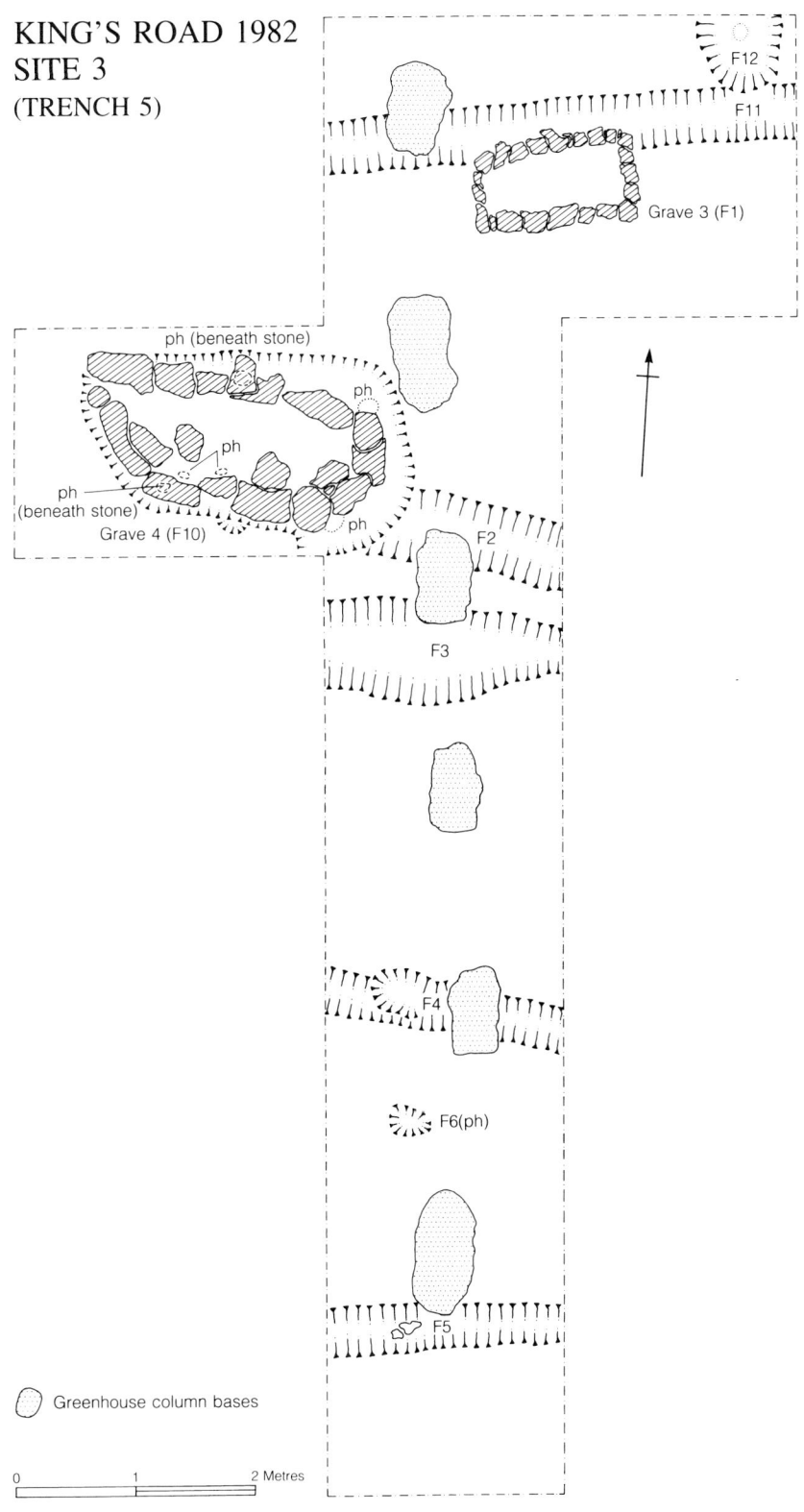

Figure 19 *King's Road, Site 3: plan.*

of local coarsewares. F5 was devoid of finds.

The fourth grave (F10) was cut into the western end of F2. It was located approximately 1.40 m south of Grave 3. The stone setting of the grave was encountered at a depth of 0.96 m beneath the modern surface, significantly deeper set than in the other examples. The grave was defined by a roughly oval stone setting measuring approximately 2.20 m by 1.10 m. The stones used in the setting were larger than those in the other graves, the largest stone on the top setting measuring 0.5 m by 0.21 m. The other stones ranged between 0.29 m by 0.22 m and the smaller ones between 0.11 m and 0.08 m. The grave was orientated east-west on the same axis as Grave 3. At the eastern end two post-holes were located just outside the stone setting. The grave pit was cut into an orange-brown clay-rich soil. Toward the lower levels of the pit the soil was softer and denser with a cheesy consistency. The fill of the grave consisted of a loosely packed, brown gritty soil. Outside the stone setting it was possible to see the line of the cut for the grave pit. A further two post- or stake-holes were situated half way along the southern edge of the grave, inside the stone setting. After the removal of the stones from the setting, two further post-holes which were square in plan were discovered.

There were very few finds. Above the grave in the modern garden soil was a single sherd of a Gallo-Roman redware flagon in a soft and friable condition. In the grave itself however, only a single flint flake was discovered. Due to the positioning of the post- and stake-holes it is possible that some type of timber setting may have formed part of the grave apparatus, as in Grave 1.

Index of features and finds from Site 3

Quantities of iron nails and other unidentifiable iron objects were found at the interface between the upper, disturbed soils and the archaeological features. Also found in this context were two fragments of resin. All of these finds must be considered as unstratified.

Feature 1: Grave 3 (Figs. 20 and 21) Late La Tène
A rectangular grave measuring 1.57 m by 0.8 m. Delineated by small stones. The fill of the grave was a gritty orange-brown soil.

Contents:

Pre-Roman pottery	Rims	Bases	Bodysherds	Remarks
Fabric 1			13	
Fabric 3			2	
Fabric LPC/3			2	
Fabric LPC/4			2	
Flint				1
Fe				3 Fe strips
				1 Fe object
Slag				1 piece
Shell				limpet

Feature 2 Iron Age
A small gully running east-west across the site, measuring approximately 0.88 m wide by 0.15-0.2 m deep.

Contents:

Pre-Roman pottery	Rims	Bases	Bodysherds	Remarks
Fabric 1			6	
Flint				1

Feature 3 Iron Age or Gallo-Roman
A small gully running east-west across the site, narrowing from 0.68 to 0.36 m in width and averaging 0.3 m in depth.

Contents:

Pre-Roman pottery	Rims	Bases	Bodysherds	Remarks
Fabric 1			18	v. abraded
Fabric LPC/3			3	v. abraded
Gallo-Roman pottery				
Gritty-ware			2	
Daub				1 lump

Feature 4 Iron Age
A small gully running east-west across the site, averaging approximately 0.53 m in width.

Contents:

Pre-Roman pottery	Rims	Bases	Bodysherds	Remarks
Fabric 2			1	
Flint				2

Feature 5 Iron Age?
A small gully running east-west across the site, averaging approximately 0.46 m in width.

Contents: Nil

Feature 6 Iron Age?
A small, roughly circular pit or post-hole, approximately 0.25 m in diameter. The fill was a dark brown gritty soil.

Contents: Nil.

Feature 10: Grave 4 (Fig. 21) Late La Tène?
A rectangular grave, measuring 2.20 m by 1.10 m. Delineated by large stones. The fill was a loose, gritty orange-brown soil.

Contents:

Pre-Roman pottery	Rims	Bases	Bodysherds	Remarks
Fabric 1			4	
Gallo-Roman pottery				
Redware			1	
Flint				1

Figure 20 *King's Road, Site 3: grave 3.*

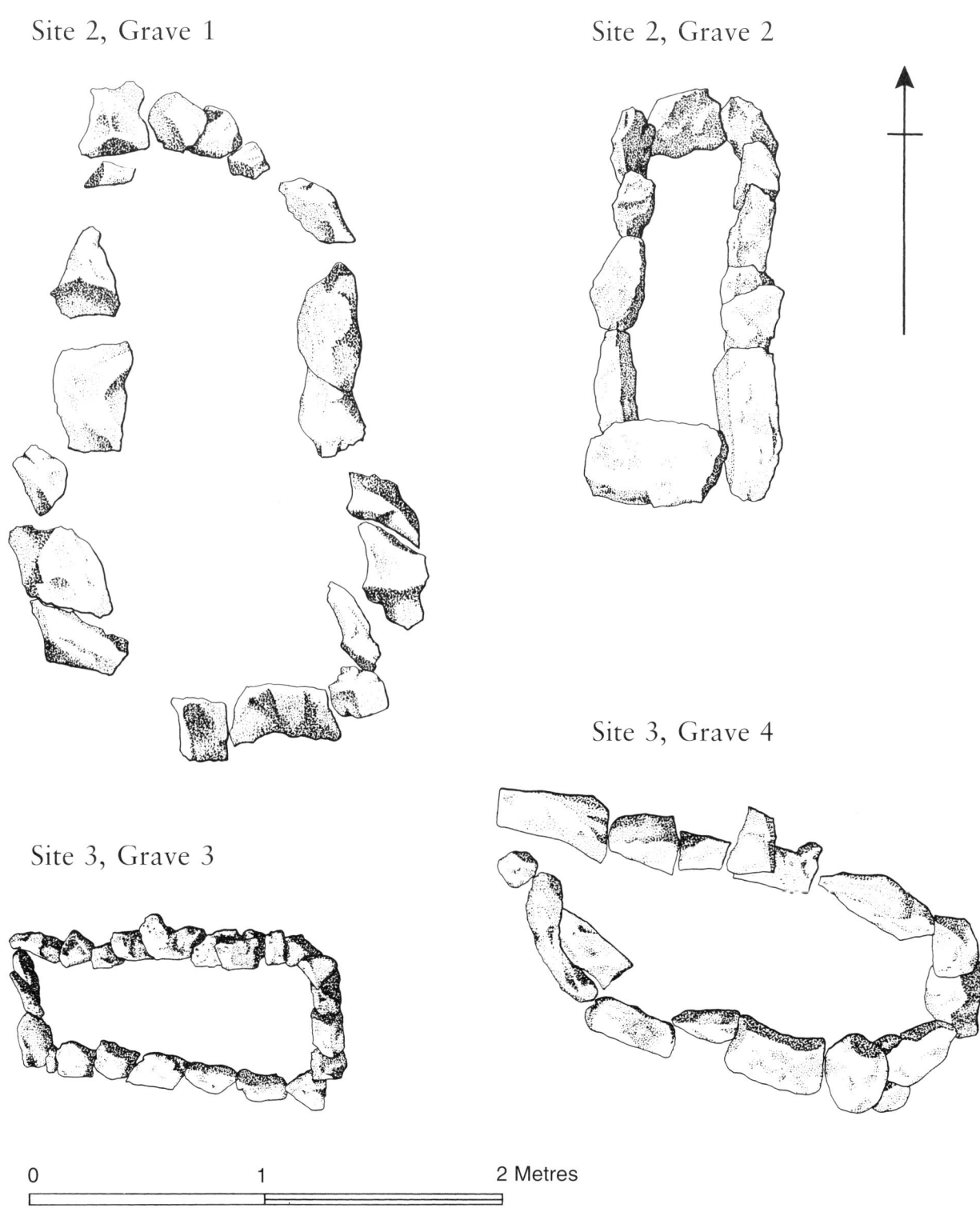

Figure 21 *King's Road, Sites 2 and 3: plans of cists.*

Feature 11 Iron Age
A gully running east-west across the site and cut by F1 (Grave 3). It measured 0.48 m across by 0.15-0.2 m deep. The fill was a gritty orange soil.

Contents:

Pre-Roman pottery	Rims	Bases	Bodysherds	Remarks
Fabric 1			6	
Flint			4	

Feature 12 Iron Age
A deep pit or post-hole approximately 1.03 m in diameter, incorporating a post-mould of darker organic soil. The fill was an orange-brown gravel.

Contents:

Pre-Roman pottery	Rims	Bases	Bodysherds	Remarks
Fabric 1			1	

Site 4 (Figs. 22-4)

Introduction

As a result of the investigations carried out on Sites 1, 2 and 3 it was obviously desirable, if possible, to examine the strip of land lying between these two areas (Fig. 5). The parcel of land in question lay immediately to the south of the recently erected Elizabeth College Boarding House and was also in the ownership of the College authorities. The intention was to use the land as a recreation area for the pupils and in fact tennis courts had already been constructed at the western end of the site. Negotiations were commenced with the College authorities and permission was readily granted for a full investigation to take place during the summer vacation of 1983.

A rectangular area of some 450 square metres was first laid out between the college building and the private garden to the south. It was later extended at the north-eastern corner to allow for a fuller examination of a timber structure. The total area of the excavation amounted to some 520 square metres.

The western end of the site had been subject to considerable dumping and levelling of builder's refuse, derived from the construction of the new college building alongside. The eastern end however had fortunately escaped much of this modern interference and in places the gravelly, natural granitic bedrock could be seen erupting through the modern topsoil and grass. There was a fall in levels from the eastern end of the site toward the west, of approximately 1.25 m. It was not known just how much modern waste had been tipped but a decision was taken to strip mechanically the western half of the area to a depth of 0.75 m. This mechanical stripping indeed saved several days of physical effort, but toward the western end still left some 0.75 m of modern builder's rubble *in situ*. The removal of this highly compacted deposit required an extended period of physical endeavour under extremely hot and dry conditions, ultimately 'wasting' several hundred volunteer hours of precious investigation time.

It is appropriate here to acknowledge the volunteer force on the excavation. It comprised roughly equal numbers of local enthusiasts and visiting volunteers from the UK, France, Switzerland and New Zealand. The weather was uncompromisingly hot during the summer of 1983 and the physical digging conditions were, in the main, extremely arduous. The team worked long and hard, without complaint and earned the genuine appreciation and thanks of all concerned for their unstinting efforts. After the initial machining was completed and the site cleaned and prepared, excavation, with the exception of the western portion, consisted totally of trowelling. At the western end, picking and shovelling was necessary in order to reach the archaeological levels.

At the eastern end of the site, the superficial deposits were shallow and features such as pits and post-holes were quickly revealed. The line of the main enclosure ditch (F17) was established after four days work and some features to its west were also uncovered. In contrast it was to be almost a fortnight before significant features were discovered at the western end. Horizontal stratigraphy was absent in all but a few limited areas, having been removed or seriously disturbed by later cultivation. In places, plough-scores and the spade-marks left by medieval cultivation were observed, cut into the natural gravels and clays.

The settlement features

The line of the main enclosure ditch (F17), which was fairly rapidly established, divided the site into an east and a west area. Clearance of the shallow overburden to the east revealed a succession of features cut into the decomposed bedrock. These were of varying nature, some well-cut and easy to define, others shallow and indistinct. The overall impression gained from the investigation of these eastern features was that they had suffered little, if any, disturbance from later activities. The main feature types include:

Scoops and worn areas
These were shallow, mostly irregular and often difficult to define positively. Some appeared in areas of significance, for example the worn depression (F134) at the postulated entrance to the round-house, or the worn surface of the trackway to the south of the gate-posts (F137).

Ditches and gullies
Defined initially by their linear nature, they were further categorized by their profile, either V-shaped or U-shaped. As a general rule, the V-shaped features were of Late Iron Age date and the U-shaped features were of later, mainly medieval, date.

Stake-holes
These, defined by their small size of between 0.05 and 0.1 m across, were mostly well-cut and often in significant patterns.

Post-holes
These were larger than stake-holes, although there were instances where a feature could have represented the remains of either a small post or a large stake. They measured between 0.15 to 1.5 m across. They were mostly, but not invariably, circular in form, well-cut,

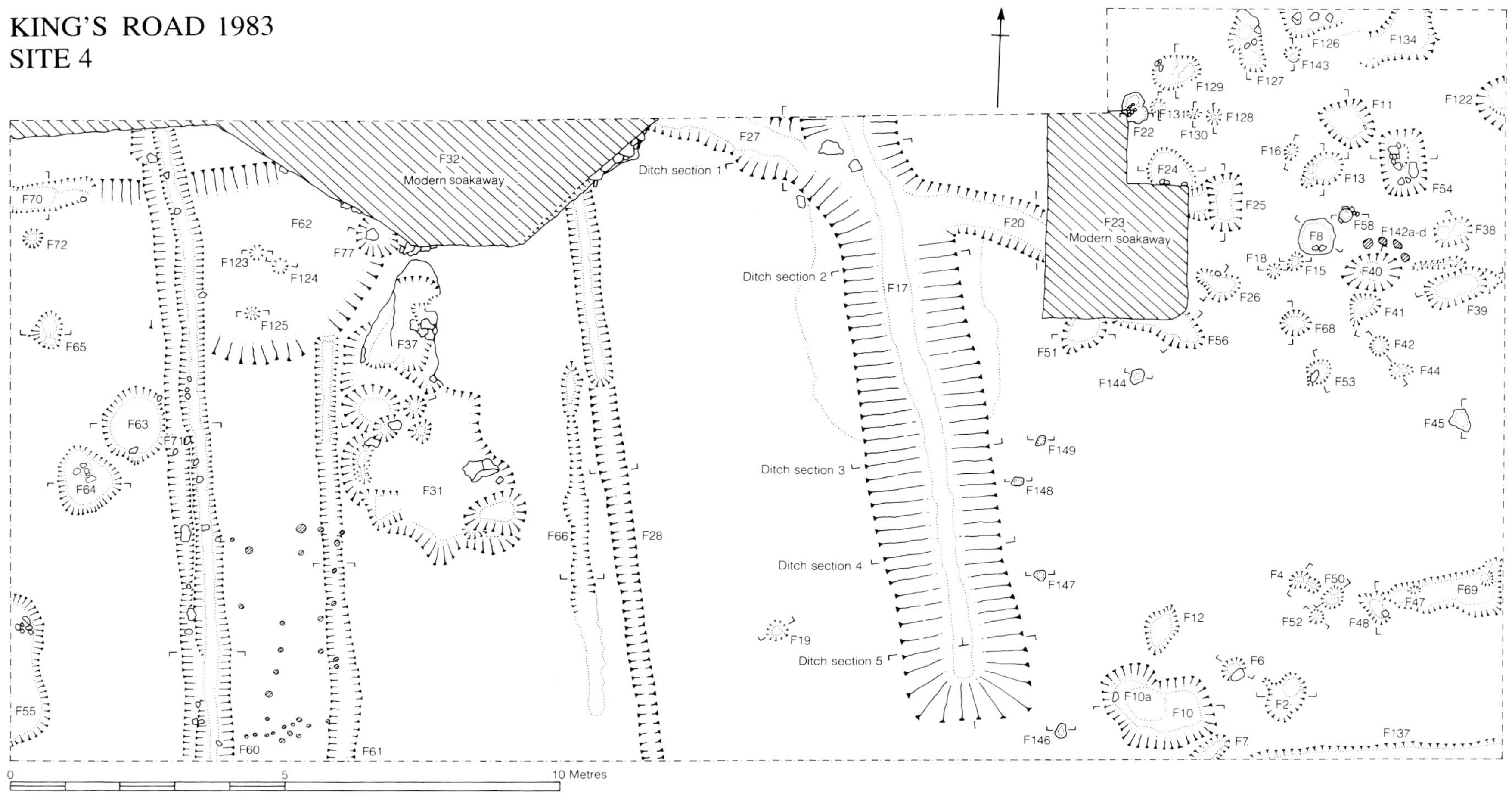

Figure 22 *King's Road, Site 4: plan.*

Figure 23 *King's Road, Site 4: general view east of the main ditch.*

with straight sides tapering to a flat or rounded base. Whilst some appeared in isolation and their purpose was unclear, others formed significant patterns, as in the round-house, the rectangular structure, the gate-posts and those situated along the inner edge of the main ditch.

Pits
Pits were defined by their size and location. They were often well-cut and rectangular, with straight sides but could also be sub-rectangular or circular in plan. Several of the features assumed to be pits had clusters of stones on their surface. Varying techniques were used to ascertain whether posts or small stakes had been cut through pit fills, but in the majority of cases no positive evidence was found.

To the west of the main ditch the features discovered were similar in nature to those at the eastern end. However, the softer, more cultivable nature of the soils here had resulted in most features being truncated to some degree, by later activities.

The main enclosure ditch (F17) ran roughly north-south across the excavated area. It was well-cut, of V-shaped profile and ended approximately 1 m short of the southern baulk. The cultivated soils of the medieval period slumped slightly into the upper profile of the ditch, which would have probably shown as a linear depression during the second to third centuries AD, when further activity took place here. The lower levels of the ditch fill contained only Late Iron Age and pre-Roman imported wares.

Some 4 to 5 m from the northern baulk, the upper layers of the main ditch contained areas of burnt clay, carbon and slag. Excavation of this area (Fig. 33) revealed an arc of post-holes set around a well-worn flat granite boulder (F29) approximately 0.6 m in diameter, which had been carefully trigged up on all sides for use as an anvil. Quantities of iron nails were found in this area, some actually adhering to the stone itself. Close to the anvil and set into a hole cut into the bedrock was the bottom two-thirds of a redware flagon, perhaps used as a quenching-pot. Also set into the upper layers of the ditch, slightly to the south of the centre of the excavated portion, was a stone setting (F133) beneath which was situated a deposit of limpet shells and animal bone (F35). The possibility exists that these features represented the remains of a grave, but no conclusive proof was obtained.

Running into the ditch from east and west, close to the northern baulk, were two gullies (F20 and F27). These had been cut after the construction of the main ditch and had deposited water-borne gravels and silts onto its, by then, considerably silted surface.

Situated along the eastern edge of the ditch and curving away to the east was a series of small, well-cut post-holes (F146, 147, 148, 149, 144). Whilst these were in an ideal position to have acted as an inner defensive palisade, they were of relatively small size and no other indications of strengthening or propping could be discerned. The presence of the massive double post-holes probably for the gate (F10, 10a) do however indicate a defensive system of some substance, presumably with associated fences or palisades. It is possible that the inner small post-holes were merely part of a fence erected to prevent cattle or people from falling into the ditch.

Immediately to the south of the termination of the main ditch and of the gate-posts was a well-worn track (F137), with clearly visible wheel-ruts worn into its surface. The southern baulk and the close proximity of the adjoining private property precluded further examination of the entrance.

With the exception of the gate-posts and the entrance track, the southern half of the area east of the main ditch revealed little of apparent significance. A scattering of post-holes some 3 to 4 m to the north-east of the gate-posts could have formed part of the entrance defences. A few indistinct scoops existed in the central portion but apart from these the area was devoid of features.

In contrast, the northern half of the area contained a variety of post-holes, pits, gullies and scoops, indicating a much more intensive use of this part of the site. The shallow gully (F20) fed into the main ditch on the slight downward slope from a setting of post-holes which formed a circle some 5 m in diameter, presumably representing a building. A modern concrete soakaway, built for the new college building to the north, lay across the western end of this feature, obliterating approximately a fifth of this structure, but sufficient remained for the basic arrangement to be discerned. At the north-eastern side of the structure lay the entrance with a well-worn, trodden path (F134) leading inside. A few small stake- and post-holes, possibly for internal fittings or roof-supports were found inside the structure. There were also two pits (F24 and F25) inside. It is of significance that the quantities of pottery and other artefacts recovered from the fill of the main ditch were considerably higher in that portion alongside the structure, than elsewhere along its length.

A series of sub-rectangular pits was situated outside and to the east of the post-built structure. One of these pits (F40) was partially surrounded on its northern rim by four stake-holes cut into the bedrock and set at an angle of approximately 60 degrees which might have provided a lean-to style of covering.

Figure 24 *King's Road, Site 4: general view west of the main ditch.*

To the south of this pit-scatter lay a rectangular five-post structure, situated some 3 m from the roundhouse. All finds from these features were of Late La Tène date.

The main ditch ran directly along a geological divide. To the east of the ditch, inside the settled area, the natural bedrock was formed of an eroded, decomposing granitic rock which was shattered and heavily fissured by both weathering and chemical action. The rock broke easily into fist-sized pieces and in places had weathered down to a pebbly pea-sized gravel. To the west the rock had further decomposed to a soft, almost silty soil, which, when damp, possessed a cheesy, slippery consistency. It is highly probable that

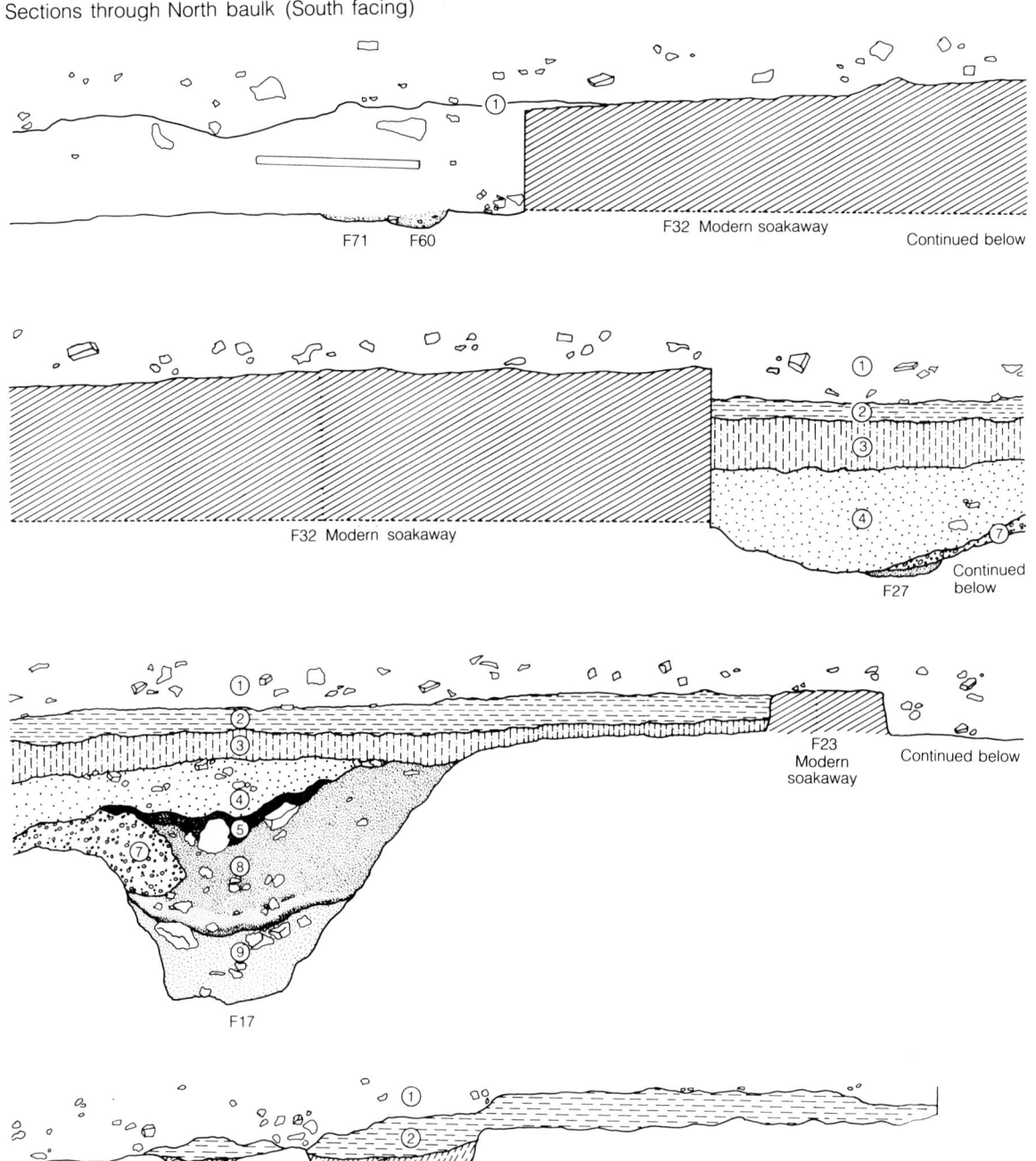

Figure 25 *King's Road, Site 4: sections.*

this dividing line was deliberately chosen by the constructors of the defences, as it would certainly have made the digging out of the ditch much less arduous.

The area immediately to the west of the ditch was, with the exception of a single well-cut post-hole (F19), totally devoid of features. It is possible, although no positive evidence for this was discovered, that this strip alongside the ditch had at one time been banked as a counterscarp, in front of the ditch. The softer, more easily worked soils here could well have been totally 'gardened' away at a later date. The surface of the clays, particularly toward the southern half of this area, showed much evidence for spade-cultivation in the form of a profusion of V- or U-shaped cuts. It is probable that this agricultural activity was medieval or later in date.

Emerging from the northern baulk was a second gully draining from the west into the main ditch (F27). It was not possible, due to the proximity of the newly erected building, to discover whether this gully emanated from a structure. Much of the face of the northern baulk to the west of the main ditch was obscured by the presence of a second large concrete soakaway associated with the new building to the north.

A series of shallow U-shaped gullies ran approximately north-south across the western half of the site (F26, 66, 61, 60, 71). F71 had been carefully recut along its length by a replacement gully (F60). The majority of these gullies produced sherds of medieval pottery indicating that they formed part of the medieval cultivation system seen in Site 1.

Lying between two of the medieval gullies, toward the northern edge of the excavated area, was a complex of pits, post-holes, stake-holes and worn areas (Fig. 35). After initial clearing this area was divided for simplicity into two main features (F31 and F37). They were probably part of a single working area and were later referred to jointly as F31/37. F31/37 contained late second to early third century Gallo-Roman pottery. A series of post- and stake-holes indicated that some form of roof-structure had existed over this working-area. At the northern tip of F37, part of the burnt clay capping of an oven survived *in situ*. The clay inside the capping had been heated until reddened and stones beneath the capping also showed signs of heating, being partially blackened by soot. The area had been slightly truncated by later activity and positive conclusions as to its possible use were not made.

Slightly to the north-west of this working-area was another large worn depression some 4 to 5 m across (F62). It contained several post-holes and may possibly have been the living-floor of another dwelling. Further to the west of F62 were several pits (F63, 64, 65).

The two features discussed above and the associated pits produced small, but identifiable sherds of late second to early third century Gallo-Roman pottery.

A complex of small stake-holes (F80-110) situated toward the southern baulk at the western end of the site (Fig. 36) possibly indicated the presence of a flimsy shelter. The holes appear to have formed three rows with an entrance mid-way along the eastern side of the structure. The western row of stake-holes had been partially removed by the medieval gully and its recut (F71 and F60). The eastern row had been cut into the silted up medieval gully (F61). Although no finds were associated with the stake-built feature, it may have been erected as late as the thirteenth to fourteenth centuries AD.

The extra time and larger work-force available for the excavations on Site 4 revealed aspects of the site's history impossible to discern during the rescue exercise on Site 1. The Late La Tène occupation of the highest part of the site appeared to be of fairly short duration, although the re-cutting of the gate-post, if it was made necessary by the deterioration of the timbers, indicates that the site was perhaps in use for a reasonable period. The earlier features and pottery discovered during the excavation of the cemetery on Sites 2 and 3 show that occupation of the area by Iron Age peoples was probably continuous between the second or third century BC until the mid first century BC.

The utilization of the area west of the main ditch during the second and third centuries AD answered the questions posed by the discovery of the samian bowl and other scraps of Gallo-Roman pottery found on Site 1. It is probable that much more evidence relating to this secondary occupation of the area lies, undisturbed, beneath the land to the west of the main site.

Medieval usage of the areas excavated seems limited to purely agricultural purposes, spade-cultivated strips of soil lying between shallow drainage gullies. The relative paucity of finds from the medieval period indicates that any domestic dwellings that might be present lie some way off from the excavated areas.

The same general picture emerges for the post-medieval period; pottery and coins dating from the seventeenth and eighteenth centuries indicate, once again, a purely agricultural use for the area.

Index of features and finds from Site 4
(Figs. 25-37)

Features considered to be isolated or not grouped in a significant fashion are listed individually. Features forming structures or considered to be part of a discrete complex are listed, as far as is possible, in their relevant groupings.

Features not listed below were those discounted for a variety of reasons as having no archaeological significance.

Features are listed in an order which roughly represents a progression from east to west.

Feature 1 Probably a natural feature
A shallow, irregular depression 0.85 m by 0.5 m in diameter by 0.1 m deep. Filled with a soft brown sandy loam.

Contents:

Pre-Roman pottery	Rims	Bases	Bodysherds	Remarks
Fabric 1			19	
Flint			1	
Slag			1	

Feature 2 Probably a natural feature
A shallow, irregular depression 1 m by 0.8 m in diameter by 0.1 m deep. Filled with a soft brown sandy loam, angular granitic fragments and pea-gravel.

Contents: Nil.

Feature 3 Modern
A small irregular pit.

Contents: Modern flower pot sherds.

Features 4, 50 and 52 Late La Tène
A group of three small post-holes. F4, 0.45 m by 0.4 m in diameter by 0.27 m deep; F50, 0.4 m in diameter by 0.2 m deep; F52, 0.25 m in diameter by 0.23 m deep. All were filled with a soft brown sandy loam; F52 contained many small rock fragments.

Contents of F4:

Daub   7

Feature 5 Probably post-medieval
Contents: Post-medieval pottery; French copper liard, *c.*late seventeenth century.

Feature 6 Late La Tène?
A well-cut post-hole situated close to the gate-posts, 0.4 m in diameter by 0.9 m deep. Filled with a soft brown sandy loam, large packing stones and many rock fragments.

Contents: Nil.

Feature 7 Late La Tène?
A short length of shallow round-bottomed gully emerging from the south baulk, close to the gate-posts. Filled with a soft brown sandy loam.

Contents: Nil.

Features 8, 11, 13, 15, 18, 22, 26, 58, 127, 129, 131 and 143 (Fig. 27) Late La Tène
A series of post-holes forming the outer perimeter of the circular structure close to the north-eastern corner of the site. Most were filled with a soft brown sandy loam with angular granitic rock fragments.

KING'S ROAD 1983
SITE 4

Section through the East baulk (West facing)

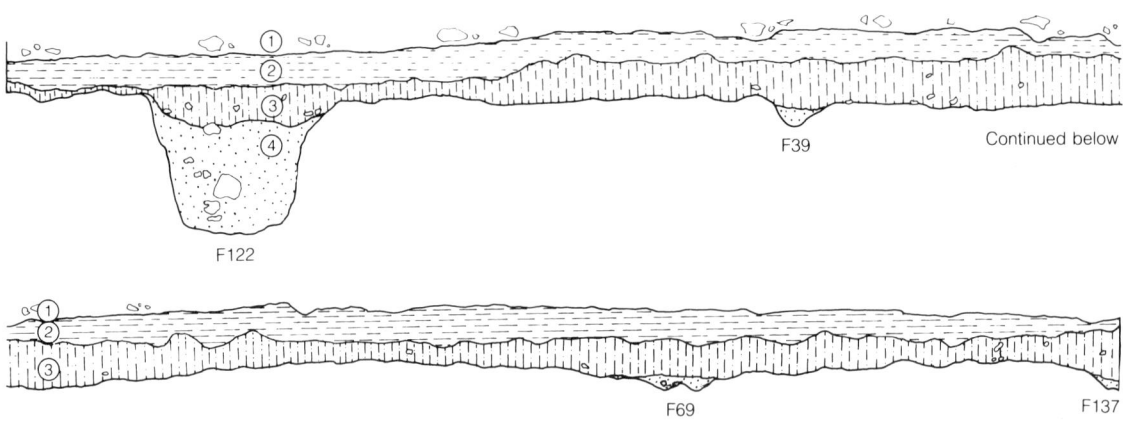

Section through the West baulk (East facing)

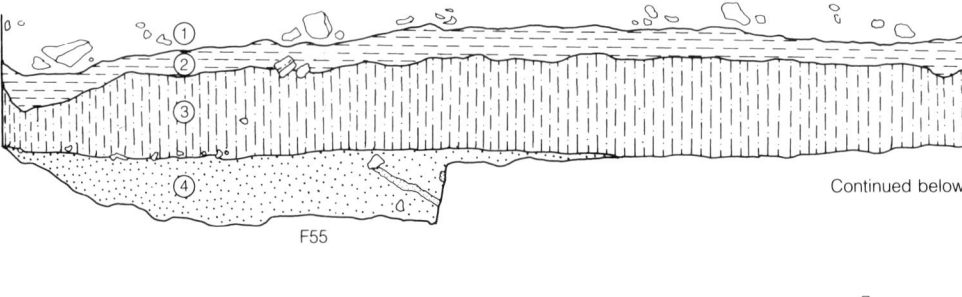

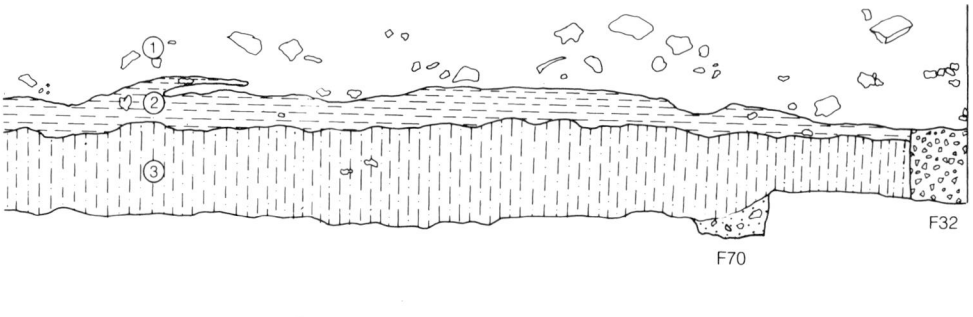

Figure 26 *King's Road, Site 4: sections.*

Feature 8
A post-hole 0.6 m by 0.7 m in diameter by 0.64 m deep, filled with a soft brown sandy loam with packing-stones. A post-mould showed as a darker stone-free area in the centre of the fill.

Contents:

Pre-Roman pottery	Rims	Bases	Bodysherds	Remarks
Fabric 1			4	
Fabric 2			3	
Fabric 3			1	
Daub			1	

Feature 11
A sub-rectangular post-hole or possibly a pit, 0.84 m by 0.9 m in diameter by 0.33 m deep. Filled with a soft brown sandy loam with packing-stones and smaller angular rock inclusions.

Contents:

Pre-Roman pottery	Rims	Bases	Bodysherds	Remarks
Fabric 1			2	
Fabric 2			9	
Fabric 3			2	
Fabric 5	1		1	
Daub			7	

Feature 13
A shallow, roughly circular post-hole, 0.6 m by 0.63 m in diameter by 0.15 m deep. Filled with a gravelly brown sandy loam; the upper layers contained some burnt clay and daub.

Contents:

Pre-Roman pottery	Rims	Bases	Bodysherds	Remarks
Fabric 1		2	2	
Fabric 2			14	
Fabric 3	1			
Fabric 5			1	
Daub			22	
Flint			1	

Feature 15
A shallow post-hole, 0.44 m by 0.35 m in diameter by 0.29 m deep. Filled with a soft brown sandy loam with much angular granitic rubble.

Contents: Nil.

Feature 18
A shallow post-hole, 0.3 m by 0.3 m in diameter by 0.15 m deep. Filled with a soft brown sandy loam.

Contents:

Pre-Roman pottery	Rims	Bases	Bodysherds	Remarks
Fabric 1			7	
Fabric 2			5	
Fabric 3		One complete profile		
Daub			2	
Flint			1	
Quern				1 fragment

Feature 22
An oval post-hole approximately 0.8 m in diameter by 0.4 m deep. Partially disturbed by the modern concrete soakaway (F23). Filled with a light brown sandy loam with granitic fragments.

Contents:

Pre-Roman pottery	Rims	Bases	Bodysherds	Remarks
Fabric 1			3	
Fabric 2			1	

Feature 26
Irregularly shaped post-hole, 0.95 m by 0.5 m in diameter by 0.42 m deep. Filled with a soft brown sandy loam with angular rock fragments.

Contents: Nil.

Feature 127
A double post-hole 1.08 m by 1 m in diameter by 0.55 m deep. Filled with a soft brown sandy loam with large packing-stones and smaller rock fragments.

Contents:

Pre-Roman pottery	Rims	Bases	Bodysherds	Remarks
Fabric 1			6	
Fabric 2			1	
Fabric 3	1		1	
Flint			1	

A single, small sherd of oxidized medieval gritty ware lay upon the top of the feature.

Feature 129
An irregular double ? post-hole, 0.8 m by 0.55 m in diameter by 0.25 m deep. Filled with a soft brown sandy loam with small granitic fragments.

Contents:

Pre-Roman pottery	Rims	Bases	Bodysherds	Remarks
Fabric 1			3	

Feature 131
A circular post-hole, 0.28 m in diameter by 0.25 m deep. Filled with a soft brown sandy loam with some rock inclusions.

Contents:

Pre-Roman pottery	Rims	Bases	Bodysherds	Remarks
Fabric 1			1	
Daub			3	

Feature 143
A small post-hole 0.17 m in diameter by 0.18 m deep. Filled with a soft brown sandy loam.

Contents: Nil.

Features 130, 128, 16, 24 and 25 Late La Tène?
Pits and post-holes situated inside the circular structure (Fig. 27).

Feature 130
A small post-hole 0.18 m by 0.1 m deep. Filled with a soft brown sandy loam; a darker central portion could have indicated a post-mould.

Contents: Nil.

Feature 128
A small post-hole 0.23 m by 0.3 m deep. Traces of a central post-mould. Filled with a soft brown sandy loam.

Contents: Nil.

Feature 16
A small pit or post-hole 0.27 m in diameter by 0.17 m deep. Filled with a soft brown sandy loam with small granitic inclusions.

Contents: Nil.

Feature 24
A shallow pit 0.98 m in diameter by 0.12 m deep. The base of this feature clearly showed the scrapes and cuts left when it was originally cut out of the bedrock. Filled with a soft brown sandy loam with angular rock inclusions and pea gravel. The feature had been partially disturbed by the modern concrete soakaway (F23).

Contents:

Pre-Roman pottery	Rims	Bases	Bodysherds	Remarks
Fabric 3		Rim and shoulder profile		4 sherds

KING'S ROAD 1983
SITE 4

Sections of features comprising the circular structure

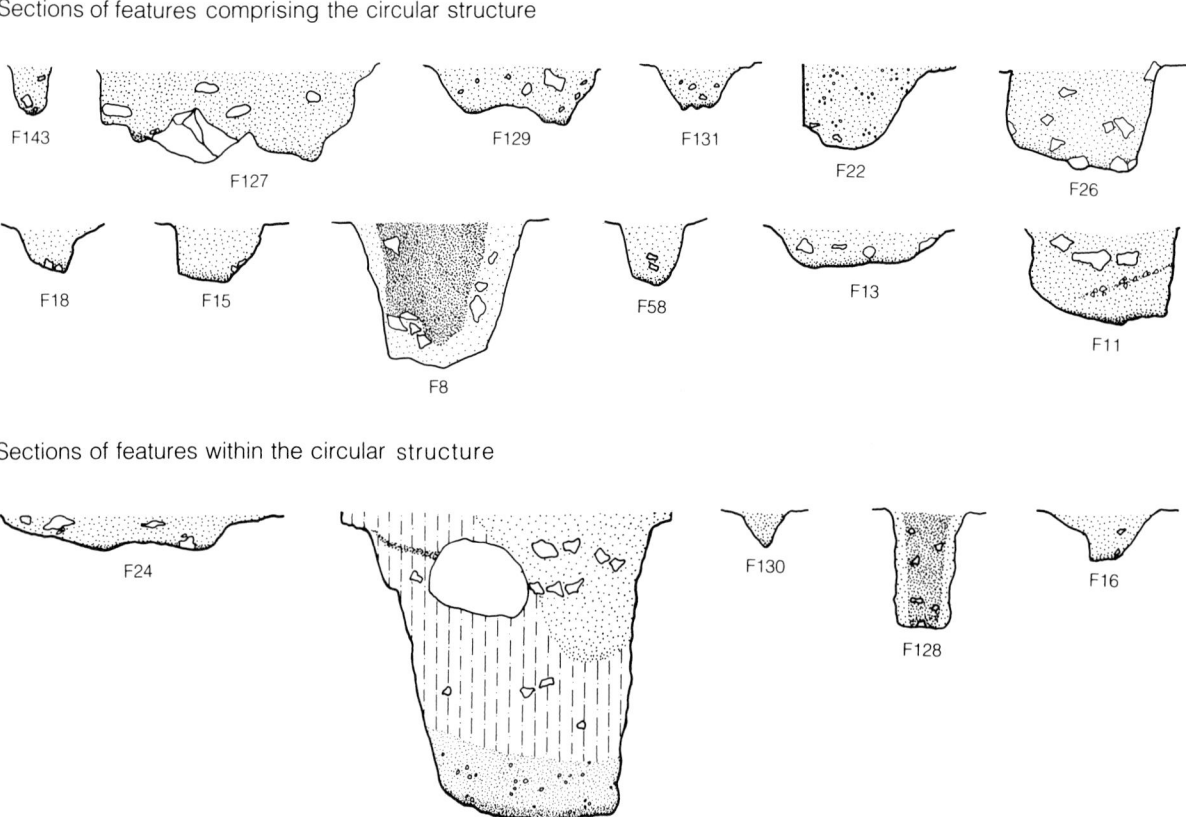

Sections of features within the circular structure

Sections of features comprising the rectangular structures

Sections through gullies

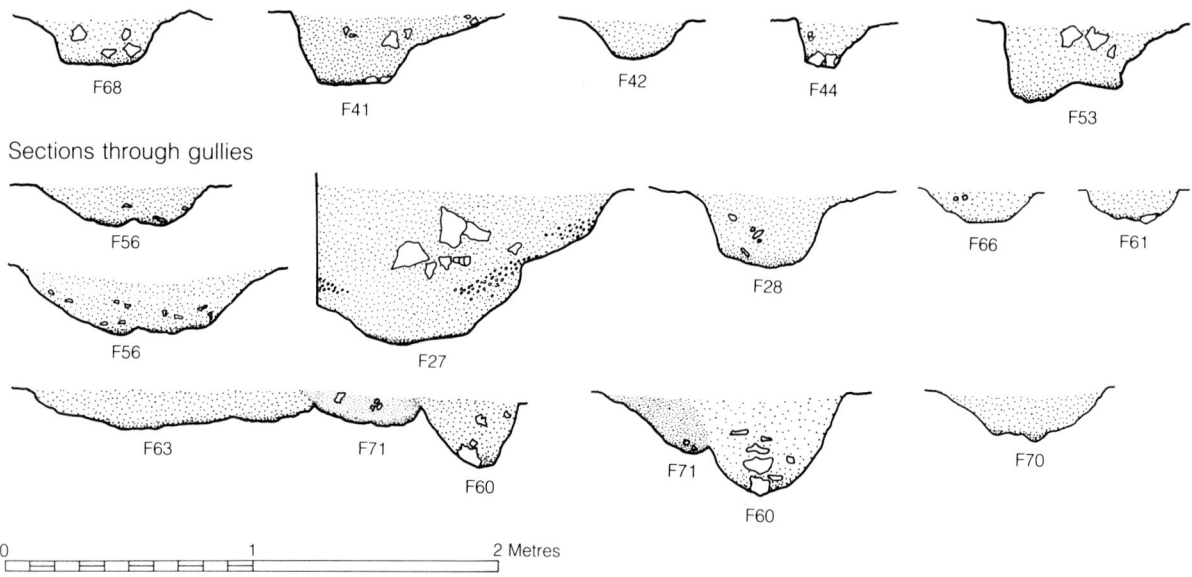

Figure 27 *King's Road, Site 4: sections.*

Feature 25
A very regular rectangular pit, sloping steeply to a flat bottom, 1.12 m by 0.65 m in diameter by 1.1 m deep. Filled with a dark brown sandy loam containing much rubble, angular rock fragments and gravel. The upper level contained fragments of daub and large sea-rolled and utilized granite boulders.

Contents:

Pre-Roman pottery	Rims	Bases	Bodysherds	Remarks
Fabric 1	2		14	
Fabric 2			1	
Fabric 3			2	
Daub				many small fragments
Utilized pebble				1

Feature 134 Late La Tène?
A worn depression at the gap indicating the entrance to the circular structure. Filled with soft brown sandy loam with some small angular granitic inclusions.

Contents: Nil.

Feature 126 (Fig. 28) Late La Tène
A rectangular pit approximately 2 m to the north-west of the circular structure and running beneath the northern baulk. It measured 1.13 m by 0.45 m by 0.45 m deep. Filled with soft brown sandy loam with some fist-sized rock inclusions.

Contents:

Pre-Roman pottery	Rims	Bases	Bodysherds	Remarks
Fabric 1			1	
Flint			2	

Feature 122 (Fig. 26) Gallo-Roman
A sub-rectangular pit or perhaps a post-hole, running beneath the eastern baulk. The portion excavated measured 0.7 m by 0.8 m deep. Filled with a very gravelly brown loam with rock fragments.

Contents:

Pre-Roman pottery	Rims	Bases	Bodysherds	Remarks
Fabric 1			7	
Fabric 2			1	
Fabric 3			1	
Fabric 5			1	
Gallo-Roman pottery				
Greyware			1	
Daub			1	
Flint			2	
Utilized stone				1 fragment

Features 54 and 54a (Fig. 28) Late La Tène
A regular rectangular pit measuring 1.16 m by 0.8 m in diameter by 0.7 m deep. A circular post-hole later cut into the pit measured 0.55 m in diameter by 0.65 m deep. Filled with a soft brown sandy loam with rock fragments and sea-worn boulders. Much evidence for post-packing on the surface, at the sides and in the base.

Contents:

Pre-Roman pottery	Rims	Bases	Bodysherds	Remarks
Fabric 2			1	
Fabric 3			1	

Feature 38 (Fig. 28) Late La Tène
A regular rectangular pit measuring 0.79 m by 0.43 m by 0.3 m deep. Filled with a soft brown sandy loam with angular rock fragments and flecks of daub.

Contents:

Pre-Roman pottery	Rims	Bases	Bodysherds	Remarks
Fabric 1			6	
Daub			9	

Features 39 and 39a (Fig. 28) Late La Tène
A rectangular pit with a shallow gully running into it on its northern edge. Traces of packing for two post-holes were encountered during its excavation but the sections provided no positive proof for this. Filled with a soft brown sandy loam with rock inclusions.

Contents:

Pre-Roman pottery	Rims	Bases	Bodysherds	Remarks
Fabric 1	1		1	
Fabric 2			2	
Fabric 3	1		1	
Utilized pebble				1

Features 40, 40b, 142a, 142b, 142c and 142d (Fig. 28) Late La Tène
An oval pit with two recuts, possibly for posts, 1.1 m by 0.82 m in diameter by 0.72 m deep. Surrounded on its northern edge by four stake-holes each cut at an angle into the bedrock to provide some form of sloping cover.

Contents:

Pre-Roman pottery	Rims	Bases	Bodysherds	Remarks
Fabric 1	1		11	
Fabric 3			2	
Fabric 5		1		
Daub			17	
Slag			1	

Features 68, 41, 42, 44 and 53 (Fig. 27) Late La Tène
A series of post-holes set out in rectangular plan, situated some 3 m to the south of the circular structure. The average diameter of the features was 0.5 m and the average depth 0.25 m. All were filled with a soft brown sandy loam with small rock inclusions.

Contents:

Pre-Roman pottery	Rims	Bases	Bodysherds	Remarks
Fabric 1			1	decorated
Fabric 3			1	
Fabric 4			1	cordoned

Feature 45 Late La Tène
A small irregular pit, 0.5 m in diameter by 0.13 m deep, close to the eastern baulk. Filled with a soft brown sandy loam with much rubble.

Contents: Nil.

Features 69, 47 and 48 (Fig. 26) Gallo-Roman
An irregular linear depression, 2.2 m by 1 m by 0.1 m deep. This feature, perhaps a gully, emerged from the eastern baulk. Toward its western end a small circular post-hole (F47), 0.25 m in diameter by 0.18 m deep, had been cut into its fill. At the western end an irregular flat-bottomed pit (F48) had also cut its fill.

Contents of F47:

Pre-Roman pottery	Rims	Bases	Bodysherds	Remarks
Fabric 3			1	grooved
Gallo-Roman pottery				
Greyware			1	
Amphora			1	

Features 10 and 10a (Figs. 28 and 29) Late La Tène
A large post-hole approximately 1.9 m by 1.55 m in diameter by 1.1 m deep. Filled with dark brown sandy loam. The recut was differentiated by its paler fill and differences in the concentrations of large packing-stones. This feature, situated close to the end of the main ditch and alongside the entrance trackway, certainly represents the northern component of the entrance gateway to the site, or at least this part of it.

Contents:

Pre-Roman pottery	Rims	Bases	Bodysherds	Remarks
Fabric 1			2	
Fabric 2			3	
Fabric 3			2	
Utilized stone				1

Feature 137 Late La Tène?
The extreme northern edge of a well-worn trackway showing traces of wheel-rutting. Only a very small part of this feature, presumably

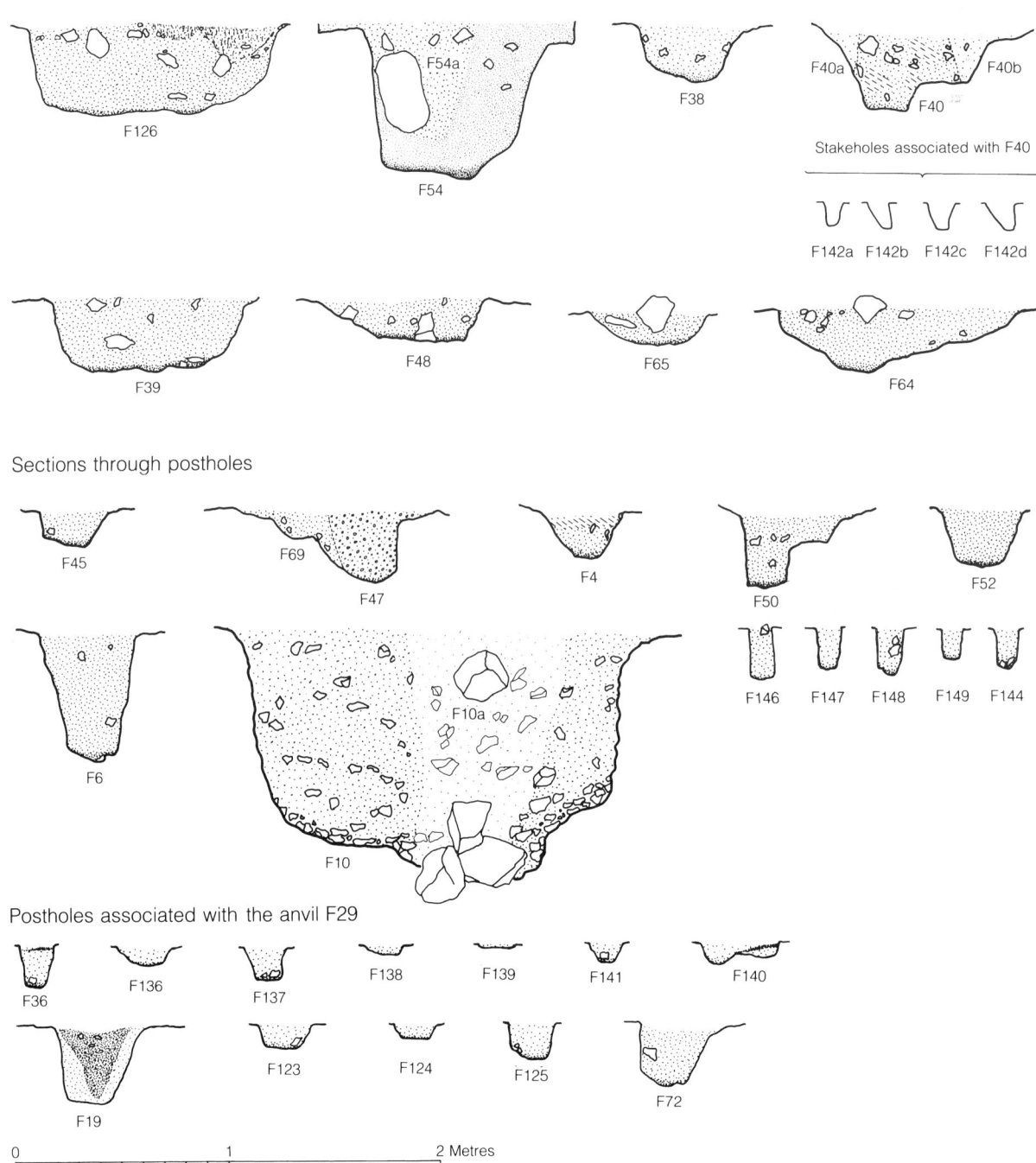

Figure 28 *King's Road, Site 4: sections*.

Figure 29 *King's Road, Site 4: F10, the double post-hole for the gate.*

an entrance into the site, could be investigated due to the proximity of the neighbouring property.

Contents: Nil.

Features 146, 147, 148, 149 and 144 (Fig. 28) Late La Tène
A series of uniformly-sized, small, well-cut post-holes situated along the eastern (inner) edge of the main ditch, averaging 0.12 m in diameter by 0.22 m in depth. All were filled with a soft brown sandy loam. Several of these post-holes were discovered on the last day of the excavation, when a heavy rain-storm showed up a variety of small features which had previously escaped notice.

Contents of F149: Fragment of iron.

Feature 51 Late La Tène?
A portion of a round-bottomed gully? or perhaps a natural feature. Much of it obscured by the modern soakaway (F23).

Contents: Nil.

Features 20 and 56 Late La Tène
A shallow gully draining away from the circular structure. Much of its length obscured by the modern soakaway (F23). At its western end it drained into the main ditch (F17). Filled with a soft brown sandy loam flecked with charcoal and daub.

Contents:

Pre-Roman pottery	Rims	Bases	Bodysherds	Remarks
Fabric 1	1		1	
Fabric 2			2	
Fabric 5			1	
Slag			1	

Feature 17 (Figs. 25, 30 and 31) Late La Tène and Gallo-Roman
This stretch of the main ditch encircling the site extended for *c*.15 m, approximately north-south across the excavated area. The width at its top varied between 2.75 m to 3 m. Its average depth varied between 1.75 m at the northern and southern ends, to 0.8 m just to the north of the central portion, where later activities had eroded the ditch shoulders. The ditch profile was V-shaped, the sides cut at an angle of approximately 50 degrees and the base slightly rounded. The southern terminal was square-cut and also sloped at an angle of 50 degrees. There appeared to be little long-term erosion of the ditch sides, the surfaces when excavated presenting, in the main, an even, fresh appearance.

The ditch was divided, for the purposes of excavation, into 2 m blocks; after sections had been drawn, the remaining upstanding blocks of fill were removed. The block of soil between sections 2 and 3 was double the size, as this stretch contained the anvil and associated working area, which was excavated separately. The illustrated sections, with the exception of the section in the north baulk (Fig. 25), do not show the superficial layers 1 to 3, which were removed before the ditch layout was established.

Stratigraphically, the fill of the ditch was similar throughout, with the exception of the north baulk, the anvil and associated working-area (F29) and the limpet-midden (F35). At the base of the ditch a small amount of pea-sized gravel derived from the sides lay in a thin lens. Above this primary silting lay a thick layer of grey silty loam with occasional angular granitic stones scattered throughout. This grey silt varied in depth from 0.5 m to 0.3 m and was covered along the entire length of the ditch by a gritty brown loam some 0.75 m to 0.3 m in depth, containing much gravel and small angular granitic stones. Above this brown loam lay a deposit of similar nature but noticeably yellower in hue. This layer which varied in depth from 0.6 m to 0.35 m, also contained small angular stones but in addition, a much higher proportion of larger angular rocks, which were rare in the lower levels of the ditch fill.

The Gallo-Roman pottery found in the ditch was confined to the interface between this yellow gravel and the later ploughsoils which lay above it. The interface was marked in most cases by no more than a general darkening of the yellow gravels, caused by a dirty, trodden and for the most part thin lens of soil rich in charcoal flecks, fragments of burnt reddened clay and thin spreads of soot.

This general pattern held good for most of the ditch but in the north baulk the section revealed a thick charcoal spread lying between the brown loam and the yellow loam. There were no obvious signs of recuts or later disturbance of the ditch fill. The overall impression was of a fairly rapid silting up of the ditch with soils and granitic gravels derived from the ditch shoulders and areas immediately adjacent to it.

Above the yellow gritty loam lay an ancient ploughsoil containing medieval and post-medieval pottery, which had sagged slightly into the compressed fill of the ditch, sealing and to a certain extent protecting the integrity of the early ditch fill. Above the ploughsoil were modern topsoils and layers contaminated by the adjoining construction work.

Careful attention was paid to the possibility that the ditch may have been a large palisade trench but no evidence of timber construction was found, either in the form of post-holes at the base or by the presence of stone packing or revetting. It appears from the sections that the ditch was intended as an open obstacle, either defensive in purpose or perhaps for the more prosaic need to keep livestock from the inner area.

The ditch lined up with the ditch terminal (F1), found when excavating Site 1, and it would appear that in this area of the site there were at least two entrances. The northern or opposing terminal of the entrance on Site 1 was not definitely identified, although the small stretch of ditch (F5) with its terminal post-holes could well have served this purpose. The need to keep to the builder's excavated areas and the shortness of time allowed on Site 1 precluded a clearer understanding of this second entrance.

Contents:

Layer 1 – Uppermost ditch fill

Pre-Roman pottery	Rims	Bases	Bodysherds	Remarks
Fabric 1	1		38	
Fabric 2	1		36	
Fabric 3		1	5	
Gallo-Roman pottery				
Greyware	1		1	
Redware			3	
Buff gritty			3	
Flagon			3	
TN Type	1		10	1 decorated
Samian	1			
Amphora			2	
Daub			5	
Utilized stone			2	
Flint			16	1 barbed and tanged arrowhead

KING'S ROAD 1983
SITE 4

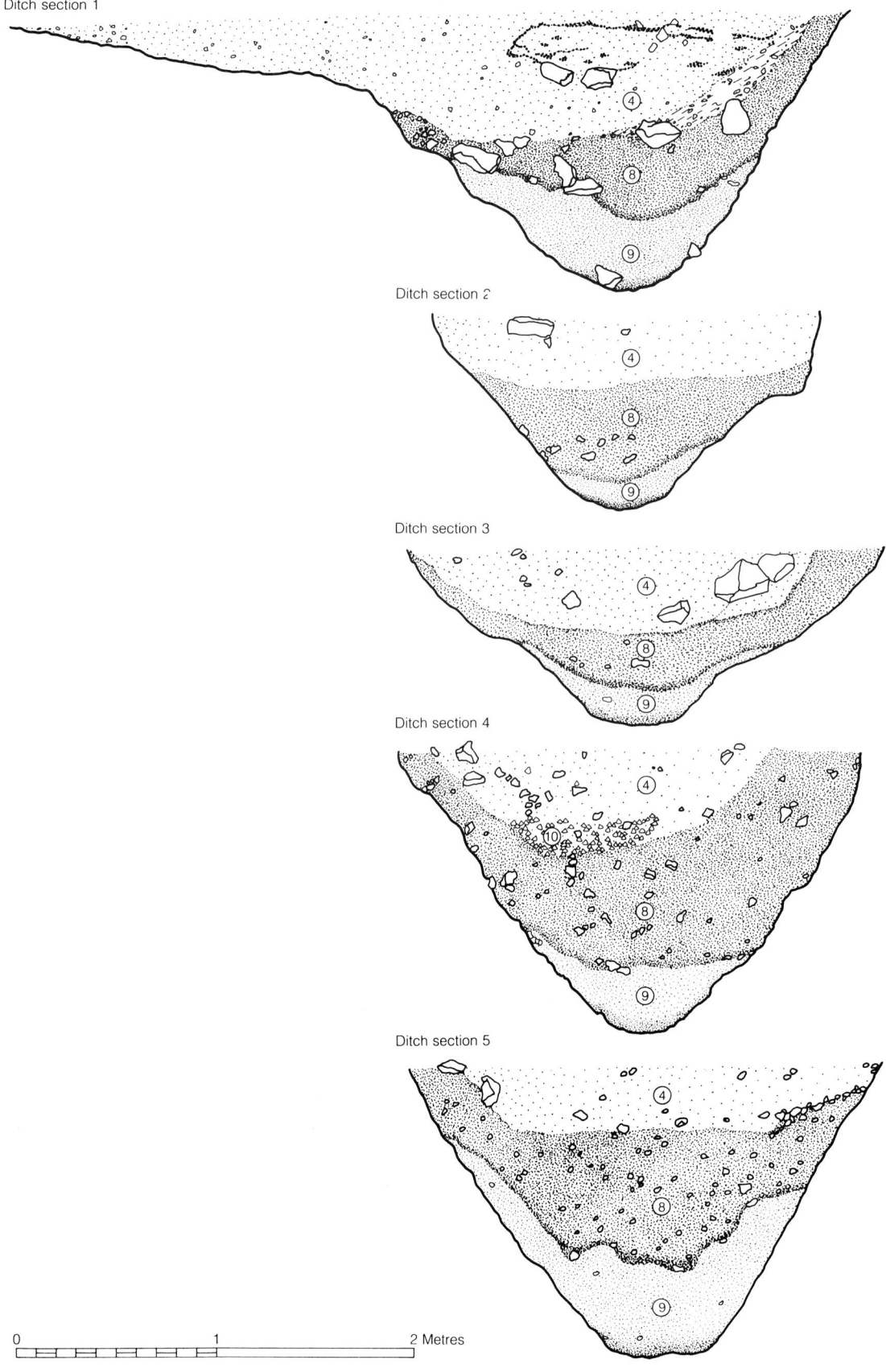

Figure 30 *King's Road, Site 4: sections.*

Figure 31 *King's Road, Site 4: F17, the main ditch, section through the north baulk.*

Layer 2   Central ditch fill

Pre-Roman pottery	Rims	Bases	Bodysherds	Remarks
Fabric 1	1	3	58	3 decorated
Fabric 2		1	29	
Fabric 3	3	2	11	1 complete profile
Fabric 4	3		10	1 cordoned
Fabric 5			2	
Fabric 7			3	
Graphite-coated			1	
Amphora			4	
Shaped clay object			1	
Daub			4	
Slag			15	
Utilized stone			3	
Bone			2	

Layer 3 – Basal ditch fill

Pre-Roman pottery	Rims	Bases	Bodysherds	Remarks
Fabric 1			20	
Fabric 2			16	
Fabric 3			5	
Fabric 4	2		6	1 almost complete pot
Amphora			4	
Daub			1	
Utilized stone			2	
Flint			14	

Features 29, 33, 36, 136, 140, 137, 138, 139 and 141 (Figs. 32 and 33)
Gallo-Roman

The shoulders of the ditch over much of the northern half of the excavated portion showed distinct signs of wear not seen at the southern end, which had sharply defined angles. The reason for this worn area became clearer once the ploughsoils were trowelled away from the uppermost ditch fill. An area containing much soot and carbon and areas of brightly reddened heated clay was revealed. Centrally situated within this area lay a large flat water-worn granite boulder (F29) (Fig. 33). It had been carefully levelled up on its north and south sides with small supporting stones. The flat stone was roughly circular with a diameter of approximately 0.8 m. Around the stone and extending to the shoulders of the ditch was a series of post-holes, three on either side (F36, 136, 140 and F137, 138, 139) and one situated centrally about 0.45 m to the south of the flat stone (F141). Set into a neatly cut pit on the western edge of the ditch, approximately 1.5 m from the stone, was the bottom half of a Gallo-Roman redware flagon. The areas of clay and carbon ended in a clearly discernible line to the south of this working-area which has been identified as a blacksmith's forge, complete with anvil and quenching-pot. Around the area and in two cases actually adhering to the anvil-stone, were quantities of nails and small unidentifiable pieces of ferrous material. This small roofed workshop belongs to the Gallo-Roman phase of the site and contained small but identifiable potsherds dating to the second or third century AD. It was possibly sited on top of the silted up ditch to take advantage of the slight depression in levels caused by the sagging of the earlier ditch fills.

Contents of F33:

Gallo-Roman pottery	Rims	Bases	Bodysherds	Remarks
Redware			1	the base and central portion of a soft redware flagon

Finds from the area surrounding the anvil stone are grouped with those from F17, layer 1.

Features 133 and 35 (Fig. 32) Late La Tène and Gallo-Roman
On the surface of the silted-up ditch, at the interface of layer 1 and the overlying ploughsoils, appeared a flattish heap of granite stones. The possibility that these might have acted as a marker for a grave was considered but no signs of any inserted feature could be seen. The stones appeared merely to rest upon the surface of layer 1. At a depth of 0.5 m beneath the stones, lying at the base of layer 1, a deposit of limpet shell and animal bone appeared. The section taken at this point showed clearly that the two features were not related in any way. Neither feature contained finds other than the shell and animal bone, which are discussed in the relevant specialist report.

Feature 19 (Fig. 28) Late La Tène
A well-cut post-hole, 0.35 m in diameter by 0.38 m deep. Filled with a soft brown sandy loam; a darker stain showing in section at the centre indicated a post-mould. Several packing stones at the base of the feature. This post-hole stands in isolation on the otherwise featureless strip of land immediately to the west of the main ditch (F17).

KING'S ROAD 1983
SITE 4

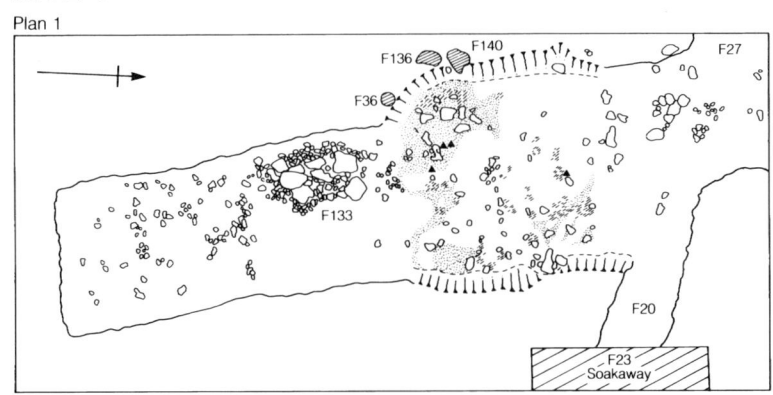

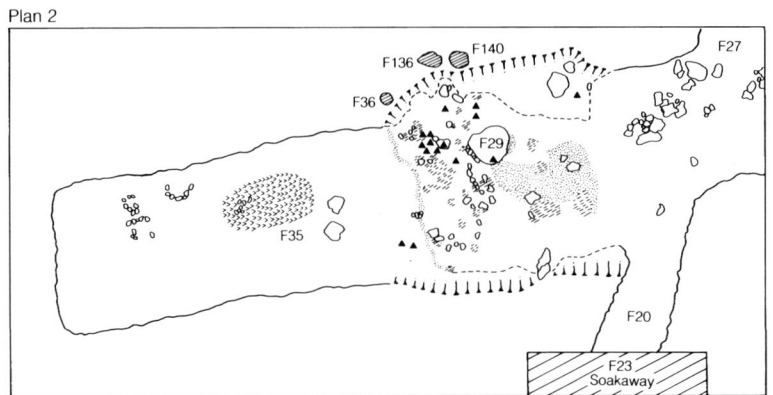

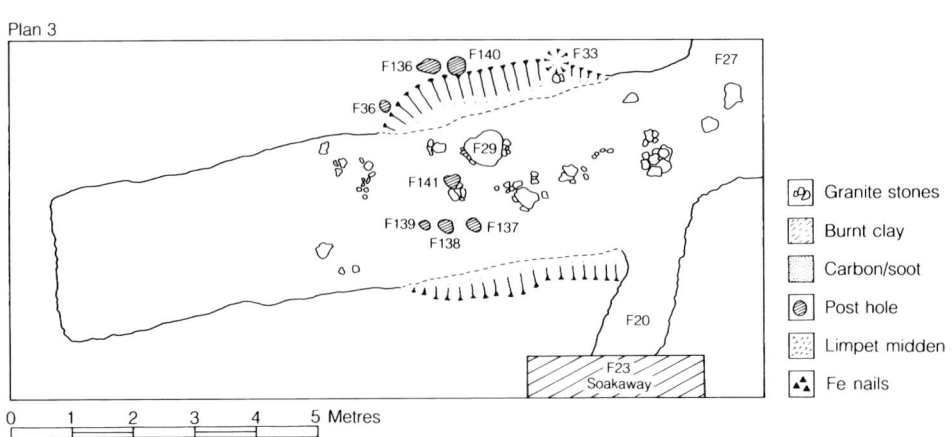

Figure 32 *King's Road, Site 4: plan of Gallo-Roman working area.*

Figure 33 *King's Road, Site 4: F29, the anvil in the main ditch.*

Contents:

Pre-Roman pottery	Rims	Bases	Bodysherds	Remarks
Fabric 2			1	

Feature 27 (Fig. 25) Gallo-Roman
A flat-bottomed gully running into the main ditch (F17) from the northern baulk of the site. The full extent of the feature is unknown. Filled with a homogeneous brown sandy loam with water-worn granite boulders. The possibility that this feature was a continuation of F20, the gully running into the main ditch on its eastern side, was discounted.

Both gullies had deposited clearly separate and recognizable gravel and silt deposits onto the fill of the main ditch.

Contents:

Pre-Roman pottery	Rims	Bases	Bodysherds	Remarks
Fabric 1			4	
Fabric 2			4	
Gallo-Roman pottery				
TN Type			1	
Greyware			1	

Features 28, 66, 61, 60 and 71 (Fig. 34) Medieval
A series of round-bottomed gullies at the western end of the site, all aligned on a north-south axis. They are aligned with the severely truncated gullies met with on Site 1 and formed part of a medieval cultivation system. The area at the southern extremity of the site between F28 and the main ditch was pock-marked by the shallow V- or U-shaped cuts caused by spade-cultivation. F71, the westernmost of the gullies had been neatly recut along its entire length by a replacement gully, F60.

Contents of F28:

Pre-Roman pottery	Rims	Bases	Bodysherds	Remarks
Fabric 1			9	
Fabric 2			3	
Gallo-Roman pottery				
TN Type			1	
Medieval pottery				
NGW	1		4	
Flint				5

Contents of F66: Nil.

Contents of F61:

Pre-Roman pottery	Rims	Bases	Bodysherds	Remarks
Fabric 1			8	
Gallo-Roman pottery				
TN Type			1	
Flagon type			1	
Medieval pottery				
NGW			3	
Flint			1	

Figure 34 *King's Road, Site 4: F28, a medieval gully, showing medieval spade cultivation traces at the top of the picture.*

Contents of F60:

Pre-Roman pottery	Rims	Bases	Bodysherds	Remarks
Fabric 1			6	
Fabric 2			2	
Gallo-Roman pottery				
Greyware	2		2	
Medieval pottery				
NGW			14	
SWF green			1	
Flint			2	

Contents of F71:

Pre-Roman pottery	Rims	Bases	Bodysherds	Remarks
Fabric 1			4	
Medieval pottery				
NGW			7	
Rouen			1	decorated, applied pad

Note on the medieval wares
The small, neat appearance of the few rim-forms in this group indicates a date spanning the period from the end of the fourteenth to the end of the fifteenth centuries AD. This would also include the single sherd of a South Western French green glazed wine jug and the decorative pad from the Rouen jug, which is parallelled by examples found at Southampton and at Paris.

Features 31 and 37, and post- and stake-holes 74, 75, 76, 78, 79, 111, 112, 113, 114, 115, 116, 117, 118, 119, 120, 121, 150, etc. (Fig. 35)
Gallo-Roman
The purpose of these two features, later considered as possibly being part of a single complex, remains unclear. That they belong to the second phase of occupation of the site is amply demonstrated by the pottery finds. F37 was situated at the northern tip of the complex and comprised an oven or perhaps a kiln of some type, with part of its clay capping still intact. Apart from potsherds, some of which had been considerably abraded, nothing to indicate the possible use of this feature was discovered. The soils inside and around the oven had been reddened by heating and there were small scraps of charcoal scattered around. Small angular granite stones were found both inside and around the feature. Whether these formed part of the capping or of an internal structure, if there was one, was unclear. The feature widened at the southern end into an irregular 'working-hollow' some 4 m by 3 m across. The southern end, divided from the narrow northern portion by a series of post- and stake-holes, was designated F31. F31 was similar in character to F37. The area had been worn away to a depth of approximately 0.45 m to 0.5 m and the depression was filled with a very dirty and greasy brown loam flecked with fired clay fragments and charcoal. A major difference however from F37 was the presence of quantities of granite stones which had been subjected to considerable heating. The stones presented a fairly random appearance, with the exception of one area close to the south-eastern extremity of the feature, where a neatly laid circle of burnt stones appeared.

The post- and stake-holes associated with F31/37 were placed roughly centrally across its middle, extending southward down its western edge. A larger post-hole (F78) appeared slightly to the north of the central row. This had been sealed by the fill of the feature and was possibly an earlier roof-support, later replaced.

This feature, whether used for domestic or industrial purposes, would appear to have had an outside oven or kiln with a roofed-over area to the south. Judging by the burnt stones and charcoal, heating also played a part in the activities undertaken under the roofed area. Just what these processes were, we were unable to discover.

Contents of F31:

Pre-Roman pottery	Rims	Bases	Bodysherds	Remarks
Fabric 1	1		2	
Gallo-Roman pottery				
Greyware			1	
Daub			1	
Slag			1	

Contents of F37:

Pre-Roman pottery	Rims	Bases	Bodysherds	Remarks
Fabric 1	5	1	45	all very small
Fabric 2			15	all very small
Fabric 3			1	
Fabric 4			18	
Gallo-Roman pottery				
Greyware			5	
Pink flagon	1	1	1	1 handle
White flagon			5	
TN type	2		14	
Samian			1	very abraded
Amphora				1 handle
Daub				2 pieces
Flint				15
Slag				6 pieces

Contents of F78:

Pre-Roman pottery	Rims	Bases	Bodysherds	Remarks
Fabric 2			3	
Flint			1	

Contents of F79:

Pre-Roman pottery	Rims	Bases	Bodysherds	Remarks
Fabric 1			8	all very small
Fabric 2			1	
Fabric 3			1	
Gallo-Roman pottery				
TN type	1			
Flint			1	

Contents of F112:

Pre-Roman pottery	Rims	Bases	Bodysherds	Remarks
Fabric 1			1	
Gallo-Roman pottery				
Gritty-buff fabric			1	

KING'S ROAD 1983 SITE 4
Features 31 and 37 the 'working area' and oven

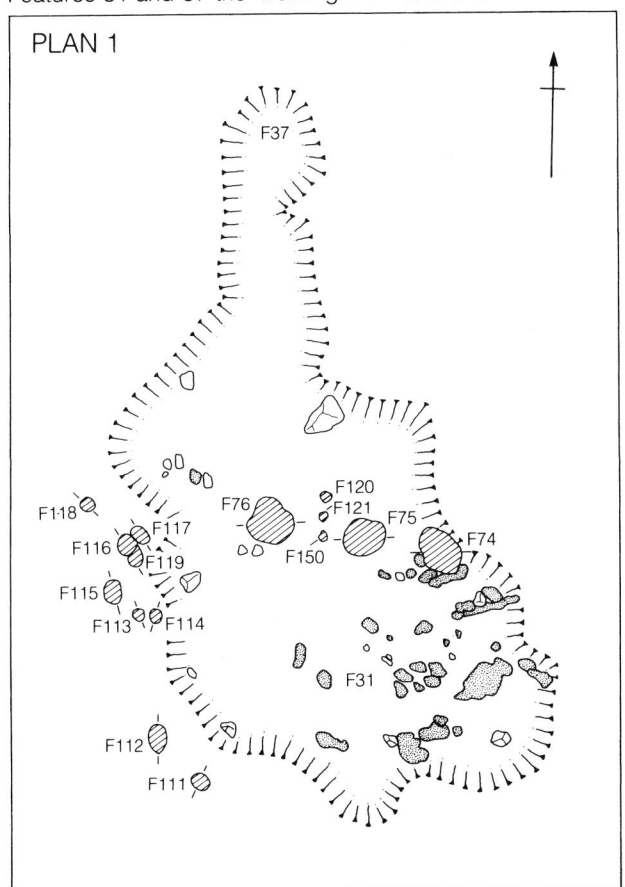

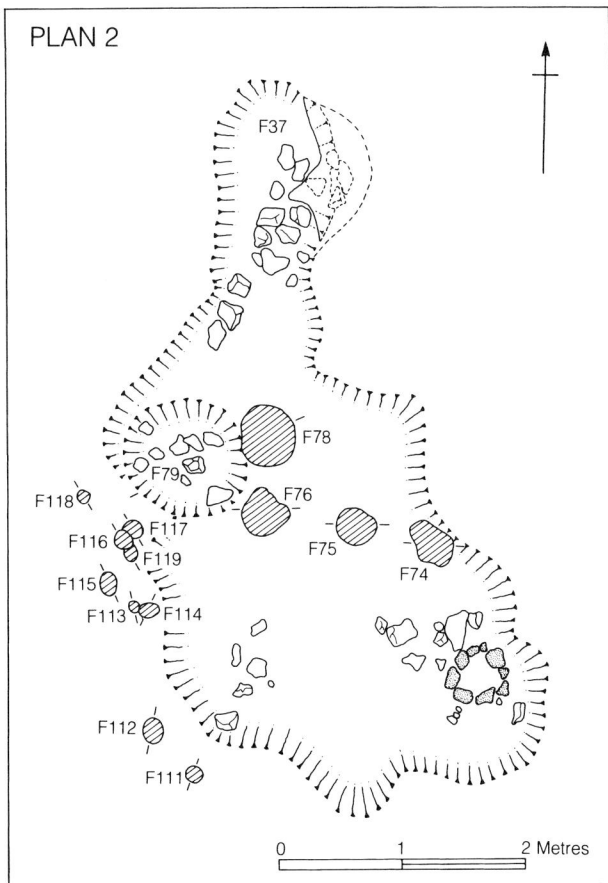

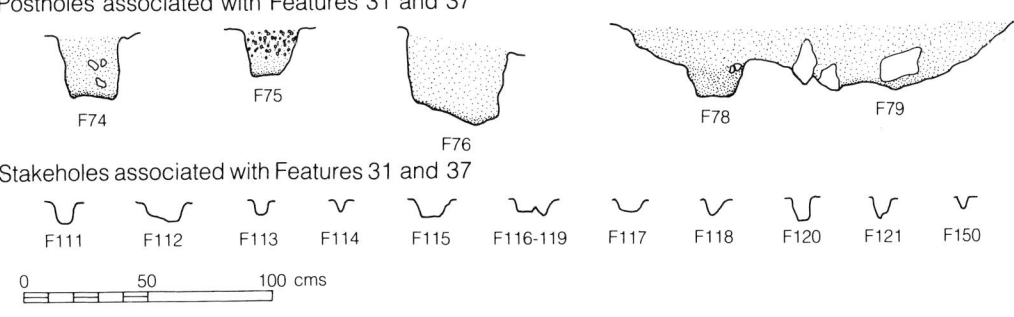

Figure 35 *King's Road, Site 4: plan of Gallo-Roman working area.*

Features 80-110 (Fig. 36) Medieval?
A flimsy building, or perhaps more accurately a shelter, constructed from small stakes and situated between gullies F61 and F60/71. The stake-holes had been cut into the fill of F61 but had been removed by the cutting of F60/71. As the gullies appear clearly to be medieval, it is possible that this slight structure belongs approximately to the same period *c*.AD 1300-1400. The stake-holes were well-cut and clear and all were filled with sandy brown loam. A small, rebated porch-like entrance was situated centrally along the eastern side of the structure.

Contents: Nil.

Features 62, 123, 124 and 125 Gallo-Roman
A large, shallow depression approximately 5 m in diameter by 0.18 to 0.25 m deep. The feature had been obliterated at its northern end by the second of the two modern soakaways (F32). The medieval gullies (F60/71 and F61) either cut through it or partially impinged upon it. The exact purpose or cause for this depression remains unclear; it was referred to during the excavation as a 'working-area' but could have possibly been the worn floor of a circular structure. Several post-holes were associated with the interior of F62. It is possible that these were posts for roof-supports; they were all severely truncated by later agricultural activity. The depression was filled with a dirty soft brown loam, almost free from rock inclusions, with smears of daub and heavily flecked with charcoal. The presence of the later Gallo-Roman pottery in its fill shows that it belongs firmly to the later phase of the site.

Contents of F62:

Pre-Roman pottery	Rims	Bases	Bodysherds	Remarks
Fabric 1			4	
Fabric 2			1	
Gallo-Roman pottery				
Greyware			1	
Fine buffware			1	

Feature 77 Medieval/Post-Medieval?
A circular pit or post-hole cut into the north-western corner of F62, adjacent to the modern soakaway (F32). Filled with a gritty soft brown loam.

Contents:

Medieval pottery	Rims	Bases	Bodysherds	Remarks
NGW			1	very small abraded sherd

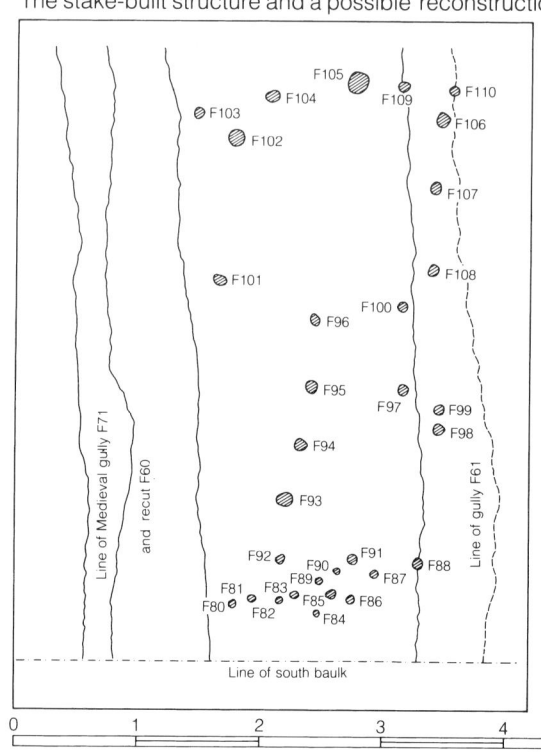
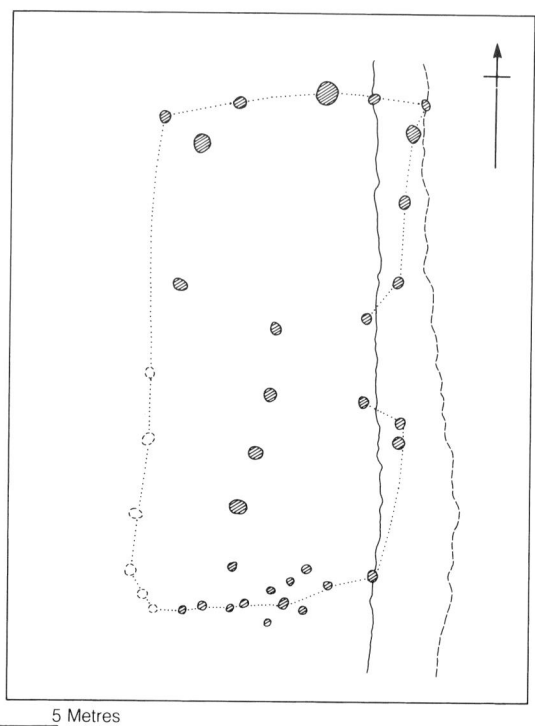
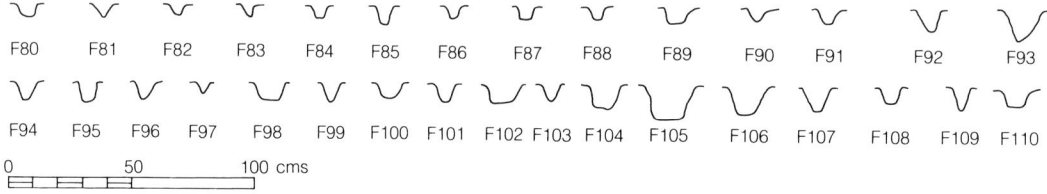

Figure 36 *King's Road, Site 4: plan of stake-built structure.*

Feature 55 Late La Tène
An elongated pit bisected by the western baulk of the site, approximately 3 m in length by 0.75 m deep. Filled with a soft brown sandy loam with rock inclusions.

Contents:

Pre-Roman pottery	Rims	Bases	Bodysherds	Remarks
Fabric 1			1	
Fabric 2			7	

Feature 64 Late La Tène
A shallow, flat-bottomed pit 1.05 m in diameter by 0.28 m deep. Filled with a soft brown sandy loam; a group of packing stones lay at its base. Truncated by later activity.

Contents:

Pre-Roman pottery	Rims	Bases	Bodysherds	Remarks
Fabric 1			12	
Slag				1

Feature 63 Late La Tène
A shallow, flat-bottomed pit 1.15 m in diameter by 0.1 m deep. Cut on its eastern edge by the medieval gully (F71). Filled with a soft brown sandy loam, a few water-worn small pebbles on its surface. Truncated by later activity.

Contents:

Pre-Roman pottery	Rims	Bases	Bodysherds	Remarks
Fabric 1			28	from same pot
Fabric 2			1	

Feature 65 Late La Tène or Gallo-Roman
A flat-bottomed, straight-sided pit 0.57 m in diameter by 0.19 m deep. Filled with a soft brown sandy loam with some possible packing stones on its surface. Truncated by later activity.

Contents: Nil.

Feature 72 Late La Tène or Gallo-Roman
A small, round-bottomed post-hole, 0.43 m in diameter by 0.24 m deep. Filled with a stone-free, soft brown sandy loam.

Contents: Nil.

Feature 70 Late La Tène
The termination ? of a shallow gully emerging from the west baulk of the site close to the north-western corner. Filled with a stone-free, soft brown sandy loam.

Contents:

Pre-Roman pottery	Rims	Bases	Bodysherds	Remarks
Fabric 1			2	
Fabric 2			1	

The pottery (Figs. 37-49)

Introduction

The pottery assemblages recovered from the King's Road excavations range in date from the later Bronze Age to the post-medieval period, but by far the greatest quantity belongs to the Late La Tène and Gallo-Roman period *c*.100 BC to AD 250.

Although the total quantity of Late Bronze Age and Early Iron Age pottery is small the fact that it has been recovered under modern conditions adds considerably to its value. Only two recently excavated sites have produced Late Bronze Age pottery, Les Fouaillages (Kinnes forthcoming) and La Banque à Barque (Hill 1990), and Early Iron Age wares were hitherto unknown.

Until recently the only Late La Tène pottery known on the island came from a series of burials discovered during the nineteenth and early twentieth centuries (described below, pp. 83-116), and from an unpublished discovery made by Lukis on Herm in the nineteenth century (described here for the first time, pp. 122-4). The excavation at the Tranquesous (Burns 1977) produced a small quantity of Late La Tène material from the earliest levels, but the site is best known for an important assemblage belonging to the earliest Roman period *c*.50 BC-AD 30.

The first century BC and early first century AD was a time when trade between Armorica and central southern Britain seems to have intensified. Detailed work in Brittany and at Hengistbury Head on the Dorset coast have allowed the identification of a range of distinctive Armorican pottery types and fabrics which were exported in quantity to Hengistbury. Some of these types have been found at King's Road, enabling a degree of precision in dating to be offered. Thin-sectioning of the Guernsey fabrics in the hope of distinguishing imports has only been partially successful because the surface geology and superficial deposits of the island are similar to those of the neighbouring Armorican peninsula. Local fabrics were also long-lived: one of the fabrics defined here as Fabric 1 began in the Early Iron Age and was still being used in second-fourth century AD contexts at La Plaiderie (St. Peter Port).

The Gallo-Roman wares and the amphorae found at King's Road added to the growing corpus of such material from the island. The excavations at La Plaiderie produced considerable quantities of late Roman wares emanating from many sources during the period second to fourth centuries AD. Further evidence from this period has been obtained from the third century AD wreck raised from St. Peter Port harbour (Rule and Monaghan 1993) and from various other marine sites situated around the east coast of the island (Burns and Burns 1986 and Monaghan 1990).

The medieval wares from King's Road are not of great significance. They are commented upon only where their presence in a feature is relevant to its dating.

Post-medieval pottery, present in the upper horizons of the site, is not discussed here. Similar wares are found in quantity on many sites throughout the island and these have been discussed at some length in previous reports. The forthcoming publication of the series of excavations at Castle Cornet will contain a comprehensive report on post-medieval pottery typical of that found on many island sites (Barton and Burns forthcoming).

In the report to follow we discuss the pottery in chronological order as follows:

Bronze Age pottery (nos. 1-8) found in ditch F10 on Site 1.

Early Iron Age pottery (nos. 176-222) found in ditch F5 on Site 2.

Late La Tène pottery (nos. 9-175) from Sites 1 and 4.

Gallo-Roman pottery (nos. 223-52) from Sites 1 and 4.

Medieval pottery (nos. 253-5) from Site 4.

Then follows a catalogue of the illustrated pottery.

The Bronze Age pottery (Fig. 40, nos. 1-8)

The recognizable Bronze Age wares found during the excavation formed only a very small proportion of the total pottery recovered. It is likely that most, if not all of the sherds, were, like the scattered flintwork, derived from original ground surface spreads, and redeposited in Iron Age features. All of the illustrated sherds were found in the main ditch (F10) on Site 1. Several undiagnostic bodysherds, possibly of Bronze Age date, were also found on the other sites. Some of these sherds may, in fact, be of Early Iron Age date.

The fabric of the Bronze Age wares was invariably fine and virtually untempered, this also being the case with the thicker sherds of cooking-pot type wares. The fabrics closely resemble those seen in the wide range of beaker-type wares in the collections of the Guernsey Museum.

The range of forms illustrated is mainly restricted to narrow-walled tall jars, perhaps of beaker form. No. 3 has a groove situated just beneath the rim. The rims are rounded and only slightly everted. Thicker bodysherds were also discovered and one base of this kind is illustrated (no. 4).

The only decoration noted on the Bronze Age wares took the form of incised grooves, both on the upper and lower portions of the vessels.

Early-Middle Iron Age pottery (Figs. 47-8, nos. 176-222)

On Site 2 an earlier phase of Iron Age occupation was demonstrated by the wares found in the primary fill of ditch F5, into which two of the later burials had been inserted. This ditch produced virtually all of the Early Iron Age wares under discussion here, although odd sherds were found in other features associated with it. The ditch lay well to the south of the main Late La Tène-Gallo-Roman occupation area.

The fabrics were, in some cases, similar to those encountered on Sites 1 and 4 and a full description of them is noted in the following section on the Late La Tène wares. Fabrics which differ from the Late La Tène typology are prefixed LPC and comprise fabrics LPC 3 to 6. In almost every case the wares from this earlier phase demonstrated a much cruder appearance and finish from those of the Late La Tène group.

The bipartite haematite-coated bowl (no. 222) is very similar in form and ware to vessels dating to the seventh-fifth centuries BC in central southern Britain. The large jar (no. 218) has its closest parallels in Brittany at about the same time.

Fabric 1

This is identical in all respects to Fabric 1 in the later La Tène series. It is a coarseware with varying proportions of quartz filler ranging in size from very small to quite large grains 5 mm in diameter. Fabric 1 differs from Fabric 2 in that it is always of a reduced colour ranging from black to light brown. Thin-sectioning indicates the use of local clays for the production of these wares (below, p. 48).

The forms met with in this fabric comprise, in the main, taller jars with slightly everted rims, similar to those found at Hengistbury Head, which are considered to pre-date the later La Tène wares (Cunliffe 1987, 217, ill. 136). The bases of several large vessels, possibly cooking-pots, were recovered.

A pierced lug (no. 183) was also found. These are well known from sites in Brittany (Daire 1992, 112-17 and Langouet 1989, 100) but until the present excavation, were unknown in Guernsey. A pedestal base from a tall narrow vessel with a pronounced omphalos was discovered. This vessel was hand-made and fairly crude in appearance (no. 190).

Decoration was absent from this ware.

Fabric 2

Fabric 2 is basically the same in composition as Fabric 1, the major difference to the eye being the fact that the wares are oxidized, ranging in colour from orange-pink to dark red.

The sherds illustrated are mainly of small size and the forms difficult to ascertain. It would appear that many of them represented small open bowls similar in form to those found among the later La Tène material.

One sherd (no. 197) was finished externally with a tooled, rilled finish.

LPC 3 (nos. 199-210)

A finely sorted fabric with very small quartz inclusions, the surfaces burnished, on occasion inside as well as externally. The colour range met with varied from dark chocolate-brown to orange-brown. Many of the sherds recovered in this fabric had suffered from the effects of the acidic soil and showed signs of weathering.

Most illustrated fragments are really too small to form any definite conclusions as to the original form of the vessels they represent. Several have vestigial bead rims and most seem to come from slightly globular jars of relatively small size. There were two lid fragments and a lid knob or handle recovered (nos. 206-8) and in general lids were more common on Sites 2 and 3 than on the other areas excavated.

Decoration was absent from this assemblage but one sherd had several incisions on its internal surface caused by knife-cuts during usage (no. 209).

LPC 4 (nos. 211-17)

A finely sorted fabric with a noticeably soapy feel. Surfaces were smoothed in all cases. Surfaces were brown, the fracture exhibiting a brown to orange colour.

The sherds recovered were all small but the forms appear to be similar to those produced in Fabric LPC 3, small closed bowls and a lid. Several rims had a vestigial bead.

Decoration was not observed in this fabric.

LPC 5 (nos. 218-19)

Fairly hard, smooth fabric with many small white grains of felspar scattered throughout with a lightish grey outer surface and darker inner surface and core. Thin-sectioning by Dr. David Williams shows a generally similar range of non-plastic inclusions described for Fabric 1 (below, p. 48), but somewhat finer-textured in this case.

Of the two sherds illustrated only one (no. 218) can be paralleled. It is a shoulder sherd with a circular concave depression at its widest point. The reconstruction illustrated is based upon a vessel found at Roz-an-Trémen, Finistère (Giot, Briard and Pape 1979, 237).

Apart from the impressed circle on the vessel above, decoration was absent in this fabric.

LPC 6 (nos. 220-1)

A hard grey, sandy fabric which is orange to orange-brown in fracture. Surface finish is rough to the touch.

Very small quantities of this fabric were recovered and it is not possible to be specific about the forms represented; one did have a vestigial bead-rim.

Decoration was absent from the sherds recovered.

Haematite-coated ware (no. 222)

A finely sorted hard sandy fabric, pale orange throughout. Traces of red haematite survive on the external surface.

The vessel represented was a small bowl with a carinated shoulder: decoration was by coating with an iron-rich slip.

Late La Tène pottery (Figs. 41-6, nos. 9-175)

The major group of pottery recovered from the King's Road excavations comprised wares from this period, which covers approximately the first half of the first century BC. Imports from Armorica were identified but they represent only a small percentage of the total assemblage. It should, however, be noted that those wares regarded as locally manufactured could well include imported varieties, since the clays from the island and those from the neighbouring Armorican peninsula are in many cases indistinguishable. The range of forms represented are very similar to those found in neighbouring Brittany and on the southern coasts of England.

Imported pottery (Fig. 41)

Rilled wares (nos. 9-11)
These were characterized by the presence of fine external rilling made on the wheel with a small pointed implement. These wares can be paralleled at Hengistbury Head (Cunliffe 1987, 235, ill. 154). A wide range of these wares were present at Le Moulin de la Rive, Locquirec, Finistère, on the north coast of Brittany (Giot, Daire and Querre 1986, 89-91, pls. 33-5).

The wares are characterized by the presence of large quantities of mica flakes in the matrix which also includes grains of felspar and quartz. The colour range varies from brown-black to a pinkish brown.

The forms represented at King's Road are of deep bowls with everted rims. One rim (no. 9) has two grooves at the top of the shoulder; the rilling is restricted to the lower half of the vessel.

Multiple fine striations made on the outer surface with a pointed tool.

Black cordoned wares (nos. 12-19 and 22-3)
Characterized by a fine black burnished finish. The wares are finely potted and great care has been taken in their manufacture. The pots bear cordons, always present above their widest girth. They were probably made in the Côtes-d'Armor and examples have been found at Alet (Langouet 1978, pl. 1) and Le Petit Celland (Wheeler and Richardson 1957, fig. 8). Large quantities have also been found at Hengistbury Head (Cunliffe 1987, 310).

The fabrics are invariably hard and finely sorted, containing quantities of grains of amphibole and felspars. Although these are almost certainly imported it should be noted that amphibole-bearing rocks are present close to St. Peter Port.

The forms represented are, in the main, shallow bowls with everted rims. There are examples of vessels with straighter sides (nos. 18 and 19) which are also probably from small bowls. One base (no. 23) appears to come from a pedestal type vessel with a pronounced omphalos.

Decoration is restricted to finely produced cordons on the upper portions of the vessels.

Graphite-coated wares (nos. 20-1)
A graphite-coated bowl was present among the rich array of grave goods found in the burial at La Hougue au Comte, discovered during the late nineteenth century (below, Fig. 71, no. 2). This form of decoration was extremely rare at King's Road, only two sherds being found. Graphite-coated wares were present in significant quantities at Hengistbury, where three different fabrics were discerned (Cunliffe 1987, 314). One sherd of graphite-coated ware was examined in the laboratory by Prof. P.R. Giot at Rennes University. He remarks that whilst, like the Breton varieties, it is rich in amphiboles, it differs in having a higher mica content. The production area of this particular variety of pottery would seem to be somewhere in the western half of Brittany, though it should be noted that the site at the Ile des Ebihens on the north coast, about 15 km west of St. Malo, has produced large quantities of the ware (Langouet 1989).

The fabrics present at King's Road were finely sorted, with few inclusions, the surfaces were black to grey-black and the fractures exhibited a grey and a brown-buff coloration.

The only vessel represented was a shallow cordoned bowl with graphite-coating around its upper part, above the cordons. Graphite-coating also extended in vertical lines on the lower half of the pot (no. 20). A graphite-coated bodysherd (no. 21) had a large cordon, pushed out from the inside. It was not possible to deduce the final form of the pot it came from.

The only decoration takes the form of graphite-coating and cordons.

Local fabrics (Figs. 42-6, nos. 24-175)

Six distinctive fabric types considered to be of local origin were discerned among the wares discovered on Sites 1 and 4. Fabrics 1, 2 and 2 sherds of Fabric 3 were also present on Sites 2 and 3. Although a comprehensive programme of thin-sectioning has not yet been carried out on the pottery, some sherds have been examined and the results are included in the respective sections. Fabrics 1 and 2, which are the most regularly met with, have a long duration, being found from the Early-Middle Iron Age until the third century AD. Positive dating is only possible where these fabrics display distinctive forms, or are otherwise securely stratified with other, more short-lived types.

Fabric 1 (nos. 24-52)
The fabric is coarse and granular and the hand lens shows angular inclusions of quartz and felspar; these inclusions range from near colourless to white. The inclusions vary in size from 1 mm to large pieces approaching 5 mm in diameter. The fabric has a colour range from brown through to black. Thin-sectioning by David Williams characterized the fabric as:

> Fairly hard gritty fabric, with one of the sherds showing a reasonably smooth outer surface. Many visible inclusions of small grains of white felspar and with the odd fragment of rock showing. The sherd has a reddish-brown outer surface and a grey inner surface and central core. Thin-sectioning and study under the microscope shows discrete angular turbid grains of partly decomposed felspar, plus fresher grains of mainly plagioclase and some potash felspar, quartz, disaggregated grains of amphibole, with occasional larger pieces made up of fibrous aggregates, a little pyroxene and some fragments of diorite(?).

The petrology closely matches the geology of the region just to the north of St. Peter Port, which has an area of gabbro surrounded by rocks of a mainly dioritic or granitic composition. Without further information, this would seem to suggest the use of local raw materials for this pottery. It is interesting to note, for example, that gabbroic clay from the Lizard peninsula in Cornwall was also utilized for prehistoric pottery, found widely distributed in south-west Britain (Peacock 1969, 41-61).

The vessels are, in the main, fairly heavily potted and coarse in appearance. Rims come in a variety of types, from slightly everted to widely flared (no. 40). Some rims have well-made beads (no. 26) but beads are mostly fairly insubstantial and crude. Two vessels (nos. 24 and 25) have a straight everted rim topping rounded bodies. One rim (no. 41) has a handle stub springing from its top. Bases are always flat. There appears to have been no attempt made to copy the imported shapes in this fabric, the vessels being either of cooking pot form or of smaller globular or ovoid drinking cups.

Decoration is scarce. One sherd (no. 38) has an applied strip with circular impressions. One rim (no. 39) has a 'pie-crust' decoration on its flat upper edge. Burnished vertical lines can be seen on one bodysherd (no. 42).

Fabric 2 (nos. 53-71)
This fabric is essentially the same as for Fabric 1. It differs only in that it has been fired in an oxidizing atmosphere resulting in a colour range from pink to dark red.

It was given a separate category to ease the task of sorting.

Once again the small size of the identifiable sherds made it difficult to be positive as to the range of forms represented.

Small ovoid drinking vessels are represented by a series of slightly everted curved rims (nos. 53-61). One rim has an internal groove and a slight bead (no. 62). Bases are mostly flat and one (no. 66) shows signs of knife-trimming externally. One base (no. 68) has a hand-built foot-ring.

Little decoration was present. Two bodysherds bore linear incised grooves (nos. 64 and 65).

Fabric 3 (nos. 72-117)
Fabric 3 is similar in some respects to Fabrics 1 and 2 but is harder, more finely sorted and always has a vesicular surface appearance. This almost certainly represents the leaching out of grains of aggregate. Vessels in Fabric 3 are present among the grave goods from the burials discovered in the nineteenth and early twentieth centuries (see p. 104) and also among the wares recovered from the Tranquesous, St. Saviour's. Thin-sectioning by David Williams leads to the following characterization:

> Hard, smoothish, somewhat vesicular fabric, with visible inclusions of small white grains of felspar, more or less darkish grey throughout. Thin-sectioning shows a similar composition of inclusions to Fabric 1 and LPC Fabric 5. The vesicles on the surfaces of these two sherds presumably represent the disintegration of some of the felspar grains, most likely due to adverse burial conditions.

The range of forms manufactured in this fabric is much more adventurous than in those preceding. The pots are also more finely made with care given to their appearance. If the fabric is indeed local the forms are possibly modelled on the imported Late La Tène wares, as the effects closely resemble the identifiable imports. Shallow bowls are commonly represented (nos. 72-103), and although there are plain examples (nos. 72, 73 and 75), these invariably possess cordons and grooves.

Some bowls have crude cordons or perhaps more correctly, corrugations giving a wreathed appearance externally (nos. 99-104). The bases found are always flat and some of the bases appear to belong to taller, more constricted jars (nos. 106-9).

Decoration on this fabric takes the form of thin burnished lines in geometric patterns (no. 105) or simply running vertically down the pot (nos. 99 and 108). Several bases had the lowest portion visibly darker, probably a result of the firing process (no. 108). Vessels with similar burnished lines were found at the Ile des Ebihens, St. Jacut de la Mer, close to St. Malo (Daire 1992, 127-8; Langouet 1989, 56, 62, 72 and 73).

Fabric 4 (nos. 118-45)

Fabric 4 is a fine hard black ware. The matrix is finely sorted with small angular grains of quartz ranging from near colourless to white. Very small mica flakes are present in small quantities. Outer surfaces are smooth and well burnished and have a colour range from very dark brown to black. There is a possible variant in this fabric; a number of sherds (in which the fabric is identical in all respects) display an oxidized colour, ranging from buff-pink to pink. These sherds (nos. 135, 137 and 138) have been included in this section but it is possible that they do in fact represent an entirely separate category.

The forms met with in this fabric appear to be shallow bowls although one vessel (no. 118) could be a deeper variety.

Rims are mostly simply everted although some are neatly turned over to produce a round bead (nos. 122-4). They are well finished, showing a high degree of skill in their manufacture.

One rim (no. 129) has an internal groove. Bases have foot-rings and can be convex or slightly concave (nos. 144 and 145).

Decoration takes the form of burnished lines either in geometric pattern (no. 139), or in pairs vertically down the pot (nos. 140-2). One bodysherd has a post-firing hole pierced through the wall (no. 142).

Fabric 5 (nos. 146-67)

This fabric is hard and sandy with a rough, but not coarse, surface feel. Inclusions consist of very small grains of quartz and felspar. The colour range is mostly grey based but can extend to greyish pink or pink-brown in the fracture.

Most of the illustrated sherds are from shallow bowls although several could represent taller, more constricted types. One rim (no. 146) appears to be hand-made with a crude attempt at a cordon just below the rim. Bases in particular have had considerable care taken in their manufacture, several have foot-rings and one (no. 157) has a circular groove cut into it.

Bases can be either flat or slightly concave.

Decoration takes the form of vertical burnished lines in pairs. One vessel (no. 160) also has the darker zone around its base, noted in Fabric 3 above.

Fabric 6 (nos. 168-75)

This fabric is finely sorted; the inclusions of white quartz are of extremely small size with only the odd larger grain present. The fabric is characterized by its smooth, soapy feel, quite unlike any other found on the excavations. Rubbing the fabric leaves the fingers with a greasy sensation, similar to that produced by the later medieval 'céramique onctueuse' produced in Brittany. In the medieval variety the presence of talc in the rock accounts for the surface feel and it is likely that this King's Road Iron Age fabric also contains talc. The colour range extends from grey-brown through to a pink-brown.

The sherds worthy of illustration were few and give little idea of the vessel forms that they came from, although once again shallow bowls with everted rims are present.

No decoration was observed on this fabric.

Quantification (Fig. 37)

The diagrams illustrate the total quantities of sherds of each type found on each site and also their weight in grammes. It can be seen that Fabrics 1 and 2 are the most common although this was not reflected in the amount of sherds suitable for illustration. Fabric 3 is only represented by two sherds on Sites 2 and 3 and these sherds were associated with the later insertion of the burials. This leads to the conclusion that Fabric 3 is purely a product of the later phase of the site, say around 100 BC.

Gallo-Roman wares (Figs. 38, 39 and 49)

The Gallo-Roman wares comprise the following groups which are considered by the specialists to whom the sherds were submitted:

Amphorae	by David Williams
Terra sigillata dish	by Brian Hartley
North Gaulish grey ware	by Mark Wood
Terra-nigra type ware	by Mark Wood
Romano-British ware	by Mark Wood
Coarse grey ware	by Mark Wood

Roman amphorae by David Williams

Dressel 1

In all 19 sherds of Dressel 1 amphorae were recovered and are listed here. Of these three have been illustrated (Fig. 38).

1. KR80/F10 (Fig. 38, A1)
   Part of a Dressel 1 rim sherd, intermediate in shape between the earlier Dressel 1A form and the later 1B (Peacock 1971, fig. 37, no. 16).

2. KR80/F1 (Fig. 38, A3)
   Part of a Dressel 1 handle, the 'chunky' nature of the sherd suggests that it is probably from the 1B form (Stockli 1979).

3. KR83/F17/B6/L3 (Not illustrated)
   Four Dressel 1 bodysherds, possibly from the same fabric as no. 2.

Site 1

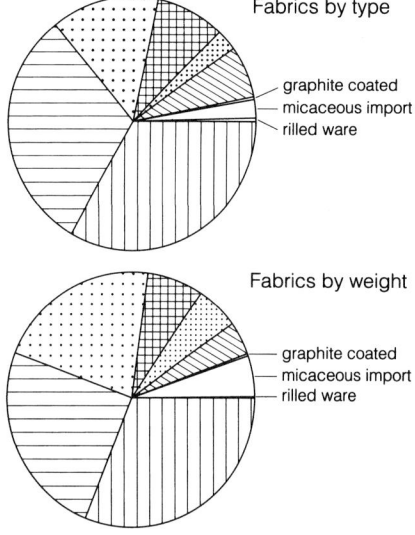

Fabric Type	Quantity	Weight
1. Fabric 1	284	2014
2. Fabric 2	263	1577
3. Fabric 3	123	1376
4. Fabric 4	77	488
5. Fabric 5	21	344
6. Fabric 6	59	276
7. Graphite Coated	2	2
8. Micaceous Import	23	359
9. Rilled Ware	2	2
Total	854	6438

Site 2

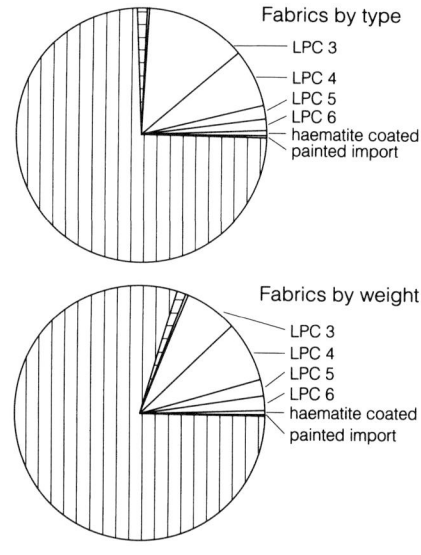

Fabric Type	Quantity	Weight
1. Fabric 1	620	5472
2. Fabric 2	11	70
3. Fabric 3	1	10
4. LPC 3	108	499
5. LPC 4	63	511
6. LPC 5	12	137
7. LPC 6	14	109
8. Haematite Coated	2	9
9. Painted Import	1	7
Total	832	6808

Site 3

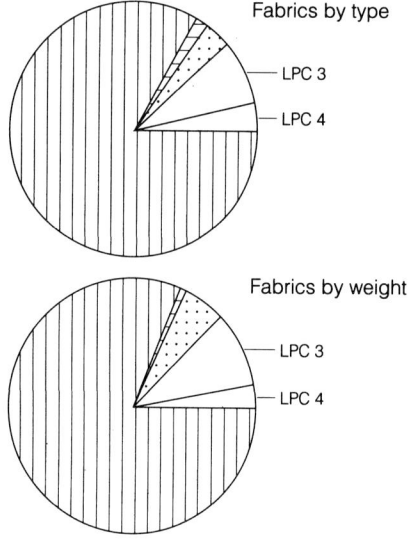

Fabric Type	Quantity	Weight
1. Fabric 1	50	231
2. Fabric 2	1	2
3. Fabric 3	2	15
4. LPC 3	5	26
5. LPC 4	2	8
Total	60	282

Site 4

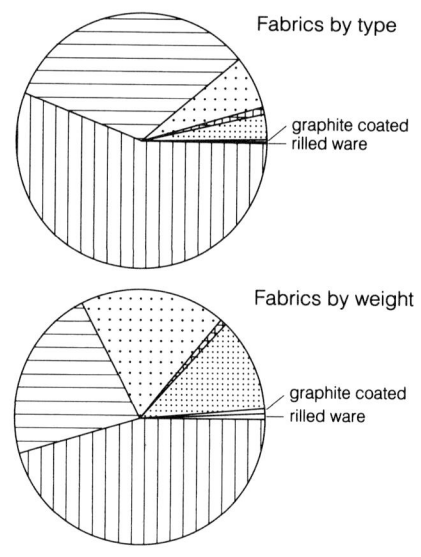

Fabric Type	Quantity	Weight
1. Fabric 1	376	2489
2. Fabric 2	221	1217
3. Fabric 3	47	1039
4. Fabric 4	5	34
5. Fabric 5	21	668
6. Graphite Coated	1	8
7. Rilled Ware	1	53
Total	672	5508

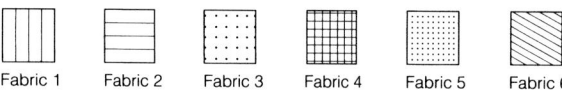

Figure 37 *Quantification of pottery fabrics.*

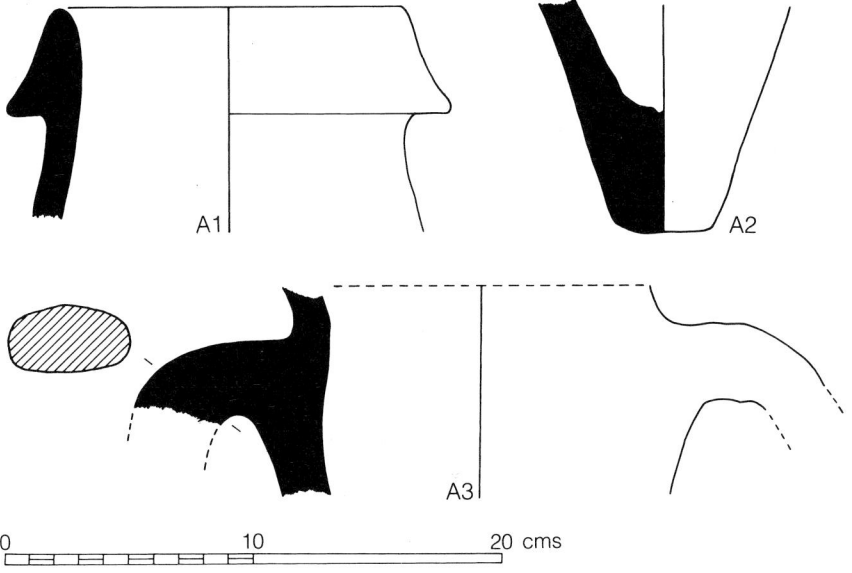

Figure 38 *King's Road: Amphorae.*

4. KR/83/F17/B5/L2 (Not illustrated)
Dressel 1 bodysherd.

5. KR83/F17/B6/L2 (Fig. 38, A2)
A small part of a Dressel 1 spike and a very friable bodysherd.

6. KR/80/F10 (Not illustrated)
Five Dressel 1 bodysherds.

7. KR83/F17/B3/L3 (Not illustrated)
Four Dressel 1 bodysherds, one in the well-known 'black-sand' fabric.

8. KR83/F47 (Not illustrated)
One Dressel 1 bodysherd.

9. KR83/F31/37 (Not illustrated)
Part of a small amphora handle, unassigned.

All the amphora sherds from the La Tène contexts on the site belong to the late Republican amphora form Dressel 1. The handle (no. 2) almost certainly belongs to the 1B type, but it is difficult to decide whether the rim (no. 1) can be assigned to the 1A form or to the 1B, and it is perhaps best regarded as belonging to the change-over period between the two forms. Dressel 1A was produced in Italy from about 130 BC (Tchernia 1983), until around the middle of the first century BC (Lamboglia 1955; Peacock 1971). Dressel 1B appears to have been made from about shortly after the first quarter of the first century BC, until the last decade of that century (Peacock 1971; Sealey 1985). The King's Road rim might tentatively be dated, therefore, c.75-50 BC.

Dressel 1 amphorae were made primarily in the Campanian, Latium and Etrurian districts of Italy and were mainly used to transport wine from those areas. Production of Dressel 1A has recently also been claimed for southern France (Sabir *et al.* 1983), though if this is true, production can only have been on a very small scale compared to the large Italian industry. Macroscopic examination of the King's Road material suggests that all the sherds are in Italian fabrics. One in particular (from no. 7), is in the distinctive 'black-sand' fabric, caused by many dark-coloured inclusions of augite in the paste. This is shown to be associated with the Pompeii-Herculaneum region of Italy (Peacock and Williams 1986, Class 3). The differences in fabric noted at King's Road suggests between five and seven Dressel 1 vessels are represented at the site.

Dressel 1 amphorae have a wide distribution and were undoubtedly one of the more important amphora forms of the Roman world. Recent excavations on both sides of the English Channel have brought to light quantities of these vessels in pre-Roman contexts, although the numbers found in Gaul far and away exceed those found in Britain (Cunliffe 1987; Peacock 1984; Fitzpatrick 1985; Galliou 1984). It should, therefore, present no surprise to find that Guernsey, given its geographical position just off the French coast, should play some part in this trade of Italian wine to Northern Europe.

Dressel 20
A single sherd of a Dressel 20 amphora was found in F20 associated with the samian bowl.

KR80/F20 (Not illustrated)
An everted rim sherd belonging to an amphora or a large flagon in a soft, sandy fabric with traces of a light pinkish slip?, on an orange body. It is difficult to be sure exactly which form is represented here, since the sherd is small and somewhat friable. It is possible that it may be related to the Gauloise series of flat-

bottomed amphorae described by Laubenheimer (Laubenheimer 1986), though it is difficult to place it with any confidence amongst the types presented here.

Author's note: Amphorae of the Gauloise flat-bottomed variety are represented among the wares discovered at La Plaiderie, St. Peter Port.

Terra sigillata dish by Brian Hartley

A complete terra sigillata dish (KR80/F21) was recovered from F21 (Fig. 39, no. 223).

This dish is a standard example of form 31R of the kind normal in Central Gaul in the mid – and late – Antonine period, but also produced at some East Gaulish potteries. Its only unusual feature lies in the nature of the stamp, which has incuse letters reading HONORATI. Such incuse stamps are very uncommon, though they appear occasionally in all the main areas of samian production.

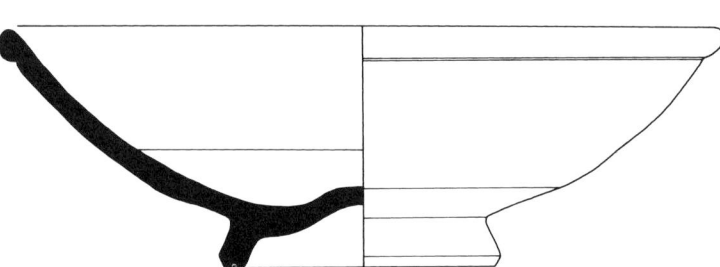

Figure 39 *King's Road: Terra sigillata dish.*

The forms, fabrics and distribution of Honoratus stamps (all from the same die), show conclusively that the potter worked in East Gaul, very probably at Trier. All the other known examples are on dishes either definitely or probably of form 32 and they come from: Altenstadt, Arnsburg-Muschenheim, Heddernheim (9), Saalburg (7) and Riederwald. Two other potters, Augustus ii (AUGUSTUS F; two examples from Dalheim) and a man who simply stamped M (only known from London), were probably associates of Honoratus, as their fabrics are similar and they stamp with incuse letters.

As for date, the dish could not be earlier than AD 160, since the form was only introduced about then, but it could be considerably later, though more probably second than third century in date.

The bowl had been broken by the weight of the overlying deposits but was complete when carefully removed by the building worker. The fabric was initially extremely soft and great care had to be exercised when handling the fragments. A long period was allowed for the fabric to dry out completely but it was still found necessary to impregnate the pieces in 10% PVA in IMS under vacuum, in order to reassemble the vessel.

The surface of the bowl exhibits a slight crazing of the glaze, but is otherwise unmarked. The foot-ring appears virtually unworn.

North Gaulish grey ware (Fig. 49) by Mark Wood

Three sherds in this distinctive fabric were recovered:

KR80/171. F21 (no. 245)
A small sherd from the neck of a beaker in a hard sandy fabric with a distinctive granular texture. The principal inclusions are fine quartz, white mica and small flecks of black iron ore.

The fabric is grey in colour and the external surface is covered in a darker grey self-slip which is burnished in thin lines which are silvery grey in colour.

This vessel dates to the second century AD and probably towards the end of that century, in view of its association with the stamped samian bowl from East Gaul. The discovery of North Gaulish grey wares at La Plaiderie, St. Peter Port (including beakers similar to this example), associated with samian wares from East Gaul, dating to the late second and early third centuries AD, would support such a date for this conical neck beaker from King's Road. Furthermore both of these wares have been found together on English sites and dated within the date-range late second/early third century. Beakers of this type (gobelet à col tronconique) were produced along with a range of other forms including dishes, bowls and jars (Bayard 1980, 189-203) in production centres (some of which have been located and excavated) in the Pas de Calais/Picardy region of northern France (Richardson 1986, 106).

KR83/197. F17/B5/L1 (no. 228)
Rim sherd from a jar in a moderately hard sandy fabric, the core of which is oxidized pale orange-buff in colour, sandwiched between thin grey fringes. Although the surfaces are worn it appears that they were originally covered in a thin dark grey self-slip. There are faint traces of burnished bands on the lower part of the external surface. The jar is similar to the prototype of the 'gobelet à col tronconique' dating to the latter part of the first century AD, as it has the short neck which is typical of such vessels (cf. Richardson and Tyers 1984, 137, fig. 2, no. 1). The fabric of this sherd differs from the previous example in having inclusions of rounded rose quartz and clay pellets. It shares these characteristics with vessels from La Plaiderie which are earlier in date.

KR83/202. F27 (no. 231)
A sherd from a beaker with a plain but slightly everted rim in a sandy and moderately hard fabric which has an orange-brown core with pale grey to off-white fringes. The external surface is covered in a smooth silvery grey slip as is the internal surface for the first centimetre or so down the rim of the vessel. Below this the interior is dark grey in colour.

The fabric contains inclusions similar to those of KR83/197 but is noticeably more fine. The small size of this sherd makes it difficult to ascribe with certainty to a particular vessel form. However it is similar to vessels from La Plaiderie which are clearly related to the carinated beaker form 120A found at Camulodunum (Hawkes and Hull 1947, pl. LVIII). Beakers of this type were produced in the potteries of North Gaul (Tuffreau-Libre 1980, 95). First century examples of this vessel form found at La Plaiderie are in a similar fabric and form to the one from King's Road. This vessel probably dates to the second half of the first century AD. There can be no doubt that this vessel like the one described above from KR83/197 share fabric similarities with vessels from the Plaiderie which are also dated to the first century. Moreover the fabric (despite its oxidized colour), the range of forms and frequently the finish of these earlier vessels are clearly related to the later products from North Gaul found in the island.

Grey ware products of the North Gaulish industries are found in England in contexts dating from the Flavian period through to the mid-third century (Richardson and Tyers 1984, 139) but the majority of the vessels that have been found would appear to have been imported during the late second/early third century, as for example those from New Fresh Wharf, London (Richardson 1986, 106), where considerable quantities of East Gaulish samian were also recovered. Despite the fact that the majority of these North Gaulish grey wares were imported into England during the period from the mid to late Empire it is worth noting that first century examples have been identified at Richborough (Richardson and Tyers 1984, 139) and now in Guernsey at King's Road (see above KR83/197 and 202) and at La Plaiderie. A beaker of North Gaulish type dating to the late first/second century has been found in Alderney (Wood 1990, 54, fig. 4, no. 17).

In addition to the beaker from King's Road (and the other vessels from North Gaul found at the same site), definite examples of North Gaulish grey wares have been discovered on two (and possibly four) further sites on Guernsey. A beaker of second century date decorated with burnished bands, similar to the example from King's Road, was recovered from the bed of the harbour at St. Peter Port (Monaghan 1990, 65) and large quantities of pottery from North Gaul have been recovered from the excavations at La Plaiderie, situated near to the modern waterfront of St. Peter Port. Of all of the 'finer' grey wares from the latter site, those produced in the potteries of North Gaul are the most common. Apart from beakers, other grey ware products of the North Gaulish industries found at La Plaiderie include dishes, bowls and jars, pentice beakers and mortaria. Terra-nigra type wares and pinch-neck flagons were also imported into the site from the potteries of North Gaul, in the period from the late first through to the fourth centuries AD. Finally, some of the material recovered from marine sites on the east coast of Guernsey, near to the ancient and modern harbour of St. Peter Port (notably Cow Bay and The North Beach) although not described as products of North Gaul are grey wares (Burns and Burns 1986, fig. 4, nos. 27, 32 and 39) and are probably from this source. The dishes nos. 27 and 39 are similar to examples found at La Plaiderie and no. 39 would appear to have burnished band decoration on the interior of the vessel. The cornice-rim jar, no. 32, is similar to vessels found at Amiens (Bayard 1980, pl. 11, nos. 43-4).

Terra-nigra type ware (Fig. 49) by Mark Wood

Rather than using such emotive terms as 'Terra-Nigra', 'Gallo-Belgic' or 'Céramique Fumigée', I have deliberately opted for the term given at the head of this section. This is probably a better policy when faced with a small number of vessels in a range of fabrics from different production centres.

Nine sherds have been recovered:

KR80/169. F10 (no. 229)
Rim sherd from a beaker with a plain rounded rim in a very hard fabric which is pale grey in colour and contains infrequent but large inclusions of iron stone as well as milky and clear quartz. The sherd retains some of its fine black slip though much of this has worn away. This vessel probably dates to the second century AD.

KR80/176. F21 (no. 227)
A very worn, sharply everted rim sherd from a jar or beaker in a fine moderately hard fabric. The fabric is quite micaceous and beige-brown in colour with grey fringes. Although the surfaces are worn, patches of a dull black slip remain. This vessel probably dates to the second century AD.

KR80/178. F12 (no. 226)
Rim sherd from a jar or bowl with a fairly thin body wall in a moderately hard sandy fabric. The rim is slightly everted while the neck below is short and near vertical and the body of the vessel curves gently downward from the neck. The fabric is non-micaceous, light grey in colour with thin paler grey fringes and has inclusions of small flecks of iron ore and clay pellets. The external surface is flaking off in laminated pieces but what remains is finely polished and near black in colour. The interior of the rim bears wipe-marks.

The form is difficult to parallel in a terra-nigra type fabric and finish but it is similar to an ovoid jar from Nijmegen, Holland (Holwerda 1941, pl. X, no. 504) and a coarseware bowl from Southampton in a grey fabric (Cotton and Gathercole 1958, fig. 24, no. 114). On these grounds, the vessel from King's Road should be dated to the late first/second century AD.

KR83/180. F31 (no. 237)
A decorated bodysherd in a hard sandy grey fabric with paler grey fringes. The fabric contains fine white mica and is similar to the fabric of KR83/190, no. 238 (see below). The surfaces are self-slipped dark grey and wiped smooth rather than burnished. The decoration of the surface which resembles a series of vertical 'teardrop' shapes may have been excised rather than

achieved by means of a roller-stamp. Nevertheless the decoration was applied after the surface was smoothed.

This kind of decoration occurs on beakers, bowls and jars found on sites in the northern area of western France (Menez 1985, types 87 and 139), where some of these vessels were undoubtedly produced. The King's Road sherd is probably from one of these production centres, which operated in the first century AD.

KR83/188. F31/37 (no. 234)
A sherd from a jar with a short everted rim and high rounded shoulder in a hard fine fabric. The fabric has a grey to dark grey core with paler grey fringes and contains moderate quantities of fine white mica. The external surface is slate-grey to near black in colour and burnished, as is the interior of the rim. Beneath this centimetre-wide zone of burnishing the interior is untreated and grey to dark grey in colour.

This vessel is similar to jars produced in a coarse grey fabric in south-western France (Santrot and Santrot 1979, 137, form 269) and to the group 3 jars produced at Usk (Greene 1979, 117). The date of the jars from these areas would support a mid- to late first century date for the example from King's Road.

KR83/190. F31/37 (no. 238)
Two joining sherds from a platter with a short vertical wall above the lower portion of the body which slopes toward the base. The junction between the upper and lower body of the vessel is marked by a slight carination. There is an indentation running around the upper body wall of the vessel which creates the impression of a rounded rim. The fabric is moderately hard, sandy and grey in colour with paler grey fringes. The inclusions are fine white mica and rounded specks of black, possibly iron ore. Both surfaces are dark grey to black in colour but in comparison to the internal surface of the vessel which has been well polished, the external surface was finished less carefully.

Platters with more pronounced rims and more curved upper body walls but made in a similar fabric to this vessel have been found in Vannes in Brittany in levels of Tiberian date (Menez 1985, 58, form 54). A probable date in the latter part of the first half of the first century AD seems likely for this vessel from King's Road.

KR83/198. F17/B2/L1 (no. 233)
A basal sherd in a micaceous fabric with a thick orange-brown core and pale grey-brown fringes. The external surface is fumed matt black whilst the internal surface is worn and dark grey in colour.

It is interesting to note that this is the only terra-nigra type vessel from King's Road in an oxidized fabric coloured orange-brown. Vessels in this fabric and colour are frequently encountered among the terra-nigra type wares from the Tranquesous and La Plaiderie in particular. Moreover, some of these are reminiscent of the North Gaulish 'grey ware' fabric and derive from that source, as for example the Flavian 'gobelet à col tronconique' from La Plaiderie, which has black surfaces. Other, more coarse fabrics, coloured orange or red, come from Breton or Norman sources. This vessel from King's Road is probably from one of the latter sources and should date to the late first or second century AD.

KR83/200. F17/B2/L1 (no. 236)
A decorated sherd with a thin body wall in a very fine, hard and slightly micaceous paste. The fabric has a thin grey-brown core with creamy buff fringes and infrequent inclusions of red iron ore. There is a fine black slip on the external surface which is decorated with well-executed judder rouletting. The interior of the sherd is also slipped but otherwise untreated. It is difficult to be certain of the vessel form to which this small sherd belongs. However, it may well be from the lower body of a beaker. In the absence of more diagnostic detail of the type of vessel this sherd represents, it can only be dated loosely, first/second century AD.

Romano-British ware (Fig. 49) by Mark Wood
KR/80/168. F10 (no. 232)
Although only the rim of this sherd is preserved along with a small portion of the body of the vessel, it looks more like a Romano-British pie dish than a vessel from the group described above. It is a pity that so little of the vessel remains as this must leave some room for doubt.

Nevertheless, the sandy grey fabric which contains some mica, as well as the technique of burnishing over a dark grey slip could indicate that this vessel is indeed a Romano-British product. It should be noted that Black-Burnished ware category two pie-dishes as well as grey ware products of the New Forest and Alice Holt industries have been found at La Plaiderie (Wood 1991, 40). This vessel dates to the second century AD.

Coarse grey ware (Fig. 49) by Mark Wood
KR80/179. F15 (no. 239)
A sherd from an everted rim jar in a coarse fabric containing inclusions of rounded white quartz. The fabric is hard, medium to dark grey in colour with grey to dark grey self-coloured surfaces. Coarse grey wares with a similar temper and imported from North Gaul have been found at La Plaiderie.

This ware is related to the first group described in this report, although the vessels in that group are noticeably finer in fabric and better finished. This vessel may have been imported from this source during the second century AD.

KR83/194. F29 (no. 230)
A worn sherd with a thick rounded rim in a soft, coarse grey-buff fabric containing frequent grey and milky angular quartz grits and some mica. The surfaces retain some patches of the self-coloured dark grey covering. It is difficult to comment upon such a small sherd, but it may be a local coarseware dating to the first or second century AD.

KR83/203. F20 (no. 241)
Rim sherd in a coarse sandy fabric which is medium grey in colour. The surfaces are self-coloured grey and are rough as some of the inclusions of clear angular quartz break the surfaces. There are numerous quartz-tempered wares found on various sites in the island which could have been produced locally or imported from neighbouring areas of Gaul. The sherd probably comes from a jar and dates to the second century AD.

Medieval pottery (Fig. 49, nos. 253-5)

Small quantities of medieval pottery, mostly in the fabric known as Normandy Gritty Ware, were found in the upper levels of the excavated areas. Only those sherds found in sealed and significant contexts are illustrated.

Catalogue of illustrated pottery (Figs. 40-9)

The catalogue is divided into the various fabric types. The listing is by illustration number. The description comprises the external appearance, the colour of the fracture and the internal appearance. Surface treatment and finish and any decoration or other noteworthy characteristics are listed. After the description will be found the sherd number, the site number and layer or feature numbers. The fabrics were examined using a X6 hand lens. Imported fabrics were, wherever possible, identified by direct comparison, either in the hand, or by reference to the published literature.

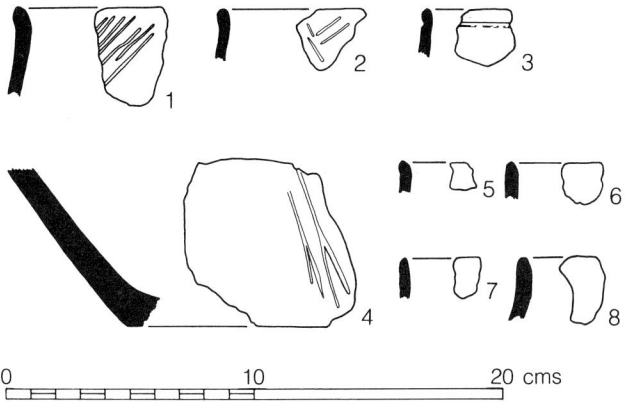

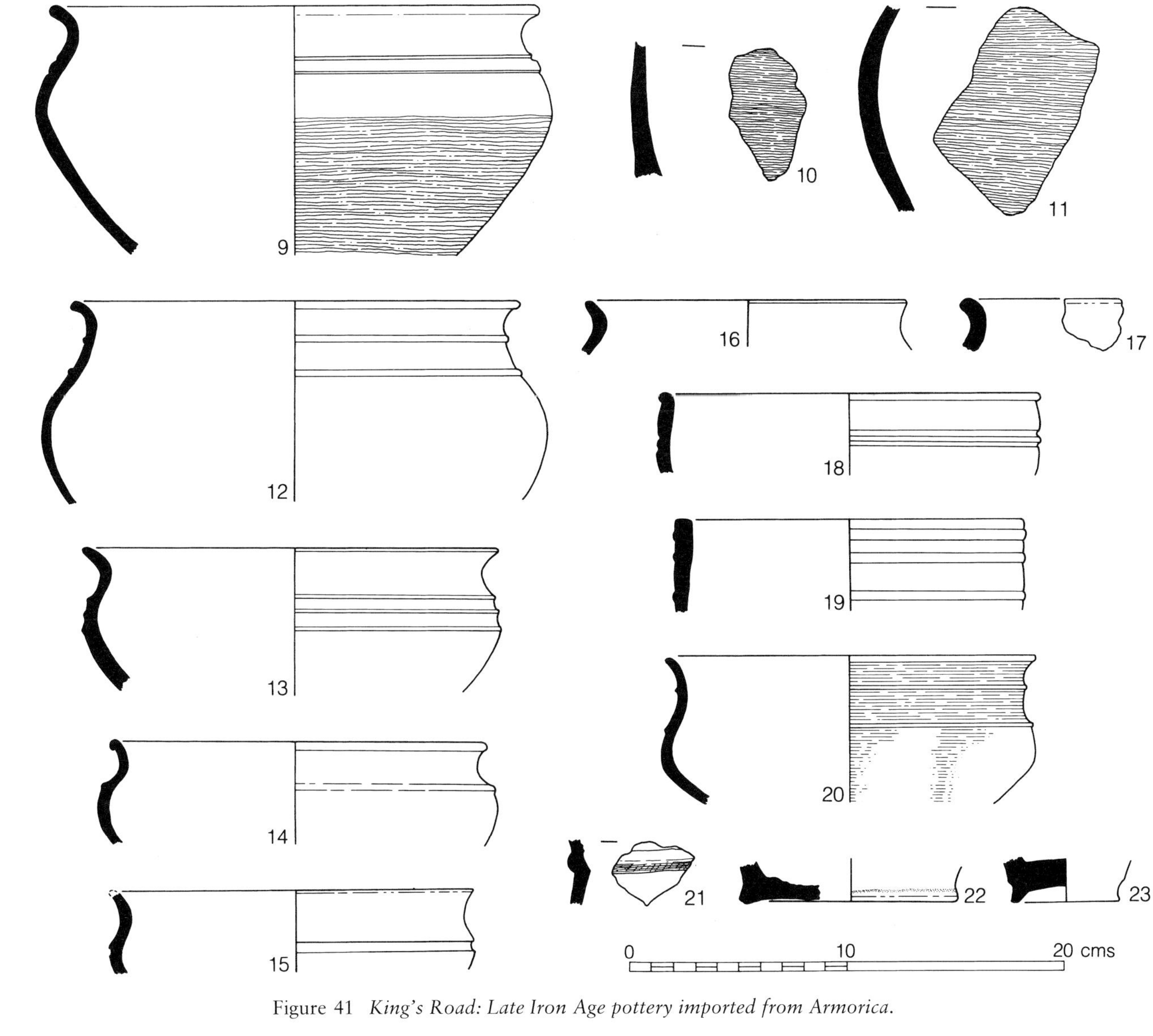

Figure 40 *King's Road: Late Bronze Age pottery.*

Figure 41 *King's Road: Late Iron Age pottery imported from Armorica.*

Bronze Age pottery from Sites 1 and 4 (Fig. 40)

1. Rim sherd, orange-brown exterior, orange fracture, orange-brown interior: diagonal incised decoration: smooth finish. 163/80. Site 1. F10.
2. Rim sherd, orange-brown exterior, orange-brown fracture, pink-grey interior: diagonal incised decoration: smooth finish. 162/80. Site 1. F10.
3. Rim sherd, orange-brown exterior, light brown fracture, orange-brown interior: smooth finish. 161/80. Site 1. F10.
4. Basal sherd, orange-brown exterior, grey-brown fracture, black interior: vertically incised decoration: smooth finish. 160/80. Site 1. F10.
5. Fragment of rim sherd, pink-brown exterior, buff fracture, pink-brown interior: smooth finish. 166/80. Site 1. F10.
6. Rim sherd, brown/black exterior, orange-brown fracture, pink-brown interior: smooth finish. 167/80. Site 1. F10.
7. Rim sherd, pink-brown exterior, buff fracture, pink-brown interior: smooth finish. 165/80. Site 1. F10.
8. Rim sherd, grey-brown exterior, orange-brown fracture, pink-brown interior: smooth finish. 164/80. Site 1. F10.

Late La Tène imported wares from Sites 1 and 4
Rilled ware (Fig. 41)

9. Rim sherd, pink to black exterior, red to black fracture, dark grey interior: micaceous: smooth burnished finish. 151/80. Site 1. F10.
10. Bodysherd, brown-black exterior, black fracture, black interior: vesicular: smooth finish. 115/80. Site 1. F10.
11. Bodysherd, black-brown exterior, grey-black fracture, grey-black interior: vesicular: some mica on surface. 116/83. Site 4. F17/B6/L3.

Cordoned and graphite-coated wares (Fig. 41)

12. Bowl, black exterior, buff-brown fracture, grey-brown interior: micaceous: fine burnish. 155/83. Site 4. F17/B5/L2.
13. Bowl, dark grey exterior, grey-buff fracture, dark grey interior: micaceous: smooth finish. 147/80. Site 1. F10.
14. Rim sherd, grey exterior, buff-pink fracture, grey interior: vesicular: smooth finish. 156/83. Site 4. F17/B6/L3.
15. Rim sherd, black exterior, pink-brown fracture, light grey interior: micaceous: very smooth burnished finish. 152/80. Site 1. F10.
16. Rim sherd, dark grey exterior, pink-grey fracture, dark grey interior: micaceous: smooth burnished finish. 148/80. Site 1. F10.
17. Rim sherd, dark grey exterior, pale grey fracture, light grey interior: micaceous: smooth burnished finish. 150/80. Site 1. F10.
18. Rim sherd, grey-black exterior, pink-brown fracture, grey-brown interior: micaceous: smooth burnished finish. 157/83. Site 4. F17/B2/L2.
19. Rim sherd, grey-black exterior, pink-brown fracture, grey-black interior: micaceous: smooth finish. 158/83. Site 4. F17/B5/L2.
20. Rim sherd, black exterior, pink-grey fracture, grey-brown interior: graphite coated: smooth finish. 153/80. Site 1. F10.
21. Bodysherd, grey-black exterior, buff-brown fracture, grey-black interior: graphite coated: smooth finish. 159/83. Site 4. F17/B5/L2.
22. Basal sherd, black exterior, pink-grey fracture, grey-brown interior: micaceous: smooth finish. 154/80. Site 1. F1.
23. Base, black exterior, orange-pink fracture, dark grey interior: micaceous: smooth finish. 149/80. Site 1. F10.

Late La Tène local wares from Sites 1 and 4
Fabric 1 (Fig. 42)

24. Rim sherd, grey-black exterior, grey-brown fracture, grey-brown interior: coarse finish. 189/83. Site 4. F31/37.
25. Rim sherd, grey-black exterior, grey-brown fracture, grey-brown interior: very coarse finish. 1/80. Site 1. F10.
26. Rim sherd with a roughly made bead rim, pink-brown sooted exterior, pink-grey fracture, grey-brown interior: very roughly finished. 19/83. Site 4. F25.
27. Rim sherd, grey-brown exterior, grey-brown fracture, grey-brown interior: rough finish. 199/83. Site 4. F17/B2/L1.
28. Rim sherd, black exterior, grey-black fracture, grey-black interior: smooth finish. 12/80. Site 1. F10.
29. Rim sherd, dark brown exterior, pink-brown fracture, dark brown interior: very smooth finish. 16/83. Site 4. F40.
30. Rim sherd, grey-brown exterior, light orange fracture, grey-brown interior: some mica inclusions: smooth finish. 13/80. Site 1. F10.
31. Rim sherd, grey-brown exterior, orange-buff fracture, grey-brown interior: some mica inclusions: smooth finish. 11/80. Site 1. F10.
32. Rim sherd, black exterior, grey-brown fracture, black interior: smooth finish. 182/83. Site 4. F37.
33. Rim sherd, grey exterior, grey-brown fracture, grey-brown interior: smooth finish. 3/80. Site 1. F10.

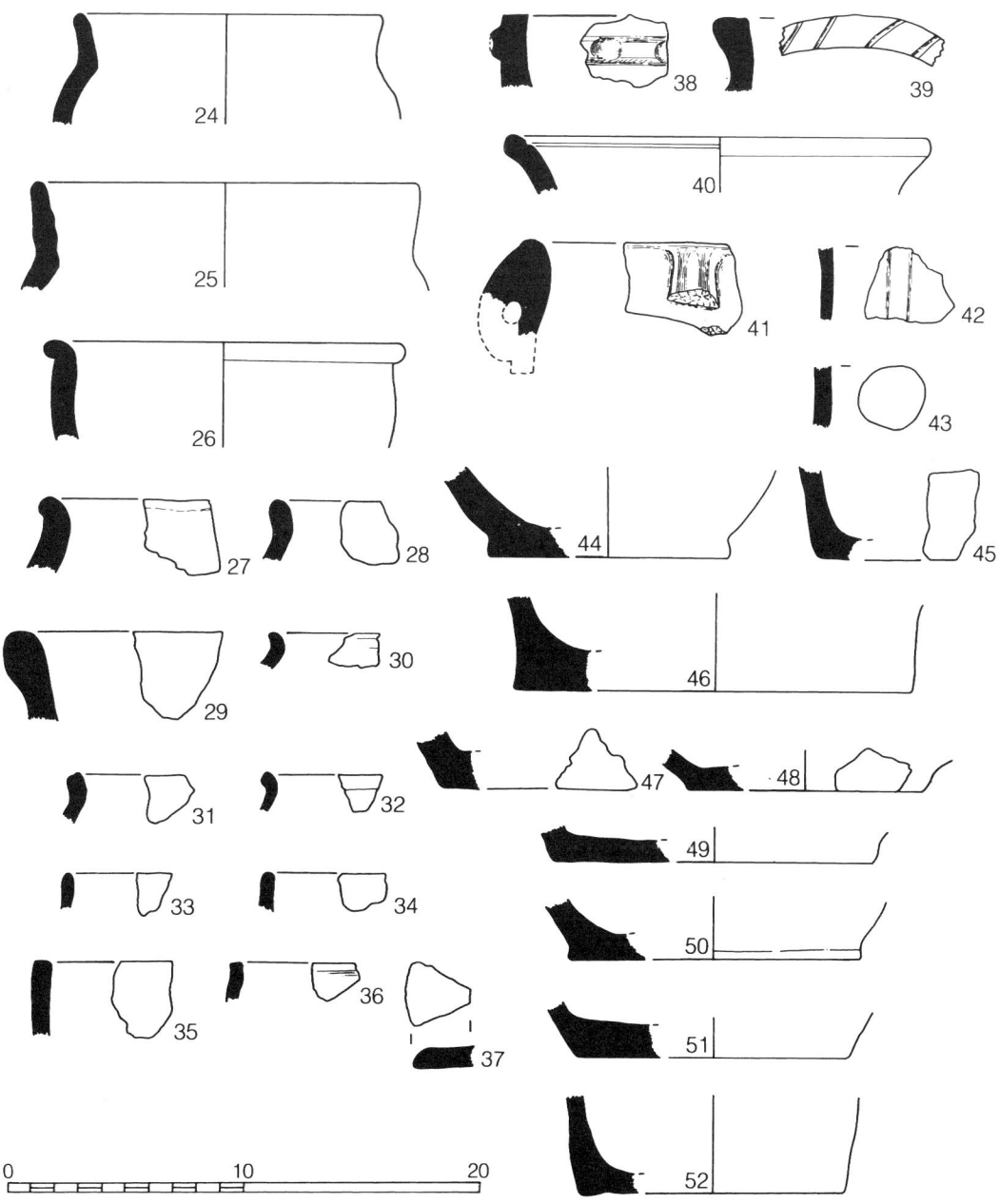

Figure 42 *King's Road: Late Iron Age local wares from Sites 1 and 4.*

34. Rim sherd, black exterior, black fracture, brown-black interior: coarse finish. 2/80. Site 1. F10.

35. Rim sherd, salmon-pink exterior, brown fracture, grey-black interior: coarse finish. 184/83. Site 4. F37.

36. Rim sherd, grey-brown exterior, brown fracture, grey-black interior: rough finish. 195/83. Site 4. F17/B5/L2.

37. Lid fragment, pink-brown exterior, grey-brown fracture, black interior: smooth finish. 193/83. Site 4. F29.

38. Bodysherd, orange-brown exterior, orange-brown to black fracture, black interior: large applied cordon with impressed decoration: coarse finish. 6/80. Site 1. F10.

39. Rim sherd, mid-brown sooted exterior, pink-brown fracture, grey-brown interior: fingernail impressed 'pie-crust' decoration on rim surface: rough finish. 21/83. Site 4. F148.

40. Rim sherd, dark brown exterior, pink-brown fracture, mid-brown interior: internally grooved: smooth finish. 15/83. Site 4. F39.

41. Rim sherd with horizontally pierced lug, brown-black exterior, salmon-pink fracture, pink-brown interior. 192/83. Site 4. F29.

42. Bodysherd, grey-brown exterior, red-brown fracture, mid-brown interior: burnished lines: coarse finish. 17/83. Site 4. F53.

43. Bodysherd (possibly re-utilized as a counter), mid-brown sooted exterior, red-grey fracture, grey-brown interior: smooth finish. 18/83. Site 4. F17/B2/L1.

44. Basal sherd, grey-brown exterior, orange-brown fracture, grey-black interior: rough finish. 191/83. Site 4. F29.

45. Basal sherd, orange-brown exterior, black fracture, brown-black interior: smooth finish. 10/80. Site 1. F10.

46. Basal sherd, pink-brown exterior, pink-brown fracture, interior surface abraded away: smooth finish. 20/83. Site 4. F17/B2/L2.

47. Basal sherd, orange-brown exterior, orange-brown to black fracture, brown-black interior: some mica inclusions: coarse finish. 5/80. Site 1. F10.

48. Basal sherd, grey-black exterior, grey-brown fracture, grey-black interior: coarse finish. 14/80. Site 1. F10.

49. Basal sherd, orange-brown exterior, orange-pink fracture, grey-black interior: coarse finish. 8/80. Site 1. F10.

50. Basal sherd, orange-brown sooted exterior, orange-brown fracture, grey interior: coarse finish. 4/80. Site 1. F10.

51. Basal sherd, grey, sooted exterior, orange-brown fracture, grey-brown interior: coarse finish. 9/80. Site 1. F10.

52. Basal sherd, grey-brown exterior, grey fracture, pink-brown interior: some mica inclusions: coarse finish. 7/80. Site 1. F10.

Fabric 2 (Fig. 43)

53. Rim sherd, orange-grey exterior, orange fracture, orange interior: smooth finish. 38/83. Site 4. F38.

54. Rim sherd, orange-grey exterior, orange fracture, grey interior: smooth finish. 24/80. Site 1. F10.

55. Rim sherd, orange exterior, orange fracture, orange-brown interior: coarse finish. 30/80. Site 1. F10.

56. Rim sherd, grey, sooted exterior, orange fracture, mid-brown interior: coarse finish. 185/83. Site 4. F37.

57. Rim sherd, buff-orange exterior, buff fracture, grey-orange interior: smooth finish. 28/80. Site 1. F10.

58. Rim sherd with vestigial bead, orange-grey exterior, orange fracture, orange-grey interior: smooth finish. 26/80. Site 1. F10.

59. Rim sherd, pink-grey exterior, pink-grey fracture, pink-grey interior: smooth finish. 32/83. Site 4. F17/B6/L1.

60. Rim sherd, orange-brown exterior, orange-brown fracture, orange-brown interior: smooth finish. 32/80. Site 1. F1.

61. Rim sherd, orange-buff exterior, orange-brown fracture, orange-buff interior: coarse finish. 23/80. Site 1. F10.

62. Rim sherd with internal lid-seating, orange-brown exterior, orange fracture, orange-grey interior: smooth finish. 207/83. Site 1. F17/B1/L1.

63. Rim sherd, chocolate-brown exterior, brown-black fracture, buff-brown interior: smooth finish. 29/80. Site 1. F10.

64. Bodysherd, pink-brown exterior, pink-brown fracture, brown interior: linear incised decoration: smooth finish. 35/83. Site 4. F17/B6/L2.

65. Bodysherd, buff-brown exterior, pink-brown fracture, grey-brown interior: one thin groove incised around girth: smooth finish. 36/83. Site 4. F17/B6/L2.

66. Pedestal-type base, orange-brown exterior, pink-grey fracture, grey-black, sooted interior: possibly knife trimmed: smooth finish. 33/83. Site 4. F17/B6/L2.

67. Basal sherd, orange-brown exterior, grey-brown fracture, dark grey interior: coarse finish. 34/83. Site 4. F17/B2/L2.

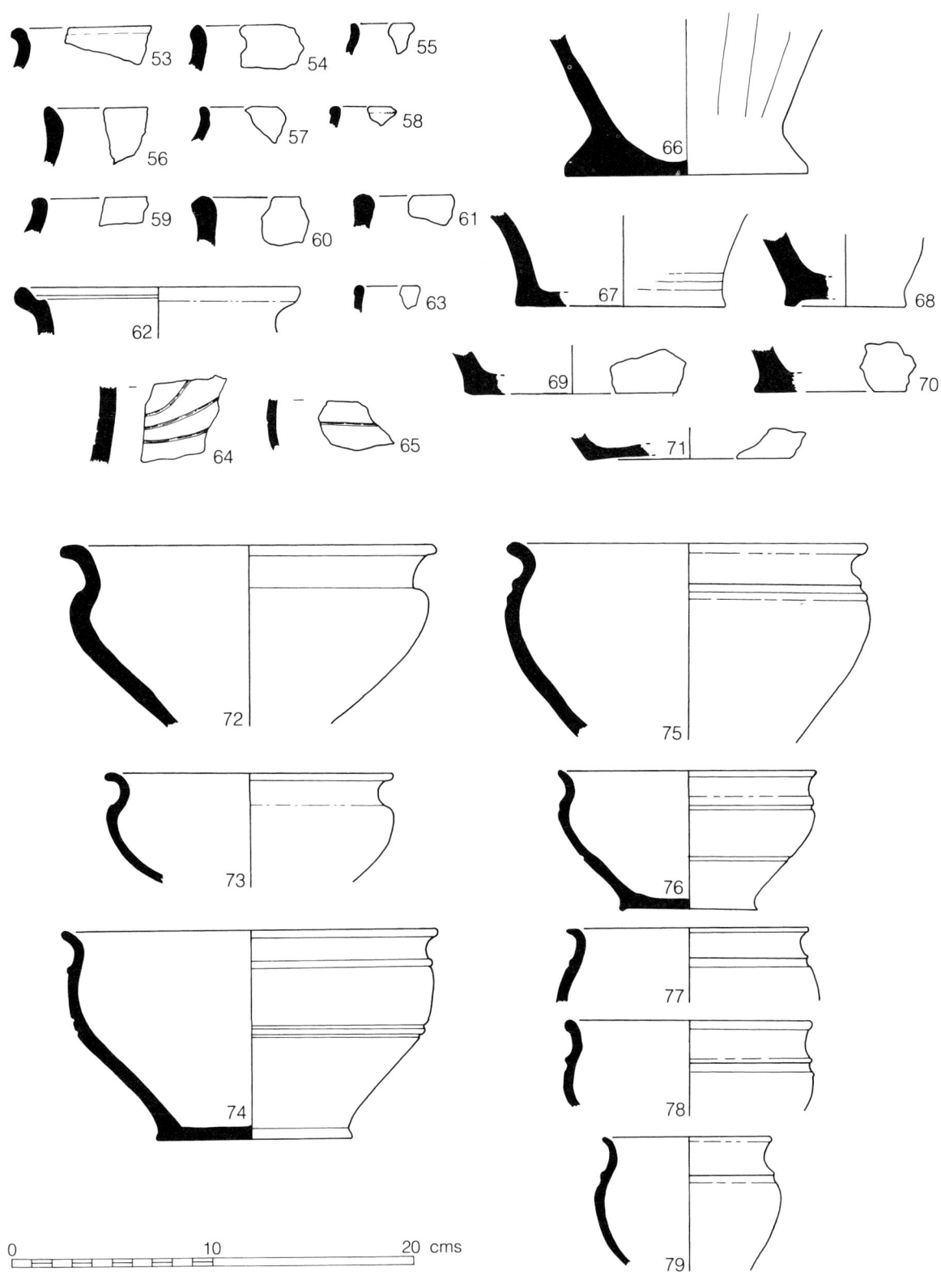

Figure 43 *King's Road: Late Iron Age local wares from Sites 1 and 4.*

68. Basal sherd, orange-brown, sooted exterior, orange fracture, orange-brown interior. A rather crude attempt has been made to hand-build a foot-ring on this vessel. 22/80. Site 1. F10.

69. Basal sherd, orange-brown exterior, orange-grey fracture, reddish-brown interior: smooth finish. 27/80. Site 1. F10.

70. Basal sherd, orange-grey exterior, orange fracture, mid-brown interior: coarse finish. 39/83. Site 4. F13.

71. Basal sherd, orange-grey exterior, orange fracture, orange-brown interior: smooth finish. 25/80. Site 1. F10.

Fabric 3 (Figs. 43-5)

72. Bowl, grey-black exterior, light grey fracture, buff-grey interior: smooth, partially burnished finish. 41/80. Site 1. F1.

73. Bowl, dark grey exterior, orange-buff fracture, orange-brown interior: smooth, partially burnished finish. 44/80. Site 1. F10.

74. Bowl, grey-black exterior, red-brown fracture, grey-brown interior: smooth finish. 74/83. Site 4. F17/B6/L3.

75. Bowl, buff-brown exterior, orange-buff fracture, buff interior: smooth finish. 43/80. Site 1. F10.

76. Bowl, grey-buff exterior, pink-buff fracture, grey-buff interior: smooth finish. 73/83. Site 1. F17/B1/L2 and B2/L2.

77. Rim sherd, grey-brown exterior, grey-brown fracture, mid-brown interior: smooth finish. 54/80. Site 1. F10.

78. Rim sherd, black exterior, pink-grey fracture, dark grey interior: smooth, partially burnished finish. 46/80. Site 1. F1.

79. Small bowl, buff to black exterior, orange-buff fracture, orange-buff interior: smooth, partially burnished finish. 48/80. Site 1. F10.

80. Jar, buff to black exterior, grey fracture, dark grey interior: internal groove: fairly smooth finish. 42/80. Site 1. F10.

81. Rim sherd, buff exterior, buff fracture, buff interior: smooth finish. 78/83. Site 4. F11.

82. Rim sherd, black exterior, grey-brown fracture, light grey-brown interior: some mica inclusions: smooth, partially burnished finish. 47/80. Site 1. F10.

83. Rim sherd, black exterior, dark grey fracture, black interior: smooth, partially burnished finish. 52/80. Site 1. F10.

84. Rim sherd, grey exterior, grey-buff fracture, grey interior: coarse finish. 50/80. Site 1. F10.

85. Rim sherd, mid-brown exterior, orange fracture, grey-brown interior: smooth finish. 56/80. Site 1. F11.

86. Rim sherd, black exterior, dark brown fracture, mid-brown interior: smooth finish. 51/80. Site 1. F10.

87. Rim sherd, grey-brown exterior, buff fracture, grey-brown interior: smooth finish. 83/83. Site 4. F17/B3/L2.

88. Rim sherd, buff-brown exterior, grey-brown fracture, buff-brown interior: smooth finish. 79/83. Site 4. F127.

89. Rim sherd, grey-brown exterior, mid-brown fracture, grey-brown interior: burnished finish. 80/83. Site 1. F13.

90. Rim sherd, black exterior, black fracture, reddish-brown interior: smooth, partially burnished finish. 53/80. Site 1. F10.

91. Rim sherd, pink-grey exterior, beige-buff fracture, pink-brown interior: very smooth finish. 70/80. Site 1. F10.

92. Bodysherd, black exterior, pink-brown fracture, pink-brown interior: fine burnished finish. 86/83. Site 4. B17/B6/L2.

93. Bodysherd, orange-brown exterior, orange fracture, orange-brown interior: smooth finish. 58/80. Site 1. F10.

94. Bodysherd, dark brown exterior, buff-pink fracture, grey interior: smooth, partially burnished finish. 59/80. Site 1. F10.

95. Bodysherd, brown exterior, pink-beige fracture, grey interior: sooted: smooth finish. 71/80. Site 1. F10.

96. Bodysherd, grey-brown exterior, pink fracture, pink-grey interior: some sooting: rough finish. 66/80. Site 1. F10.

97. Bodysherd, black exterior, buff fracture, grey-black interior: smooth finish. 62/80. Site 1. F10.

98. Bodysherd, black exterior, chocolate-brown fracture, brown-black interior: smooth finish. 61/80. Site 1. F10.

99. Bowl, grey-black exterior, grey fracture, grey-brown interior: vertical zones of burnishing: sooted. 75/83. Site 4. F24.

100. Rim sherd, grey exterior, orange-buff fracture, dark grey interior: smooth finish. 45/80. Site 1. F1.

101. Rim sherd, orange-grey exterior, pink-buff fracture, grey interior: smooth, partially burnished finish. 49/80. Site 1. F10.

102. Rim sherd, grey-brown exterior, pink fracture, buff-brown interior: sooted: smooth finish. 77/83. Site 1. F17/B5/L2.

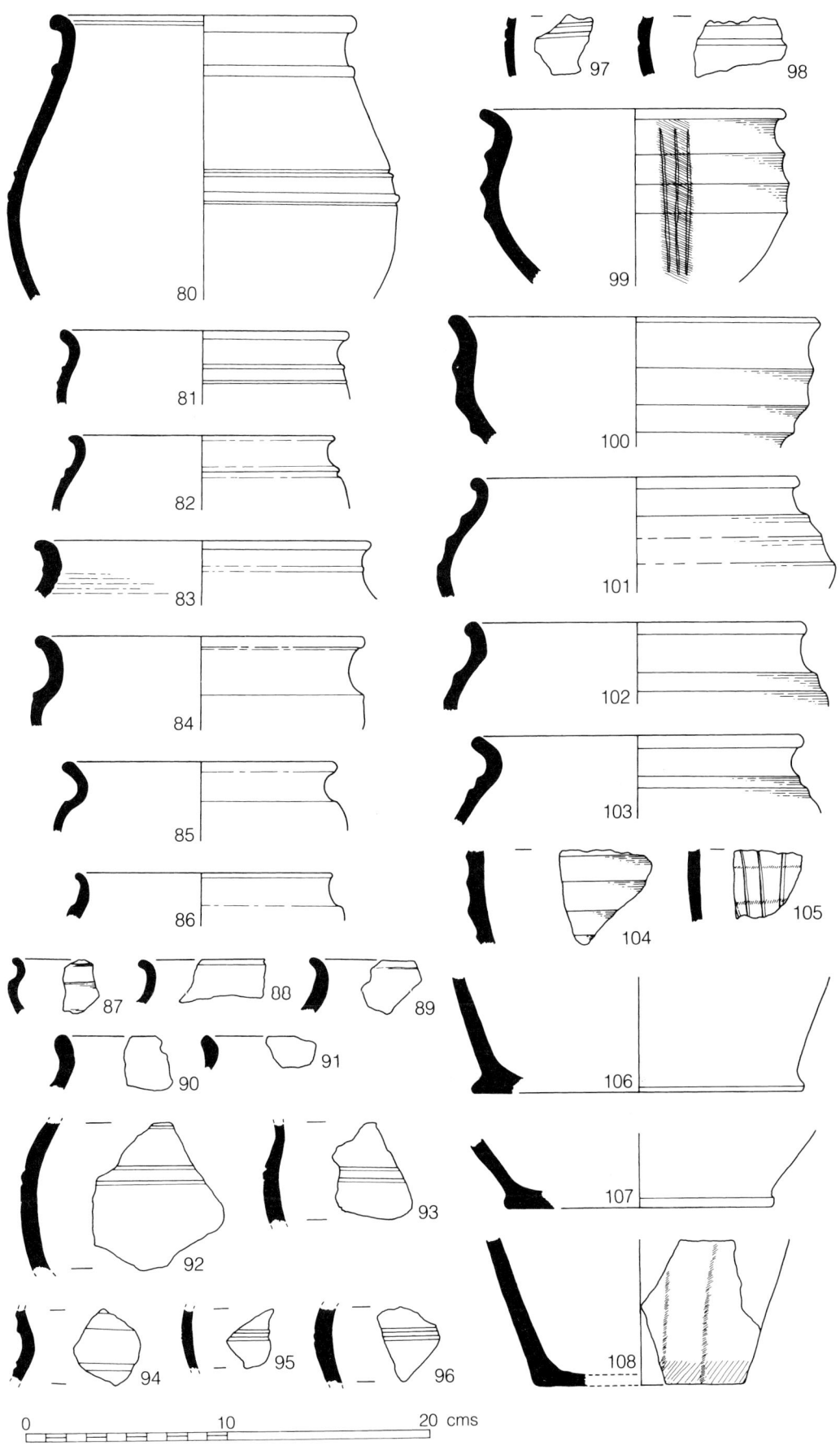

Figure 44 *King's Road: Late Iron Age local wares from Sites 1 and 4.*

103. Rim sherd, grey-brown exterior, pink-brown fracture, grey-brown interior: smooth finish. 76/83. Site 4. F17/B6/L3.

104. Bodysherd, grey-black exterior, pink-buff fracture, grey-brown interior: smooth finish. 81/83. Site 4. F17/B4/L1.

105. Bodysherd, grey-brown exterior, mid-brown fracture, grey-brown interior: burnished lines around girth: vertical tooled grooves down body: rough finish. 85/83. Site 4. F17/B5/L2.

106. Basal sherd, mid-brown exterior, orange-brown fracture, orange-brown interior: smooth finish. 64/80. Site 1. F10.

107. Basal sherd, black exterior, pink-brown fracture, brown-black interior: smooth, partially burnished finish. 57/80. Site 1. F10.

108. Basal sherd, grey-brown exterior, black to pink fracture, orange-brown interior: vertical burnished lines: dark zone around base: rough finish. 82/83. Site 4. F17/B3/L2.

109. Basal sherd, grey-black exterior, pink-brown fracture, grey-black interior: rough finish. 84/83. Site 4. F122.

110. Basal sherd, black exterior, pink-grey fracture, black to beige interior: pronounced concentric grooves on base: smooth burnished finish. 67/80. Site 1. F10.

111. Basal sherd, grey exterior, grey fracture, pink-grey interior: rough finish. 69/80. Site 1. F10.

112. Basal sherd, orange-brown exterior, dark brown fracture, orange-brown interior: coarse finish. 83/80. Site 1. F10.

113. Basal sherd, pale orange-buff exterior, orange-grey fracture, light brown interior: smooth finish. 60/80. Site 1. F10.

114. Base, brown-black exterior, grey fracture, grey-black interior: some mica inclusions: rough finish. 65/80. Site 1. F10.

115. Basal sherd, brown-grey exterior, grey fracture, dark grey interior: rough finish. 72/80. Site 1. F10.

116. Basal sherd, orange exterior, chocolate-brown fracture, pink-brown interior: rough finish. 68/80. Site 1. F10.

117. Basal sherd, grey-black exterior, beige fracture, beige interior: smooth finish. 63/80. Site 1. F10.

Fabric 4 (Fig. 45)

118. Rim sherd, dark grey exterior, pink-grey fracture, dark grey interior: some mica inclusions: smooth finish. 88/80. Site 1. F10.

119. Rim sherd, dark grey-brown exterior, dark grey fracture, chocolate-brown interior: some mica inclusions: smooth finish. 92/80. Site 1. F10.

120. Rim sherd, chocolate-brown exterior, black fracture, grey interior: some mica inclusions: smooth finish. 90/80. Site 1. F10.

121. Rim sherd, dark grey exterior, light brown fracture, dark grey-brown interior: smooth finish: 93/80. Site 1. F10.

122. Rim sherd, black exterior, pink-grey fracture, dark grey interior: smooth burnished finish. 91/80. Site 1. F10.

123. Rim sherd, dark brown exterior, grey-brown fracture, dark brown interior: burnished finish. 107/83. Site 4. F17/B5/L2.

124. Rim sherd, greyish-beige exterior, pale beige fracture, greyish-beige interior: smooth finish. 98/80. Site 1. F10.

125. Rim sherd, dark grey exterior, pink-brown fracture, dark grey interior: smooth finish. 96/80. Site 1. F10.

126. Rim sherd, black exterior, beige fracture, black interior: some mica inclusions: smooth finish. 87/80. Site 1. F10.

127. Rim sherd, black exterior, brown to black fracture, black interior: some mica inclusions: smooth finish. 102/80. 102/80. F10.

128. Rim sherd, black exterior, pink-grey fracture, dark grey interior: some mica inclusions: smooth burnished finish. 89/80. Site 1. F10.

129. Rim sherd, brown to black exterior, dark brown fracture, black interior: internal groove: burnished finish. 108/83. Site 4. F25.

130. Rim sherd, beige-brown exterior, light beige fracture, beige interior: smooth finish. 99/80. Site 1. F10.

131. Rim sherd, black exterior, grey-brown fracture, black interior: smooth finish. 92/80. Site 1. F10.

132. Bodysherd, black exterior, beige fracture, grey interior: cordoned: smooth finish. 100/80. Site 1. F10.

133. Bodysherd, grey-black exterior, grey-black fracture, grey interior: cordoned: smooth finish. 109/83. Site 4. F17/B5/L2.

134. Bodysherd, grey-black exterior, grey-black fracture, grey interior: cordoned: smooth finish. 110/83. Site 4. F17/B2/L2.

135. Bodysherd, salmon-pink exterior, beige fracture, salmon-pink interior: cordoned: smooth finish. 112/80. Site 1. F10. Possibly Gallo-Roman.

136. Bodysherd, grey-black exterior, beige fracture, grey-black interior: smooth finish. 95/80. Site 1. F10.

137. Bodysherd, salmon-pink exterior, salmon-pink fracture, salmon-pink interior: cordoned: smooth finish. 113/80. F10. Possibly Gallo-Roman.

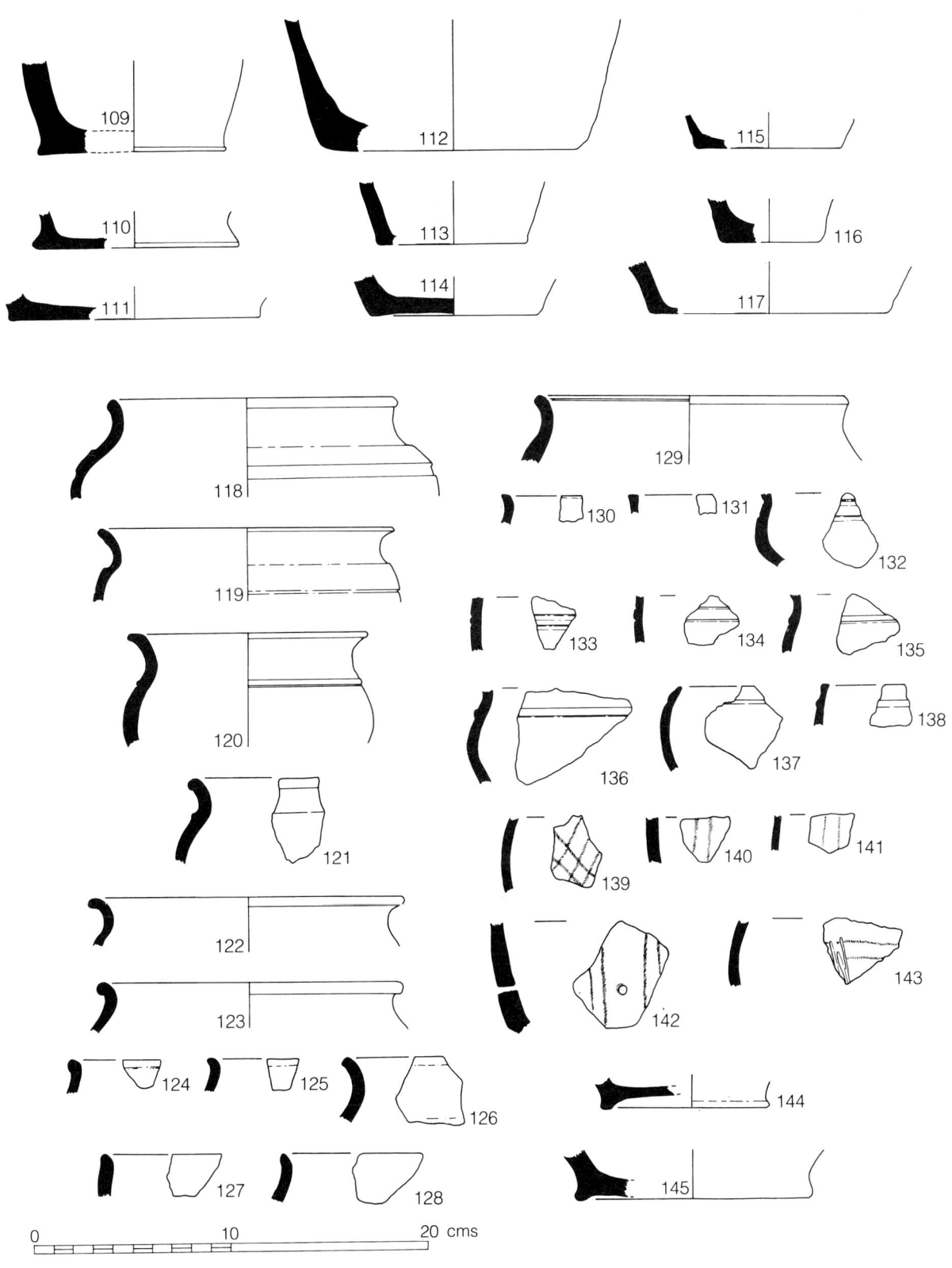

Figure 45 *King's Road: Late Iron Age local wares from Sites 1 and 4.*

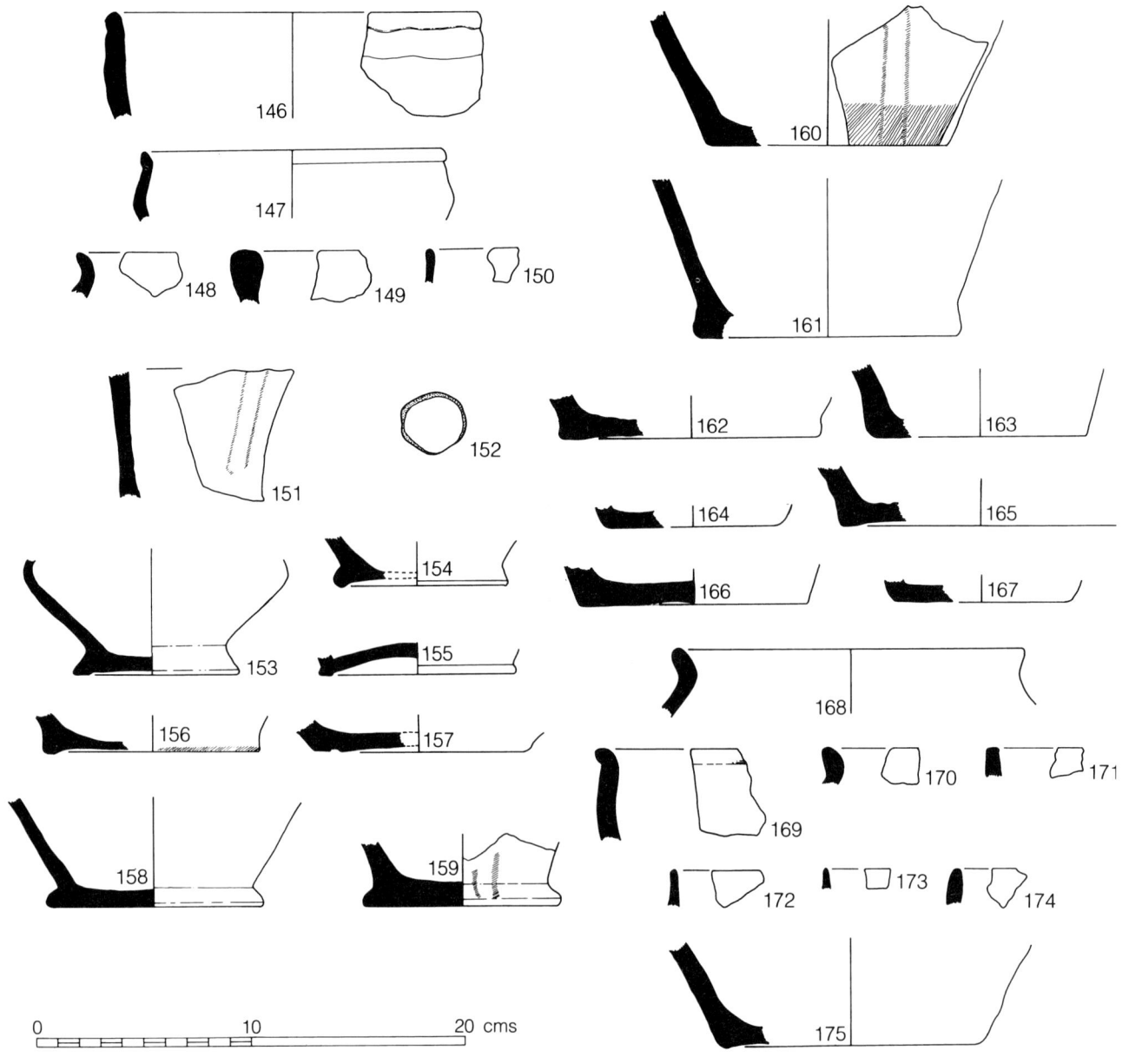

Figure 46 *King's Road: Late Iron Age local wares from Sites 1 and 4.*

138. Bodysherd, salmon-pink exterior, salmon-pink fracture, salmon-pink interior: cordoned: smooth finish. 111/80. Site 1. F10. Possibly Gallo-Roman.

139. Bodysherd, orange to black exterior, beige to black fracture, orange to black interior: lattice burnishing: smooth finish. 106/80. Site 1. F1.

140. Bodysherd, beige to grey exterior, dark grey fracture, grey-brown interior: vertical burnished decoration. 101/80. Site 1. F10.

141. Bodysherd, black exterior, beige fracture, grey interior: vertical burnished decoration: smooth finish. 103/80. Site 1. F1.

142. Bodysherd, black exterior, pink-beige fracture, pink-brown interior: pierced with hole: vertical burnished decoration: smooth finish. 105/80. Site 1. F1.

143. Bodysherd, black exterior, pink-beige fracture, brown to black interior: horizontal burnished decoration: vertical incised decoration: smooth finish. 104/80. Site 1. F10.

144. Basal sherd, light salmon-pink exterior, salmon-pink fracture, light salmon-pink interior: smooth finish. 114/80. Site 1. F10. Possibly Gallo-Roman.

145. Basal sherd, brown exterior, beige-brown fracture, beige interior: neat, well-made foot-ring: smooth finish. 94/80. Site 1. F10.

Nos. 135, 137, 138 and 145 have been included in the listing of Fabric 4 pottery. They are of identical composition and display typical Late La Tène characteristics, such as shape and cordons. However they are generally of much more delicate and careful workmanship and all are of an untypical salmon-pink colour. It is possible that they are a colour variant of Fabric 4, but as all are from F10, the enclosing ditch, it is also possible that they are from the Gallo-Roman deposits which lay on the upper horizon of the ditch. The machining of this part of the site makes such an eventuality quite possible.

Fabric 5 (Fig. 46)

146. Rim sherd, grey exterior, pink-grey fracture, pink-grey interior: hand-made with a very crude finish. 138/83. Site 4. F17/B6/L3.
147. Rim sherd, pink-brown exterior, light pink-brown fracture, pink-brown interior: smooth finish. 117/80. Site 1. F10.
148. Rim sherd, grey-black exterior, pink fracture, pink-brown interior: rough finish. 118/80. Site 1. F10.
149. Rim sherd, beige-grey exterior, beige-grey fracture, beige-brown interior: smooth finish. 119/80. Site 1. F10.
150. Rim sherd, pink-brown exterior, buff-pink fracture, salmon-pink interior: smooth finish. 121/80. Site 1. F10.
151. Bodysherd, grey interior, red-brown fracture, pink-brown interior: vertical burnished decoration: smooth finish. 128/80. Site 1. F10.
152. Bodysherd, buff-brown exterior, pale buff fracture, grey-brown interior: possibly re-utilized as a counter: rough finish. 136/83. Site 4. F17/B2/L2.
153. Base, grey-brown exterior, orange-brown fracture, mid-brown interior: some mica inclusions: shallow, flat foot-ring: smooth finish. 131/83. Site 4. F17/B5/L2.
154. Basal sherd, grey-brown exterior, buff-brown fracture, grey-brown interior: shallow, flat foot-ring: smooth finish. 134/83. Site 4. F13.
155. Base, grey exterior, pink-beige fracture, reddish-brown interior: omphalos type: smooth finish. 126/80. Site 1. F10.
156. Basal sherd, grey-black exterior, pink-beige fracture, pinkish-brown interior: smooth burnished finish. 124/80. Site 1. F10.
157. Basal sherd, grey-brown exterior, pink-buff fracture, pink-grey interior: some mica inclusions: shallow groove on base: smooth finish. 133/83. Site 4. F40.
158. Base, grey-black exterior, grey-black fracture, grey-black interior: some mica inclusions: smooth finish. 129/83. Site 4. F17/B5/L2.
159. Base, grey-brown exterior, pink-brown fracture, grey interior: vertical burnished lines: rough finish. 135/83. Site 4. F17/B5/L2.
160. Basal sherd, buff-brown exterior, pink-brown fracture, grey-brown interior: vertical burnished lines with darker zone at base: some mica inclusions: smooth finish. 130/83. Site 4. F17/B2/L2.
161. Basal sherd, dark grey exterior, buff fracture, pink-brown interior: smooth finish. 125/80. Site 1. F10.
162. Basal sherd, orange-pink exterior, orange-pink fracture, pink-grey interior: some mica inclusions: smooth finish. 122/80. Site 1. F10.
163. Basal sherd, grey exterior, grey-black fracture, buff interior: smooth finish. 137/83. Site 4. F17/B6/L4.
164. Basal sherd, pink-beige exterior, orange-brown fracture, grey interior: rough finish. 127/80. Site 1. F10.
165. Basal sherd, grey-black exterior, pink-brown fracture, brown-black interior: smooth finish. 120/80. Site 1. F10.
166. Basal sherd, grey-brown exterior, buff-brown fracture, grey-brown interior: rough finish. 132/83. Site 4. F17/B6/L3.
167. Basal sherd, grey exterior, pink-beige fracture, pink-orange interior: rough finish. 123/80. Site 1. F10.

Fabric 6 (Fig. 46)

168. Rim sherd, pink-brown exterior, red-brown fracture, grey-brown interior: smooth soapy finish. 145/80. Site 1. F10.
169. Rim sherd, pink-brown exterior, pink-buff fracture, pink-brown interior: smooth soapy finish. 139/80. Site 1. F10.
170. Rim sherd, pink-brown exterior, buff fracture, pink-brown interior: smooth soapy finish. 141/80. Site 1. F10.
171. Rim sherd, pink-brown exterior, grey-brown fracture, grey-brown interior: smooth soapy finish. 142/80. Site 1. F10.
172. Rim sherd, pink-brown exterior, red-brown fracture, pink-brown interior: smooth finish. 143/80. Site 1. F10.
173. Rim sherd, dark grey exterior, pink-brown fracture, pink-brown interior: smooth finish. 144/80. Site 1. F10.
174. Rim sherd, grey-brown exterior, beige fracture, pink-grey interior: smooth soapy finish. 140/80. Site 1. F10.
175. Rim sherd, grey-brown exterior, pink-brown fracture, pink-brown interior: rough finish. 146/80. Site 1.

Early to Middle Iron Age pottery from Sites 2 and 3 (Figs. 47-8)

Fabric Type 1 (Fig. 47)

176. Jar, orange-brown exterior, orange-brown fracture, dark brown, sooted interior: rough finish. 214/82. Site 2. F5.
177. Rim sherd, orange-black exterior, orange-black fracture, black interior: rough finish. 216/82. Site 2. F8.
178. Rim sherd, orange-brown exterior, mid-brown fracture, orange-brown interior: rough finish. 212/82. Site 2. F5.
179. Rim sherd, orange exterior, orange-brown fracture, chocolate-brown interior: micaceous: smooth finish. 218/82. Site 2. F8.
180. Rim sherd, grey-brown exterior, orange-brown fracture, light brown interior: rough finish. 219/82. Site 2. F5.
181. Rim sherd, buff-brown exterior, dark grey fracture, orange to grey interior: rough finish. 224/82. Site 2. F5.
182. Rim sherd, mid-brown exterior, brown fracture, orange-brown interior: smooth finish. 221/82. Site 2. F5.
183. Horizontally pierced lug, orange-brown exterior, orange-brown to black fracture, orange-brown interior: smooth finish. 223/82. Site 2. F5.
184. Lid sherd, pale orange exterior, bright orange fracture, orange-brown interior: rough finish. 217/82. Site 2. F4.
185. Bodysherd, mid-brown exterior, orange-brown fracture, orange-brown interior: carinated: rough finish. 211/82. Site 2. T3/L3.
186. Basal sherd, mid-brown exterior, orange-brown fracture, grey-brown interior: rough finish. 213/82. Site 2. F5.
187. Basal sherd, mid-brown exterior, mid-brown fracture, orange-brown interior: rough finish. 210/82. Site 2. F8.
188. Basal sherd, mid-brown exterior, orange-brown fracture, abraded, buff interior: sooted: rough finish. 222/82. Site 2. F5.
189. Basal sherd, orange-brown exterior, orange fracture, orange-brown interior: rough finish. 220/82. Site 2. T3/L3.
190. Pedestal base with thumb impressions on footring, orange-brown exterior, orange-brown fracture, orange-brown interior: sooted: rough finish. 215/82. Site 2. F5.

Fabric Type 2 (Fig. 47)

191. Rim sherd, brown exterior, grey-brown fracture, grey-brown interior: sooted: very smooth finish. 232/82. Site 2. T3/F5.
192. Rim sherd, orange-brown exterior, light orange-brown fracture, grey-brown interior: smooth finish. 227/82. Site 2. T2/F5.
193. Rim sherd, mid-brown exterior, mid-brown fracture, orange-brown interior: smooth finish. 225/82. Site 2. T3/L5.
194. Rim sherd, buff-pink exterior, buff fracture, buff-orange interior: rough finish. 231/82. Site 2. T3/F5.
195. Rim sherd, dark buff exterior, buff-grey fracture, orange-buff interior: micaceous: smooth finish. 226/82. Site 3. T5/F4.
196. Lid sherd, light grey exterior, pink-grey fracture, dark grey interior: smooth finish. 233/82. Site 2. T3/F5.
197. Bodysherd, dark brown exterior, mid-brown fracture, orange interior: tooled finish similar to rilled ware. 228/82. Site 2. T3/F5.
198. Basal sherd, dark orange-brown exterior, orange-brown fracture, orange-brown interior. 230/82. Site 2. T3/F5.

Fabric Type LPC/3 (Fig. 47)

199. Jar, dark grey-brown exterior, light brown fracture, dark chocolate-brown interior: bead rim: smooth finish. 241/83. Site 2. F5.
200. Rim sherd, black exterior, orange-brown fracture, grey-brown interior: smooth finish. 236/82. Site 2. F5.
201. Rim sherd, black exterior, orange-brown fracture, orange-brown interior: smooth finish. 245/82. Site 2. F5.
202. Rim sherd, dark chocolate-brown exterior, black fracture, brown to black interior: smooth finish. 244/82. Site 2. F10.
203. Rim sherd, grey-brown exterior, orange-brown fracture, black interior: smooth finish. 237/82. Site 2. F5.
204. Rim sherd, grey-brown exterior, orange-brown fracture, brown interior: smooth finish. 238/82. Site 2. F5.
205. Rim sherd, black exterior, brown fracture, black interior: smooth finish. 239/82. Site 2. F5.
206. Lid sherd, black exterior, black fracture, black interior: burnished, with added vertical burnished lines. 235/82. Site 2. F5.
207. Lid sherd, orange-brown exterior, orange fracture, black interior: sooted: smooth finish. 240/82. Site 2. F5.
208. Lid knob, black exterior, brown fracture, black interior: burnished on both surfaces: smooth finish. 234/80. Site 2. F5.

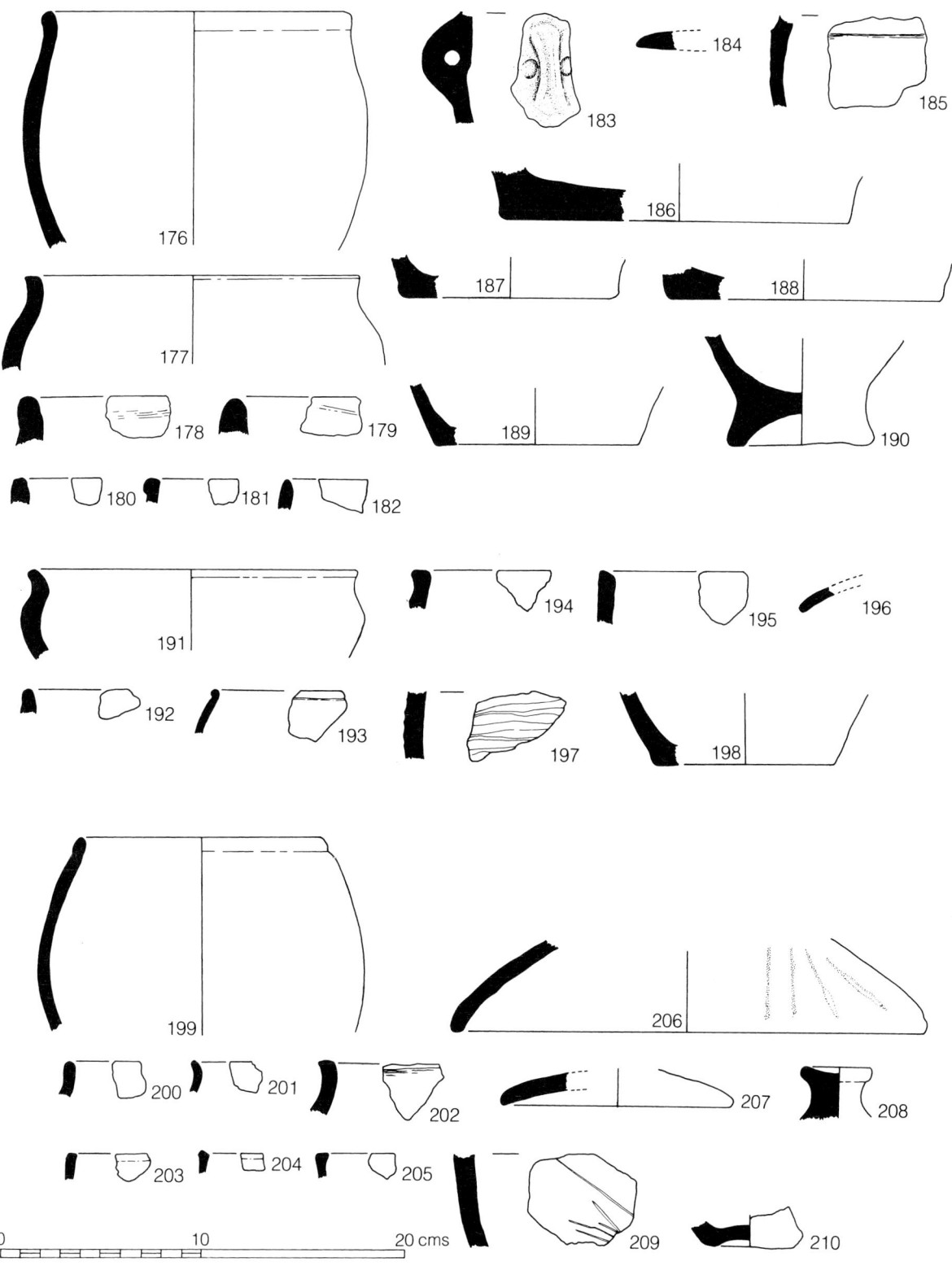

Figure 47 *King's Road: Early to Middle Iron Age wares from Sites 2 and 3.*

209. Bodysherd, orange-brown exterior, chocolate-brown fracture, grey-brown interior: sooted: knife-cuts on internal surface. 242/82. Site 3. F4.
210. Basal sherd, dark grey exterior, orange-brown fracture, dark grey-brown interior: omphalos type: smooth finish. 243/82. Site 2. F5.

Fabric Type LPC/4 (Fig. 48)
211. Rim sherd, black exterior, mid-grey fracture, black interior: smooth finish. 247/82. Site 2. F5.
212. Rim sherd, light brown exterior, orange fracture, buff-brown interior: smooth finish. 250/82. Site 2. F5.
213. Rim sherd, dark grey exterior, orange-brown fracture, grey-brown interior: smooth finish. 251/82. Site 2. F5.
214. Rim sherd, dark chocolate-brown exterior, orange-brown fracture, brown interior: smooth finish. 252/82. Site 2. F5.
215. Rim sherd, brown to black interior, light orange fracture, grey-brown interior: smooth finish. 253/82. Site 2. F5.
216. Rim sherd, black exterior, dark orange-brown fracture, black interior: slight bead on rim: smooth finish. 248/82. Site 2. F5.
217. Lid sherd, dark orange-brown exterior, orange-brown fracture, black interior: smooth finish. 249/82. Site 2. F5.

Fabric Type LPC/5 (Fig. 48)
218. Bodysherd, brown exterior, dark grey fracture, orange-brown interior. This shoulder sherd has a circular depression impressed into it. It belongs to the series of tall situlate jars found in Brittany. The drawing has been modelled upon the jar from Roz-an-Trémen, Finistère (Giot *et al.* 1979, 237). 254/82. Site 2. F5.
219. Rim sherd, dark grey exterior, mid-brown fracture, black interior: smooth finish. 255/82. Site 2. F5.

Fabric Type LPC/6
220. Rim sherd, orange-brown exterior, orange-brown fracture, pale orange-brown interior: bead rim: very smooth finish. 256/82. Site 2. F5.
221. Basal sherd, orange-brown exterior, orange-brown fracture, black interior: rough finish. 257/82. Site 2. F5.

Haematite-coated ware (Fig. 48)
222. Rim sherd, pale orange exterior, pale orange fracture, orange interior: traces of haematite coating on exterior: abraded. 258/82. Site 2. F5.

The Gallo-Roman pottery from Sites 1 and 4
(Fig. 49)

Fuller descriptions on illustrated sherds marked with an asterisk will be found in the reports by Mark Wood (pp. 52-5). The complete samian bowl, no. 223, is commented upon separately in the note by Brian Hartley (p. 52).

223. *Samian bowl, form 31R, bearing stamp with incuse lettering, HONORATI. 177/80. Site 1. F21.
224. *Abraded samian base, either form 15/17 or 18. 196/83. Site 4. F17/B6/L1.
225. *Abraded samian rim, either form 18 or 18/31. 181/83. Site 4. F37.
226. *Rim sherd, terra-nigra type, black exterior, pale grey fracture, dark grey interior: smooth finish. 178/80. Site 1. F12.
227. *Rim sherd, grey ware, abraded dark grey exterior, pale grey fracture, pale grey interior: smooth finish. 176/80. Site 1. F21.
228. *Rim sherd, terra-nigra type, dark grey exterior, pink-buff fracture, grey-brown interior: smooth finish. 197/83. Site 4. F17/B5/L1.
229. *Rim sherd, terra-nigra type, abraded dark grey exterior, pale grey fracture, pale grey interior: smooth finish. 169/80. Site 1. F10.
230. *Rim sherd, terra-nigra type, grey-black exterior, pale grey fracture, grey-black interior: abraded, smooth finish. 194/83. Site 1. F29.
231. *Rim sherd, terra-nigra type, grey exterior, pale grey fracture, grey interior: smooth finish. 202/83. Site 4. F27.
232. *Rim sherd, grey ware, dark grey exterior, pale grey fracture, dark grey interior: possibly Romano-British. 168/80. Site 1. F10.
233. *Base, terra-nigra type, black exterior, orange-brown fracture, dark grey interior. 198/83. Site 4. F17/B2/L1.
234. *Rim sherd, terra-nigra type, grey-black exterior, pale grey fracture, grey-black interior. 188/83. Site 4. F31/37.
235. Base of strainer, terra-nigra type, grey-black exterior, pale grey fracture, grey-black interior: smooth finish. 205/83. Site 4. F29.
236. *Bodysherd, terra-nigra type, rouletted decoration. 200/83. Site 1. F17/B2/L1.
237. *Bodysherd, terra-nigra type, grey exterior, buff fracture, grey interior: seed pattern decoration. 180/83. Site 4. F31.

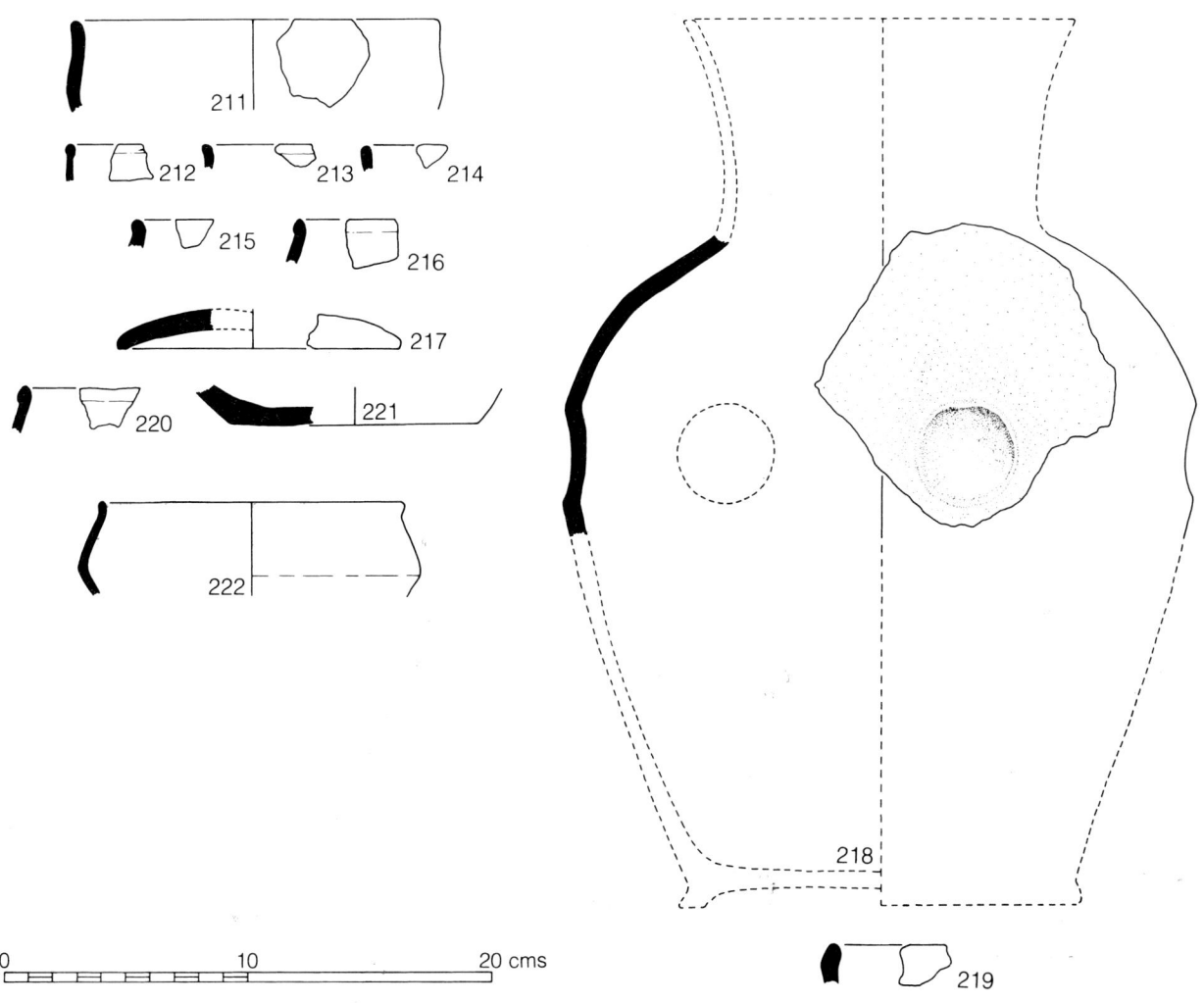

Figure 48 *King's Road: Early to Middle Iron Age wares from Sites 2 and 3.*

238. *Rim sherd, terra-nigra type, grey-black exterior, pale grey fracture, grey-black interior: smooth finish. 190/83. Site 4. F31/37.

239. *Rim sherd, grey ware, grey exterior, grey fracture, pale grey interior: abraded, smooth finish. 179/80. Site 1. F15.

240. Rim sherd, grey ware, light grey exterior, light grey fracture, light grey interior: abraded. 172/80. Site 1. F21.

241. *Rim sherd, grey ware, grey throughout: sandy finish. 203/83. Site 4. F20.

242. Basal sherd, terra-nigra type, abraded dark grey exterior, mid-grey fracture, mid-grey interior: smooth finish. 170/80. Site 1. F10.

243. Basal sherd, grey ware, dark grey exterior, mid-grey fracture, dark grey interior: smooth finish. 173/80. Site 1. F21.

244. Base, grey ware, grey throughout: micaceous: rough finish. 204/83. Site 4. F31.

245. *Bodysherd, grey ware, grey exterior, black fracture, grey interior: bands appearing silver-grey, burnished around girth. 171/80. Site 1. F21.

246. Rim sherd (of beaker?), orange-brown exterior, brown fracture, orange-brown interior: micaceous: smooth finish. 168A/83. Site 4. F31/37.

247. Rim sherd, pink-buff exterior, salmon-pink fracture, pale buff interior: smooth finish. 175/80. Site 1. F21.

248. Flagon base, redware, soft oxidized red fabric throughout. Approximately half of the lower portion of this vessel was set into the soil close to the anvil in F17. 206/83. Site 4. F33.

249. Handle, pale buff oxidized fabric throughout. 186/83. Site 4. F31/37.

250. Ribbed handle fragment, pale buff soft oxidized fabric throughout. 183/83. Site 4. F37.

251. Flagon base, pale buff-pink fabric throughout, thin white slip applied externally: micaceous. 187/83. Site 4. F31/37.

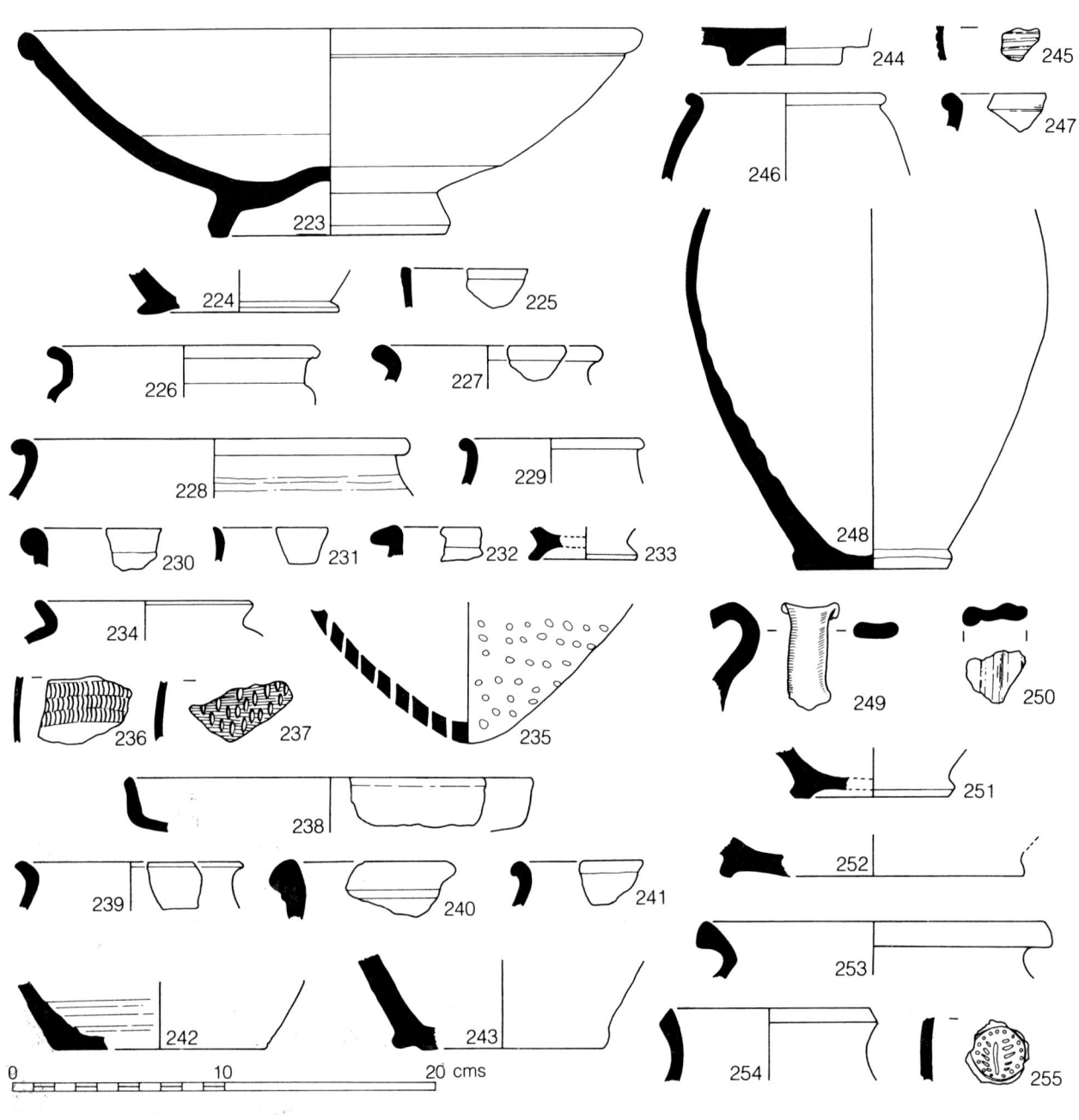

Figure 49 *King's Road: Gallo-Roman and medieval pottery.*

Medieval pottery from Site 4 (Fig. 49)

252. Basal sherd, black exterior, orange-brown fracture, black interior: micaceous: smooth finish. (This sherd is similar to Fabric Type 4 and is possibly redeposited in the later context.)

253. Rim sherd from cooking-pot, pale creamy buff fabric throughout, clear grains of sand and white quartz erupting through the surface. Normandy Gritty Ware, fourteenth or fifteenth century AD. 209A/83. Site 4. F28.

254. Rim sherd from a pitcher, creamy buff fabric with erupting sand grains. Normandy Gritty Ware, fourteenth or fifteenth century AD. 209/83. Site 4. F60.

255. Decorative applied pad from a Rouen-type jug. White clay on a buff, red-slipped body. 208/83. Site 4. F60. Identical decoration can be seen on Rouen jugs found in Paris and at Southampton (Nicourt 1986, 249, no. 3; Platt and Coleman-Smith 1975, 133, no. 976, these last considering their sherd to be of thirteenth century date).

Small finds

Apart from the objects found with the warrior burial (below, pp. 85-92) small finds were not prolific. Items are listed and discussed here according to material. Opportunity has also been taken to list and illustrate eight polished stone implements recovered over the years from the King's Road area.

Copper Alloy objects (Fig. 50)

Only two fragmentary copper alloy objects were found during the excavations. No. 1 appears to be part of a buckle. No. 2 is a small piece of bronze sheet pierced for attachment, perhaps to a leather belt or garment.

1. Buckle fragment? Site 4. F10.
2. Pierced sheet. Site 1. F10.

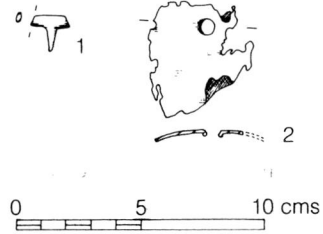

Figure 50 *King's Road: objects of copper alloy.*

Iron objects (Fig. 51)

With the exception of the iron objects present in Grave 1 on Site 2, metal objects of any type were uncommon finds at King's Road. They consisted in the main of nails, ranging in size from 100 mm to 50 mm. There were a few flat pieces, possibly parts of blades and a variety of small lumps of indeterminate form. In all cases the iron objects had suffered from the acidic soils of the site and were in poor condition. The three metal strips from Grave 3 on Site 3 are all similar in size and shape; they all have mineralized wood traces adhering and presumably form part of the surviving fittings from a box or similar object.

1. Nail. Site 4. F17/B6/L2.
2. Nail. Site 4. F17/B5/L1.
3. Nail. Site 1. F10.
4. Nail. Site 4. F17/B4/L2.
5. Nail. Site 4. F17/B6/L2.
6. Nail. Site 4. F26.
7. Nail. Site 4. F29.
8. Nail. Site 2. F1.
9. Nail. Site 4. F17/B4/L2.
10. Nail. Site 2. F5.
11. Nail. Site 4. F17/B4/L2.
12. Nail. Site 4. F17/B4/L2.
13. Blade? Site 4. F10.
14. Blade? Site 1. F10.
15. Blade? Site 4. F53.
16. Blade? Site 4. F54.
17. Rivet? Site 2/L3.
18. Strip. Grave 3. Site 3.
19. Strip. Grave 3. Site 3.
20. Strip. Grave 3. Site 3.

Objects of Shale (Fig. 52)

These were rare and fragmentary finds; two bracelets were represented, one from Site 2, the other from Site 4. Site 4 also produced part of a turned shale bowl from the main ditch.

Shale bowls modelled upon contemporary pottery forms are known from other pre-conquest deposits (Cunliffe 1982, fig. 15). Two other shale bracelet or armlet rough-outs, one from St. Peter Port Harbour and one from Herm, are illustrated below (Fig. 82).

1. Bracelet fragments. Site 4. F17/B3/L2.
2. Bracelet fragment. Site 3. F8.
3. Rectangular fragment. Site 4. F17/B6/L2.
4. Bowl fragment with cordon. Site 4. F17/B4/L2.

Ceramic spindle-whorls (Fig. 53)

Site 1 produced three clay spindle-whorls and a stone loom-weight in close association, this perhaps denoting a dedicated textile-working area. Two of the whorls were specifically made for the purpose, the others were manufactured from re-utilized pottery

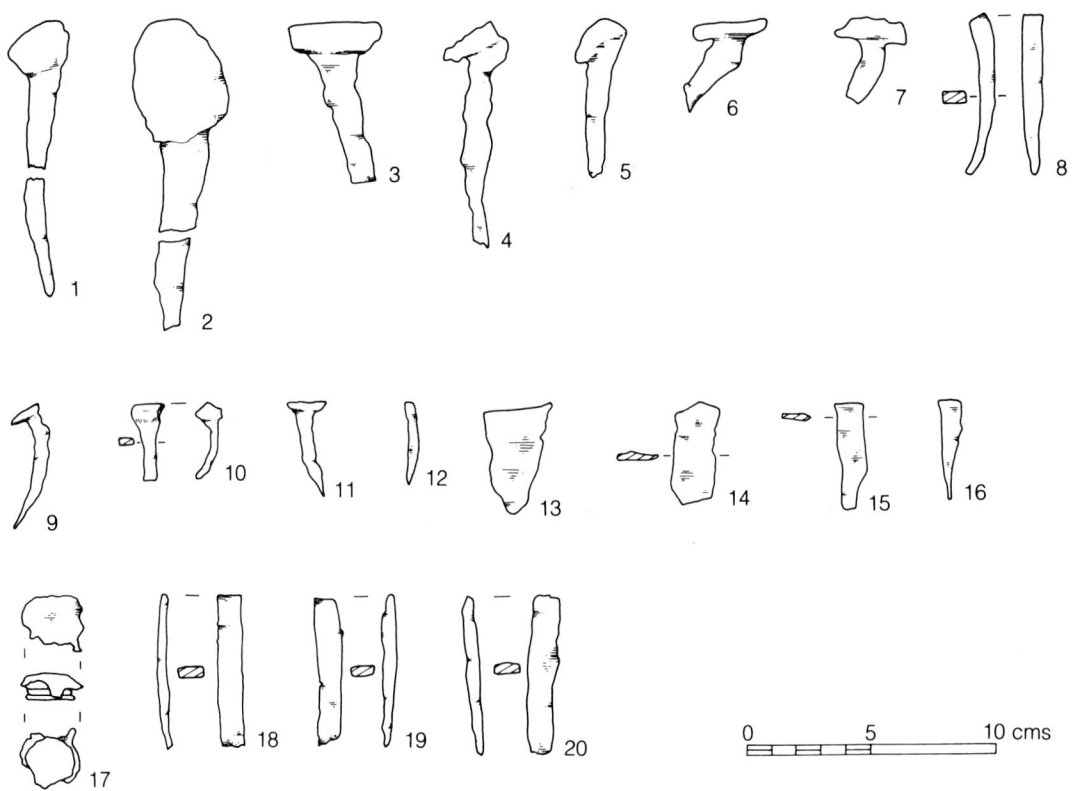

Figure 51 *King's Road: objects of iron.*

sherds. Two shaped fired-clay objects were also discovered on Site 1; their purpose or function is unclear, although they appear to have been carefully shaped into their final form.

1. Spindle-whorl. Made in Fabric 1. Site 1. F10.
2. Spindle-whorl. Made in Fabric 2. Site 2. F5.
3. Spindle-whorl. Re-utilized sherd of Fabric 2. Site 1. F10.
4. Spindle-whorl. Re-utilized amphora sherd. Site 1. F10.
5. Shaped clay object. Site 1. F10.
6. Shaped clay object. Site 1. F10.

Utilized Stone objects (Fig. 54)

(The identifications of the rock and mineral types have been made by Alan Howell, Guernsey Museum.)

Whilst it is apparent that shape, size and texture were taken into consideration when selecting the raw materials for the manufacture of the various tool types found at the site, it is difficult to discern any regular or significant patterns. The main tool types, as might be expected, are of simple design and have much in common with utilized stone implements found on Neolithic and Bronze Age sites throughout the island. With this in mind and considering the more identifiable

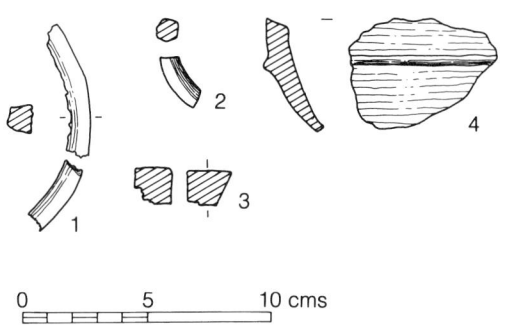

Figure 52 *King's Road: objects of Kimmeridge shale.*

Neolithic and Bronze Age artefacts found during the excavations, it is highly probable that some of the tools listed here are residual in the later Iron Age contexts. Similar raw materials can be readily collected from the island's beaches today.

The surviving fragments of querns, which are with one possible exception of the saddle type, have, not surprisingly, been selected for their abrasive qualities. Granodiorites from the Bordeaux exposures on the north-east coast of the island are present, as are examples from the Cobo rocks on the west coast.

The tool types present on the site include rubbers, grinders, hammers, whetstones and smoothing stones. There is a single example of a loom-weight and a much burnt stone with an hourglass perforation which is possibly a fragment of a tuyère.

The collection fits in well with assemblages from other Late Iron Age sites, for instance the finds from Hengistbury Head (Cunliffe 1987, ill. 123).

Catalogue of utilized stone objects

1. Elongated pebble fragment abraded on its surviving end, the other (broken) end is rubbed into two opposing planes. There are slight indentations pecked into one side of the central portion. A sandstone with similarities to that from Alderney.

   Site 4. F17/B6/L3.

2. Elongated pebble fragment with depressed and smoothed central portion, abraded on surviving end. A dual-purpose whetstone/grinder. Well cemented and tough quartzite.

   Site 4. F17/B5/L2.

3. Elongated pebble of triangular section, rubbed into opposing planes on its surviving end. A dolerite, possibly local.

   Site 4. F25.

4. Elongated pebble of roughly triangular section, two scars remain from flakes detached from its larger end. A biotite/granite gneiss, probably local.

   Site 1. F21.

5. Trapezoidal pebble, slight indications of wear on one edge and on its 'base'. Perhaps used as a smoother. A very fine-grained sandstone or quartzite.

   Site 1. F21.

6. Triangular beach pebble, rubbed into two opposed planes on the larger end. A veined microdiorite or dolerite of probable local origin.

   Site 1. F10.

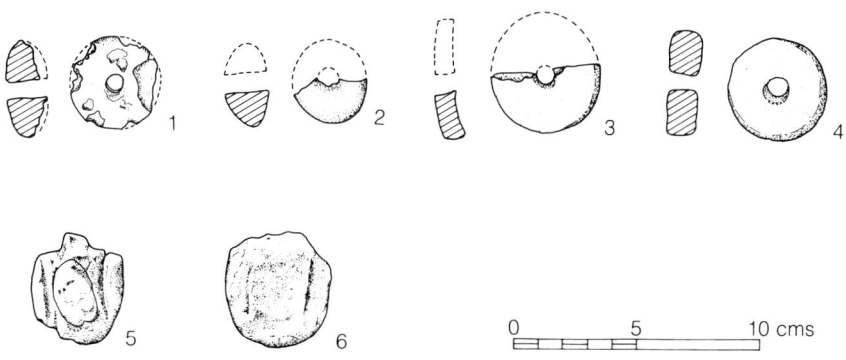

Figure 53 *King's Road: objects of baked clay.*

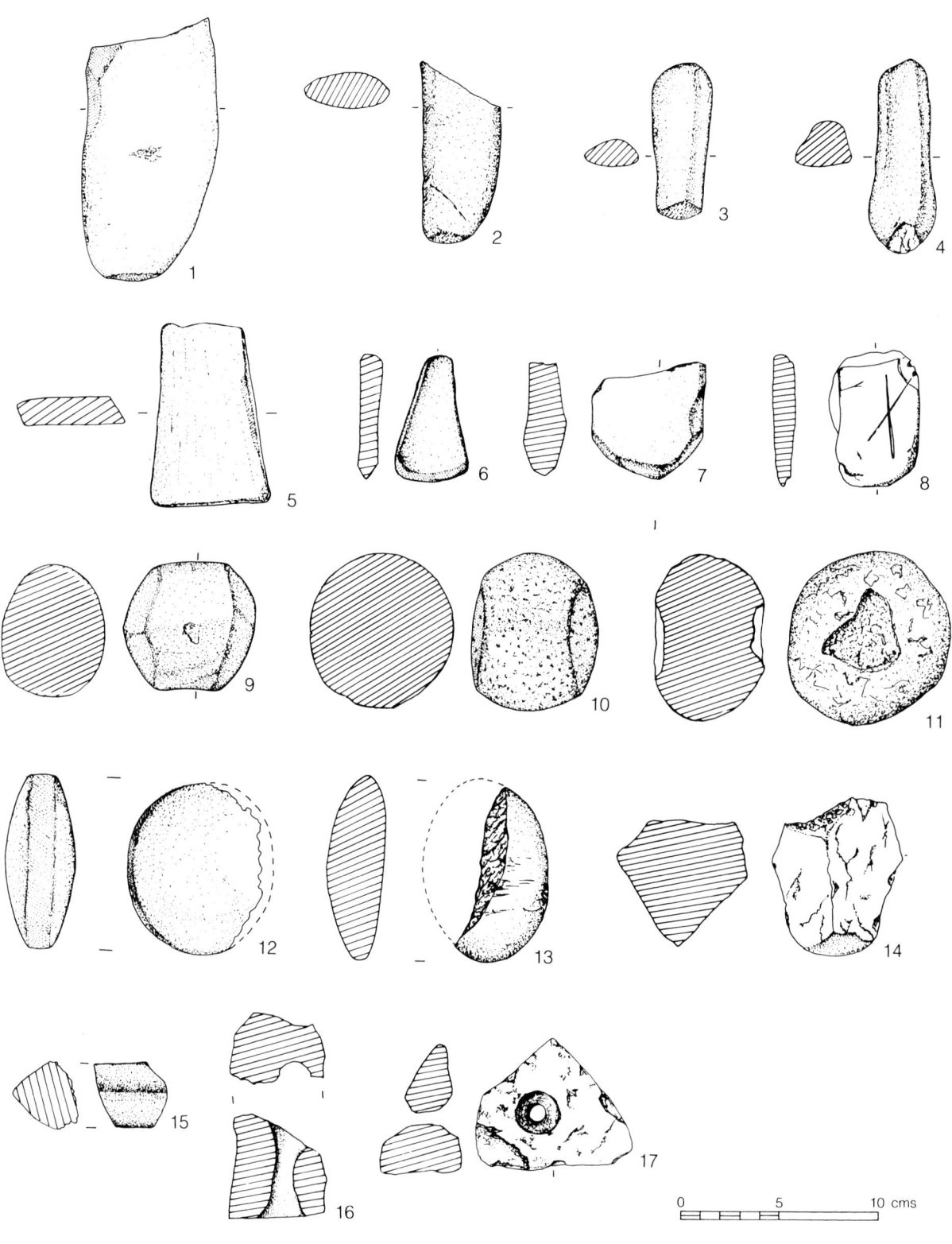

Figure 54 *King's Road: utilized stone.*

7. Pebble fragment of roughly rectangular section, rubbed on its surviving end into several opposed planes. A poorly cemented sandstone.

   Site 4. F17/B5/L2.

8. Sea-washed? pebble with knife? cuts on both sides. A slaty meta-sediment, unlikely to be local.

   Site 4. F10.

9. Spherical pebble, rubbed into several opposed planes at either end. A porphyritic micro-granite granophyre, possibly local.

   Site 1. F10.

10. Spherical pebble, rubbed flat on both sides. A local granodiorite, possibly Bordeaux diorite.

    Site 1. F10.

11. Spherical pebble, hammered on both sides. Vein quartz as at Marble Bay, St. Martin's.

    Site 1. F10.

12. Flattened spherical pebble, rubbed flat around what survives of its edges. Quartzite.

    Site 1. F10.

13. Oval pebble fragment, utilized on central face and on surviving central edge. A very fine-grained holocrystalline igneous rock with feldspars and altered? horneblende, possibly of volcanic origin.

    Site 1. F10.

14. Pebble of roughly triangular section, worn and hammered on its smaller end. Vein quartz, as at Marble Bay, St. Martin's.

    Site 3. F5.

15. Small fragment, detached from a larger stone rubber? Mica lamprophyre, local.

    Site 1. F19.

16. Fragment of stone with an hourglass perforation. Perhaps part of a tuyère or a loom-weight. This rock has been subjected to very high temperatures altering and concealing its mineral appearance. Fibrous actinolite.

    Site 4. F10.

17. Triangular stone with an hourglass perforation, possibly a loom-weight. A soft, greasy micaceous rock, possibly a soapstone. The rock has been burnt and could be a local amphibole, actinolite-rich rock which can change to soapstone after heating.

    Site 1. F10.

Quern fragments (Not illustrated)

Saddle-quern fragment of pinkish rock, possibly Cobo adamellite from the west coast.

Site 3. F8.

Fragment from the upper part of a rotary quern, sooted. A granodiorite of the Bordeaux diorite group.

Site 4. F17.

Saddle-quern fragment, local granodiorite, possibly from the Bordeaux group in the north of the island.

Site 4. F10.

The Flintwork (Fig. 55) by Ian Kinnes (illustrations by Jenny Grant)

There is no positive evidence that this small quantity of material represents an assemblage (47 struck pieces). It derives either from unstratified deposits or is apparently residual in Iron Age contexts. The sharper or finer edges normally show damage, as likely to be the result of movement within the ground as original utilization.

As is normal to Channel Islands flintwork, there are real difficulties in providing a date. The raw material is consonant with local beach pebbles where both nodular size and fissile quality form a natural restriction on the possible range of forms and the quality of the end-product.

Both flake and blade production are attested in roughly a 5:1 proportion by cores and debitage. There seems to be an incipient trend in the islands from early Neolithic blade industries to Chalcolithic flake-dominated, but groups such as this cannot be securely located. Certainly, there is no indication of the early tradition of narrow blade manufacture from prismatic cores.

The identifiable implements are all consonant with a later Neolithic-Chalcolithic attribution: barbed and tanged arrowheads and steeply retouched scrapers. The transverse arrowhead might be earlier but does appear, not apparently as a residual, in stratified assemblages such as Les Fouaillages and La Hougue Catelain (Hill 1990). Notable amongst the scrapers are three examples (Fig. 55, nos. 4-6) which represent a distinctive characteristic of beach-pebble material: simply, in primary core preparation, one end is removed as a slice to provide a platform; the slice, rather like the top of an egg, is then given simple marginal trimming to form the scraper. The other tools represented, knife, awl and notched flake (spoke-shave?) are unsurprising in such a group.

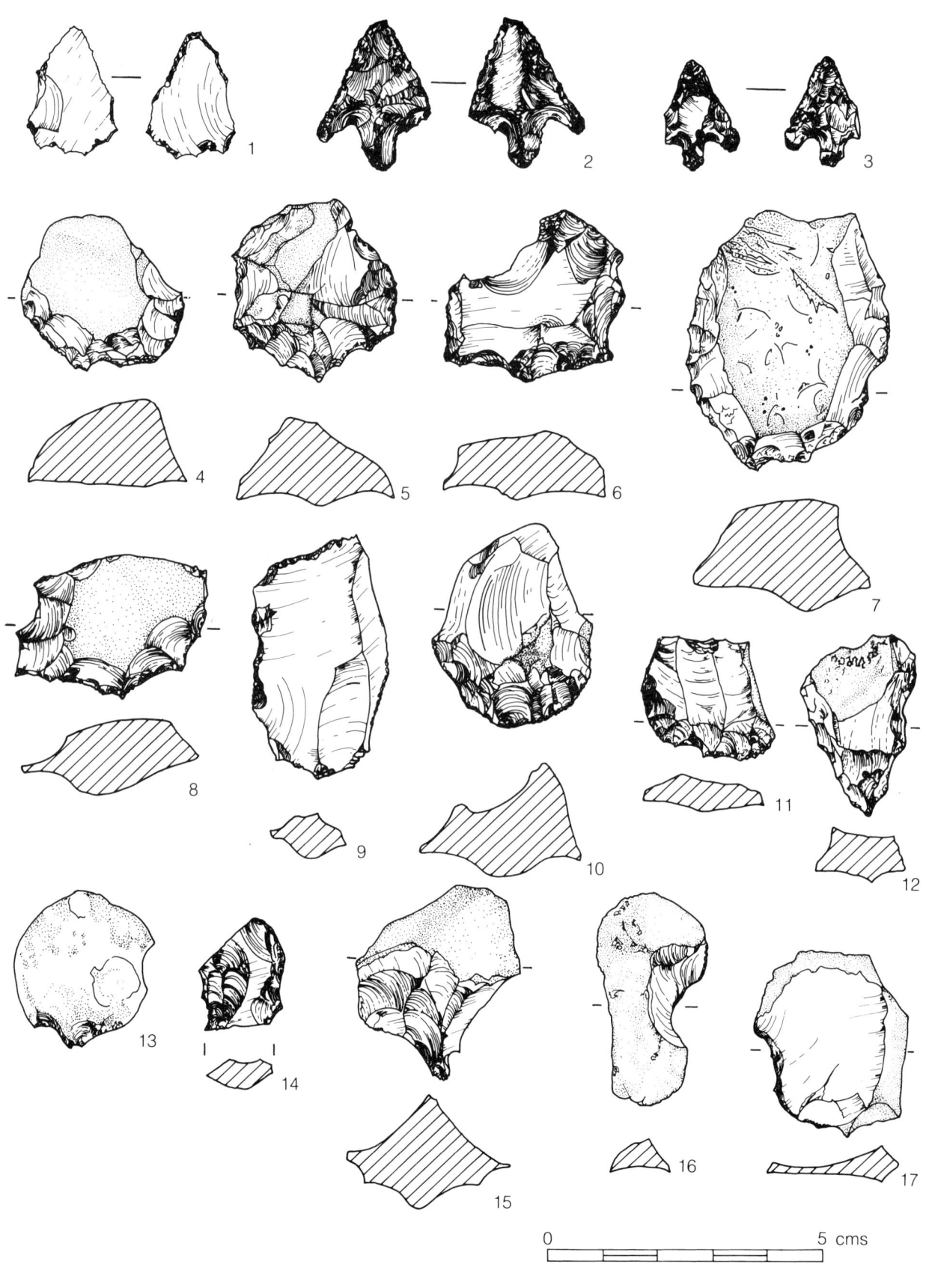

Figure 55 *King's Road: worked flints.*

All are, or could be consonant with a later Neolithic-Chalcolithic date. On-site working is demonstrated by the presence of cores and debitage. Raw material derives from beach-pebbles involving some collection and transport to the site. The tool types present the usual domestic activity, although the impact fracture on the point of one arrowhead (Fig. 55, no. 2) hints at greater drama.

Catalogue of illustrated flint (Fig. 55)

1. Transverse arrowhead on flake, fine steep retouch to triangular form, edge damaged.
    L 22: W 16: Th 3   Site 4. F127

2. Barbed and tanged arrowhead, fine all over pressure flaking on ventral with limited on dorsal; one barb broken; point lacking by impact fracture.
    L 25: W 19: Th 5   Site 4. F17/B2/1

3. Barbed and tanged arrowhead, coarse all over pressure flaking on dorsal and partial on ventral; one barb broken.
    L 19: W 15: Th 5   Site 4. F17/B1/1

4. Horse-shoe scraper on core-trimming flake, fine steep marginal retouch.
    L 28: W 24: Th 15   Site 2. F4

5. Horse-shoe scraper on core-trimming flake, fine steep marginal retouch, heavy edge damage.
    L 34: W 30: Th 18   Site 4. F29

6. Horse-shoe scraper on core-trimming flake, irregular marginal retouch.
    L 27: W 27: Th 10   Site 4. U/S

7. Horse-shoe scraper on flake, coarse steep retouch, platform butt.
    L 44: W 35: Th 15   Site 4. F17/B3/1

8. End-and-side scraper on flake, coarse steep marginal retouch, platform butt.
    L 30: W 22: Th 14   Site 4. U/S

9. End-and-side scraper on flake, fine steep marginal retouch, platform butt.
    L 43: W 25: Th 7   Site 2. T3. U/S

10. End-scraper on flake, fine steep retouch.
    L 36: W 31: Th 19   Site 2. F5

11. Side scraper on flake, coarse irregular retouch, platform butt.
    L 43: W 25: Th 7   Site 2. T3. U/S

12. Scraper fragment, fine steep retouch, platform butt broken.
    L 31: W 20: Th 8   Site 3. F1

13. Scraper fragment on flake, fine steep retouch, broken.
    L 32: W 30: Th 12   Site 4. U/S

14. Knife fragment on blade, fine steep retouch, snapped.
    L 18: W 14: Th 4   Site 4. F29

15. Awl on blade core remnant, point worn by abrasion.
    L 28: W 35: Th 20   Site 4. F8

16. Notched flake, fine steep retouch.
    L 39: W 19: Th 9   Site 2. F5

17. Worked flake, fine retouch.
    L 33: W 29: Th 6   Site 4. F28

Other flintwork (Not illustrated)

3 flake core remnants	Site 3. F11; Site 4. F29
1 blade core-rejuvenation flake	Site 3. F5
1 core-trimming flake	Site 2. F8
21 primary flakes	Site 2. F5, F9, F10 Site 4. F13, F17, F122, F127
4 blades	Site 2. F5 Site 4. F12, F17
5 thermally fractured	Site 2. U/S Site 4. F122

Catalogue of antiquarian finds from the King's Road area (Fig. 56)

(Geological appraisals by Alan Howell.)

1. Ground and polished stone 'pick-axe'. Found at Courtil de la Rocque à L'Or, Vauquiédor, St. Peter Port.

    Serpentine rock, a highly altered basic rock with, in this example, a high percentage of magnetite. This material could occur within the mineralization zones of the St. Peter Port gabbro or perhaps in Sark. However a source in one of the classical serpentine areas such as the southern Loire or the Lizard peninsula is more likely.
    Collection No. GMAG 3507b.

2. Ground stone 'pick-axe'. Found at Courtil de la Rocque à L'Or, Vauquiédor, St. Peter Port.

    A dolerite or similar igneous rock, with a somewhat weathered appearance. The felspars are somewhat brownish and the ferro-magnesian materials also look somewhat altered. Probably from the Channel Islands.
    Collection No. GMAG 3507a.

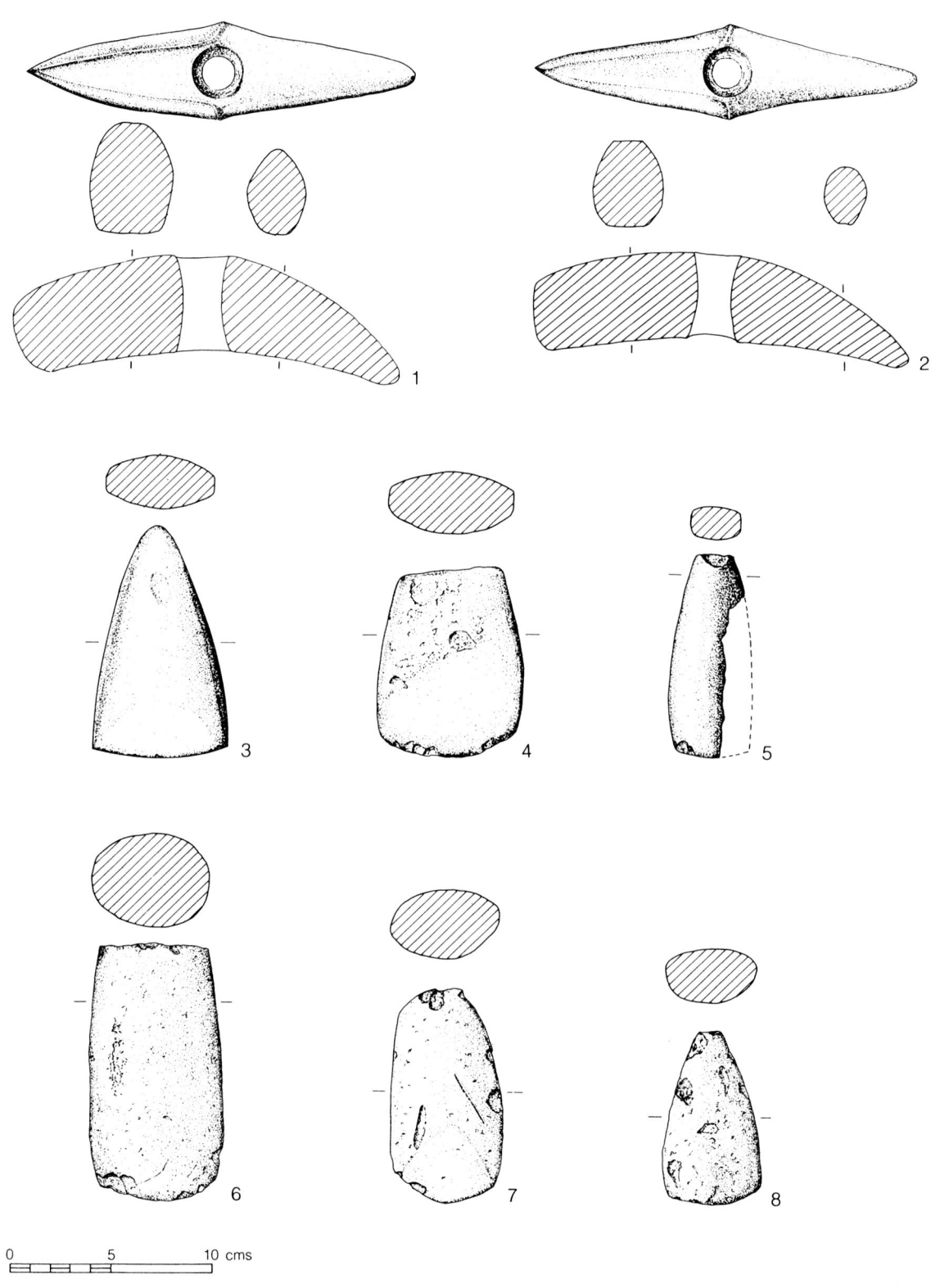

Figure 56 *Stone implements from the King's Road area.*

3. Ground and polished stone axe-head. Found at Mount Row, St. Peter Port.

    A dolerite or similar igneous rock, with rather porphyritic texture and a certain amount of mineral alteration. Possibly from the Channel Islands.

    Collection No. GMAG 2618.

4. Ground and polished stone axe. Found at Havilland Hall, St. Peter Port.

    A dolerite or similar igneous rock with a rather porphyritic texture. Probably from the Channel Islands.

    Collection No. GMAG 2786.

5. Ground and polished stone axe-head. Catalogued as from King's Road, but also labelled Bordeaux (an area on the north-east coast of the island), thus exact provenance unsure.

    A very fine-grained material, difficult to identify on macroscopic evidence alone, it may be a metasediment of some kind, or possibly an aphyric igneous rock. Possibly from the Channel Islands.

    Collection No. GMAG 2749.

6. Ground stone axe-head. Found at Courtil à L'Or, King's Road, St. Peter Port.

    A dolerite or similar igneous rock, with a somewhat porphyritic texture and lath-like amphiboles. This specimen has been identified by Charles-Tanguy Le Roux as being of Dolerite Type A, the source being Sélédin à Plussulien, Côtes-d'Armor, Brittany.

    Collection No. GMAG 2749.

7. Ground stone axe-head, plough-scarred. Found at Queen's Road, St. Peter Port and bears a label 'Neolithic celt 27.7.(18)97. On Mr Wm. Carey's land at Queens Rd'.

    A fine-grained dolerite with a rather felted texture. The ferro-magnesian minerals show evidence of alteration, perhaps to actinolite. Quite probably from the Channel Islands.

    Collection No. GMAG 2784.

8. Crudely manufactured ground stone axe-head, plough scarred. Found at La Grande Marche (King's Road).

    A dolerite with a rather finer grained texture than example no. 7. The ferro-magnesian and felspar minerals show less evidence of alteration. Quite probably from the Channel Islands.

    Collection No. GMAG 2618.

Author's note: A source at Le Pinacle, Jersey, has been suggested for the axes of porphyritic dolerite, but it is more probable that they were manufactured from separate sources in the various islands.

Specialist reports

Slag by Chris Salter

Approximately 650 grammes of slag were recovered during the excavation, with the material being equally divided between the two main phases (see Table 1). The external and internal morphology of the slag was entirely consistent with material being formed during iron-smithing. The larger bun-shaped pieces of slag were almost certainly formed during the welding process, when the forge-hearth is run at rather higher temperatures than is the case for simple forging (metal-shaping). A number of the samples were heavily abraded. This suggests that some of the slag was in a secondary deposit, or at least spent some time in an environment where the slag was subjected to abrasive wear, such as a floor or a plough-soil.

No micro-slag such as hammer-scale, or millimetre-sized slag was recovered, although this should have occurred in large quantities around the hearth, anvil and in the quench-pot, if it is such. [Author's note: There was a thick layer of charcoal distributed around the anvil-stone and also deposits were present in the base of the pot, but unfortunately none were collected for expert analysis]. The recent excavations at Maiden Castle produced over 20 kg of hammer-scale in the sample taken from the floor of the forge at the Eastern Gateway. The low amount of slag found would also reinforce the idea that this smithy was a very peripheral affair, temporarily set up for the production of some immediately needed artefact, such as the nails found on the site. On the other hand, the nails may well have been the raw material for the smith. In general, the amount of slag found is fairly typical of many Iron Age rural settlements in Britain (Case *et al.* 1965). Another possibility is that the floor of the forge was kept clean and the main deposit of slag was deposited elsewhere. The evidence from other sites, however, for example those at Bryn y Castell, Cracwellt and Maiden Castle, is that the slag was moved as short a distance as possible, if at all. At Maiden Castle, the charcoal, hammer-scale and slag built up into a floor over 100 mm thick. The find of a stone anvil is unusual although an example, together with two hammer-stones, was recovered at Bryn y Castell, Gwynedd in Wales (Crew 1987).

In summary, the material indicates two very short-lived episodes of iron-working activity, involving iron welding as well as forging. Unless the majority of the slag had been removed from the site, which would seem unlikely, the quantity of iron processes must have been very small, probably for a specific purpose.

The slags, in general, were of the iron oxide-fayalite-glass type typical of British Iron Age iron-working slags. They exhibit primary globular wustite and dendritic wustite and/or magnetite, overgrown by long thin fayalite laths in a 'glassy' potassium-calcium iron alumino-silicate, with more magnetite precipitating out of the glass. Sample KR5 from F29, though, consisted mainly of primary fayalite in the glassy matrix. The potassium to calcium ratio was unusually high compared with many British iron-working slags. This may be a reflection of the composition of the charcoal used.

Table 1. Samples submitted

Feature No.	Description	Qty	Weight (gms)	No.
Late Iron Age. Phase 1				
KR83/F1	Small irregular piece of high-density slag	1	26	7b
KR80/F6	Slag flow with small quartz crystals partially absorbed	1	1	12
KR80/F16	Fragment of bun-shaped slag with included quartz pebbles	1	69	8
KR83/F40	Thick bun-shaped slag	1	203	9
Second-third century AD. Phase 2				
KR83/F17/L2	Small fragment of slag with smooth flow surfaces	1	20	7a
KR83/F17/L2	One large and one very small quartz slag aggregate	2	60	13
KR83/F17/L2	Fragments of slag, probably hearth bottom	4	23	2
KR83/F17/L2	Two very small sinter-type slag fragments and hammer-scale	2	1	14
KR83/F29/L1	Fragmented portion of bun-shaped slag flow	1	74	5
KR83/F29/L1	Fragments of lining reaction product	3	13	15
KR83/F29/L1	Slag fragment	1	14	16
KR83/F31	Reaction between hearth-lining and slag	1	41	17
KR83/F31/37	Worn fragment of flat bun-shaped slag	1	62	10
KR83/F31/37	Small fragments of blue/grey high density slag with high pore content	2	14	18

Animal Bones by Jennifer Coy

Author's note: Bone from prehistoric deposits in Guernsey suffers greatly from the acidic nature of the granite-derived soils. In most cases all traces of such deposits have completely disappeared over time. However when deposits of bone are found in conjunction with shell, in the case of island sites this being mainly marine crustacea, survival can occur.

The two deposits discussed here occurred in conjunction with such shell deposits. In the main these comprised the common limpet, *patella vulgaris* but a few winkles, *littorina littoralis* and ormers, *haliotis tuberculata* were also present.

Three groups of bone are discussed. The first is from Site 1, F1, the second a small deposit from F10, the enclosure ditch and the third group is from Site 4, F35, which was a shell-midden in the fill of the enclosure ditch, F17.

Site 1, F1

This small collection of 47 fragments is worthy of documentation as it represents a rare find of bones from an Iron Age context in Guernsey.

The fragments were identified to domestic species as shown in Table 2. Bones unidentifiable to species were divided into 'C-size', those from 'cattle-sized' mammals – cattle, horse or red deer and 'S-size', these, whilst probably from sheep, could be from goat, pig or roe deer. One 'C-size' sacral fragment is probably horse.

The few measurements taken from these relatively well-preserved bones are given in Table 3 and represent small stock with delicate limbs. These individuals are small even for Iron Age stock, but there are parallels this small from Iron Age settlements in Wessex and in other parts of Europe.

Ageing and minimum number of individuals
Cattle jaws and teeth represent animals c.2 years of age, although one may be older. The radius and ulna suggest a somewhat older animal. The sheep metatarsal represents an animal over 2 years of age. A minimum of two cattle, one sheep and one pig is therefore represented with the possibility of one horse.

Butchery and usage
There are fine knife-cuts on cattle mandible, scapula, os coxa and ulna. Fourteen 'S-sized' fragments in F1 and those in F10 are calcined.

Table 2. Identification of the fragments

	Cattle	C-size	Sheep	Pig	S-size
Site 1, F1					
mandible	1				
maxilla	1				
premaxilla				1	
scapula	1				
radius + ulna	1				
os coxa	1				
metapodial			1		
vertebra		3			
loose teeth	2				
long bone frags					14
unidentifiable		5			13
Totals	7	8	1	1	27
Site 1, F10					
long bone frags					3

Table 3. Measurements in millimetres

species	bone	description	*v.d.D.	mm
Cattle	mandible	height in front of M_2		51.3
	scapula	greatest length processus artic.	GLP	70.4
		breadth glenoid cavity	BG	50.9
		length glenoid cavity	LG	58.8
	os coxa	length acetabulum incl. lip	LA	63.9
	rad/ulna	greatest breadth proximal	Bp	58.5
Sheep	metatarsus	greatest length	GL	118.0
		proximal breadth	Bp	18.5
		proximal depth	PD	17.0
		min. breadth diaphysis	SD	9.2
		distal breadth	Bd	19.8
		+this gives withers height of		53 cm

References: * (von den Driesch 1976)
+ (Teichert 1975)

Site 4, F35

A number of fragments were cleaned of soil and dried slowly in air, before being identified as to species and anatomical element, where possible. They were recorded using the site block and layer numbers. Forty-three of them were mammalian fragments, probably all from domestic horse, cattle, sheep and pig (Table 4).

The horse teeth and jaw remains could all come from the same individual head. Horse was probably eaten at this period but as only jaw remains were found, it is impossible to tell in this particular case. None of the bone fragments in this collection show butchery, probably because most are badly eroded.

The cattle metatarsus is from a calf and the vertebrae are from a skeletally immature animal with unfused epiphyses. The sheep or goat remains are more likely to be from the former species as goats are rare finds in the Iron Age, but only the radius is anatomically identifiable to sheep. This bone, the vertebrae, two of the maxillae and a rib classified to 'S-size', are all from immatures. The two maxillae are from different individuals of a similar age, with all the milk molars in wear and the first permanent molar erupting. The third maxilla is from an adult with all three permanent molars erupted.

The pig femur is from a skeletally immature animal and it is not possible to tell whether this is from a wild or domestic form. The two fragments may belong to the same bone.

At least two of the fragments tabled under 'C-sized' in Table 4 are very large and amorphous. There is a possibility that they might in fact be from a whale and this should be borne in mind for future finds. The cortex appears to be very thin, but it is difficult with such eroded material, to be sure how much of this is due to erosion.

Table 4. Identification of the fragments: Site 4, F35

	Horse	Cattle	C-size	Sheep/Goat	Pig	S-size	Total
cranium		1		1			2
maxilla				3			3
mandible	1						1
vertebra		3	3	2			8
rib						3	3
scapula						1	1
radius				1			1
femur					2		2
metapodial		1					1
loose teeth	6	3			1		10
long bone frag						2	2
fragment			9				9
Total	7	8	12	7	3	6	43

Molluscs by Jessica Winder and Mike Allen

The following were identified:
cepea nemoralis A catholic species of land mollusc found in woods, hedges, scrub and grassland.
littorina littoralis The flat periwinkle, a marine winkle.
patella vulgata The common limpet.
haliotis tuberculata The ormer, modern specimens show the same 'ornamentation' and growth ridges.

Discussion

The excavations at King's Road have helped to enlarge the body of knowledge relating to the later Iron Age, enhancing the results gained from the excavation of the settlement site at the Tranquesous.

King's Road itself provided clues that the area had been used during the later Neolithic and the Bronze Ages. The antiquarian finds and the pottery and flintwork recovered during the excavations must not be considered as unduly significant. It is true to say that virtually every excavation undertaken on the island reveals artefactual evidence relating to those early periods. No evidence of actual occupation has been found *in situ* and the finds, mostly redeposited, are more likely to represent sporadic, non permanent usage of the area.

The early phase of the Iron Age site represented by the ditches on Sites 2 and 3 have not been fully investigated and its possible layout and purpose are not understood. It is however of some significance that it lies so close to the later site and surely demonstrates a degree of continuity of occupation in the area. It is from the early phase on Site 2 that the only convincing traces of a palisade slot in the bottom of a ditch (F5) were discovered. The ditches on Sites 1 and 4 showed no evidence for palisades or fences placed within them, in fact on Site 4 the fence seems to have been placed immediately inside the inner edge of the ditch, as evidenced by the row of post-holes discovered there. This situation was also seen at the Tranquesous where post-holes were found along the edge of the ditch. It is possible therefore that palisades placed within a deep ditch are an earlier feature not found on the later sites. The series of graves from Sites 2 and 3 were later insertions into the earlier horizons and can probably be associated with the occupation of Sites 1 and 4. The presence of the sherds of Type 3 vesicular ware associated with the burials but otherwise absent from Sites 2 and 3, further reinforces this argument.

Sites 1 and 4, essentially parts of the same settlement, provided the major evidence for the layout of the site and the way of life of its Late La Tène inhabitants. There are several striking similarities with the site at Le Braden close to Quimper in Brittany (Le Bihan 1984 and 1986). A small blacksmith's forge was situated in one of the ditches at Le Braden as was the case with F29 in the main ditch on Site 4. There were several graves under stone settings discovered at Le Braden and it is possible that the stone setting (F35), situated in the main ditch on Site 1, was also a grave, although no visible evidence of an interment or cremation could be discerned. The single circular post-built house on Site 4 is in the British tradition of circular dwellings but it is of note that a circular building was also present at Le Braden. The excavator of the French site notes this building as running against the normal tradition of rectangular dwellings in western France. It would seem perhaps that the Guernsey site and the settlement at Le Braden lie at the interface between the two traditions.

It is quite within the bounds of possibility that there was a regular sea-borne connection between the sites on the western and northern coasts of neighbouring Brittany and that at King's Road. Strong similarities in pottery styles existed on the later site at the Tranquesous and that at Alet, close to St. Malo, indicating that trading links at least were in existence. Whether these links were stronger with tribal or even family ties is wholly unknown.

Some of the daily activities at King's Road were revealed by the excavations: cattle and other livestock were reared, wheeled transport was used and metal-working and textile weaving were undertaken. Wine was imported probably by sea via neighbouring western Brittany. The burial has provided important information on clothing, weaponry and personal equipment as well as fresh evidence for the burial practices of the period. No evidence for pottery production was found on that portion of the site excavated but it must be noted that the greater part lies unexcavated, and very probably undisturbed, in the surrounding area.

The evidence from Sites 1 and 4 indicate a fairly short life for the settlement; there are very few instances of later Iron Age features intercutting. It is possible that the site at the Tranquesous which follows on chronologically from that at King's Road provided the next home for the inhabitants and their descendants from the earlier site.

In common with many sites of the Late La Tène period, the King's Road site appears to have been re-used once more at some time during the late second or early third century AD. There is no firm indication that the site remained in continuous use up to this later occupation and evidence for structures of the later period was absent from that part of the site which was examined. By this time the entrepôt at La Plaiderie was functioning and the island had been drawn into the Roman sphere of influence, forming a link in the sea-borne trade between Gaul and Britain.

The island and its archaeologists can be thankful for the happy geological and geographical circumstance which placed it in position. Trade between its neighbouring land masses, from the earliest periods in its history to the present day, have made it a desirable and profitable place in which to live. Those who take the ferries from St. Malo to the island and on to the south coast of England are travelling an enduring, tried and tested journey.

The Iron Age Burials of Guernsey

by Barry Cunliffe

Introduction

In 1848 F.C. Lukis published his paper entitled *Sepulchral Caves in the Isle of Guernsey* (Lukis 1848) in which he discussed a distinctive type of burial monument, essentially a long cist about 7 ft. in length built of two parallel rows of upright stones capped with horizontal slabs. Twenty such cists had been reported to him: he described five of them, a single cist at Les Issues found in 1818, a group of three which he examined at Le Catioroc in 1845 and a single example at Les Adams excavated in the same year. A few years later he described a fourth cist unearthed at Le Catioroc in 1851 (Lukis 1853). Several others were found subsequently. Of those recorded, the cist at La Hougue au Comte, discovered in 1885, produced an impressive range of grave goods (Derrick 1906) while a small cemetery of at least five examples were uncovered at Richmond between 1900 and 1905 (Anon. 1901).

By the time that Colonel de Guérin published his paper on the Bronze and Iron Age occupation of Guernsey (de Guérin 1918) more had come to light. In addition to those mentioned he lists two at La Hougue de Noirmont, Vale, one at Pulias, St. Sampson's and one in the churchyard of St. Saviour's.[1] The total would therefore seem to be 31.

There matters rested until 1982 when the excavation at King's Road, St. Peter Port produced a further four cist burials one of which contained warrior equipment.

Although the majority of the Guernsey cists were empty when found, eight (probably nine) produced grave goods of late pre-Roman Iron Age date and of these seven (probably eight) contained one or more swords. It would seem reasonable therefore to suggest that these long cists may represent an Iron Age burial tradition comparatively widespread on the island. Skeletal remains were rarely found but the absence of cremations and the coffin-like proportions of the cists suggests that the rite was one of extended inhumation, the lack of skeletons being the result of acid soil conditions, but at Les Adams part of a skull and an arm bone were recovered with grave goods. The description is vague but would fit an extended inhumation. It was this burial which Kendrick identified, wrongly, as coming from Lihou Island.

The Guernsey Iron Age cist burials have received comparatively little attention. Apart from the admirable summary given by Kendrick (1928, 190-8), which was illustrated with sketches of some of the objects, the finds have never been adequately published. The current state of research and in particular the discovery of the King's Road cemetery makes a more extended treatment desirable.

The present paper is divided into two sections: the first gives a full description of the material as it now survives, or was recorded before loss, while the second offers a discussion of the historical and cultural context of the burials. All the finds were cleaned and studied in the Laboratory of the Institute of Archaeology, University of Oxford by Sarah Watkins and Esther Cameron. Ms. Cameron has contributed observations on the organic residues preserved in the corrosion products of the iron artefacts and Dr. Gilmour offers a comment on the metallurgy of the swords.

Descriptions of the principal burials

The cemetery at King's Road, St. Peter Port

In 1982, during a rescue excavation carried out on a development site at King's Road, St. Peter Port, four burials were discovered and were carefully excavated by a professional team. The context details of the graves have been described in the excavation report above. Here only a brief summary is required.

The four burials, presumably extended inhumations, were laid in rectangular graves cut into the natural decayed granite (above, Fig. 21). In all four cases the graves were demarcated with large granite boulders. The bodies had entirely decayed, leaving no trace, but in grave 1 an internal timber structure composed of four upright posts was recorded together with evidence for a timber lining to the grave. This grave was evidently that of a warrior who was provided with equipment appropriate to his status. Grave 1, the warrior burial, is considered in detail here: the other graves are described in the excavation report above.

Grave 1: the warrior burial (Figs. 15-17)

The grave pit measured 2.6 m long by 1.9 m wide at its broadest. Its sides were almost vertical and it was cut to a depth of 1.25 m below the surface of natural. For the most part the grave had been dug into the filling of ditch F5 but both ends extended beyond the limits of the ditch.

Within the grave pit a four-post structure had been erected before the burial was laid in position. The structure was represented by four post-holes cut into the bottom of the grave:

ph 1 (SE corner) cut to a depth of 0.12 m below the grave bottom. Filled with grey/brown silty clay with a stone boulder *c*.0.10 m across towards the centre.

ph 2 (SW corner) cut to a depth of 0.22 m below the grave bottom. Filled with grey/brown silty clay with some charcoal flecks.

ph 3 (NE corner) cut to a depth of 0.22 m below the grave bottom. Filled with mottled black/brown silty clay.

ph 4 (NW corner) cut to a depth of 0.25 m below the grave bottom. Filled with blackish-brown silty clay. Towards the bottom was an iron nail beneath a large boulder *c*.0.22 m across.

Although the post-holes were not traced through the filling of the grave pit as it was being excavated the spatial relationships of the posts, the grave pit and the burial suggest that the posts were probably standing upright when the body was laid in position and the grave filled. It will be apparent from the plan that the hilt end of the sword lay over the edge of ph 1. If it is assumed that the posts were some centimetres less in diameter than the post-holes then the sword hilt could have been lying against the side of the post.

Another factor which argues in favour of the posts standing upright at the time of the grave filling is the relationship of their supposed positions to the stone curb described below: the stones appear to have been laid to avoid the posts. Only the NW post-hole was partially overlapped by a stone but the stone could have slipped into the void after the post was removed or had rotted.

The exact nature of the timber structure is impossible now to determine. The positions of the sword and the spear and the anticipated length of the body (assuming a normal size and an extended inhumation burial) would argue against any vertical boarding between the northern or southern pairs of posts, but beneath the burial deposit was an organic-rich layer 0.02-0.05 m thick derived largely from the decay of the body, including the total disintegration of the bones. In places however there were indications of timber graining suggesting that the body may have been laid on a floor of timber planks. A rather more substantial timber stain 1.2 m long and 0.2 m wide occurred between the two western posts above the level of the body, though its original function must remain unknown. What is clear, therefore, is that the vertical timbers retained planking which lined the sides of the grave. It may be that the substantial timber lying within the grave fill was a revetting plank which had become dislodged. The possible implications of this will be considered below. Around the upper part of the grave a curb of granite boulders *c*.0.3-0.4 m across had been placed outside the timber lining.

Of the body itself nothing remained, the acidity of the soil being such that even the bones had disintegrated leaving some small cavities in the lowest filling of gritty sand. We may assume, however, from the position of the grave goods that the body was extended lying on its back with head to the south. The weapons buried with the dead person would suggest that the body was male. On his right side was an iron sword in an iron scabbard. Towards the hilt end was a leather pouch containing a razor and a pair of shears. Close by was an amber bead presumably once tied to the sword hilt. Some traces of a leather strap or belt were found over where the upper abdomen of the body is thought to have been. Across the body had been placed the shield represented now by its iron boss with nearby staining suggestive of leather or wood. The right edge of the shield would have covered the sword. Beneath the left edge was a copper alloy ring, the size and position of which would suggest it may have been a finger ring worn by the deceased. The spear, represented now by the iron spearhead, was placed on the left hand side of the body. Roughly in the position of the right hand side of the chest was an iron fibula and a number of other small iron items.

The grave pit above the body was filled with orange-brown clayey soil. While the structure of the grave pit and the disposition of the body and grave goods can be described with some precision, the processes involved in the act of burial must, of necessity, remain obscure. We can be sure, however, that the timber-lined grave pit, probably with its stone curb, was constructed first and the body of the deceased warrior with his equipment was later laid out on the bottom. Finally the grave was filled or allowed to fill. While the sequence is clear the time intervals involved and the associated rituals are not. It may be that the processes of construction, deposition and refilling followed closely one upon the other as would today be the case, but it is equally possible that considerable time intervals intervened. It could, for example, be that the body was laid out within the grave beneath the four-post structure and that it remained uncovered while a series of ritual activities took place. It may even have been that the four-post structure provided a platform for activities associated with the burial rites. Another alternative is that the body may have been exposed on the raised platform for a liminal period before the remains were placed in the timber-lined grave beneath. How long the body remained exposed before soil washed in or the grave was refilled raises a further interesting question. These are, of course, speculations difficult or impossible to test but it is right that questions and possibilities of this kind should be raised if only to remind us that the past cannot always be interpreted by direct reference to the present.

While timber structures in or closely associated with graves of the Mid-Late La Tène period are not common in Europe, a number of examples have been recorded in northern France, and have been brought together in a general discussion by Alain Villes (Villes 1983). The nearest parallels to the King's Road grave are three graves found at Champlay (Yonne) (Merlange 1979), in each of which was discovered a four-post structure, set up in the bottom of the grave, in a manner closely comparable to King's Road grave 1. The structures are interpreted as having stood well above the ground surface to form a mortuary house or possibly a platform for excarnation. It may well be that the ritual involved was originally more widespread than it at present appears to be.

The grave goods

Immediately following the discovery of the grave the writer, accompanied by Sarah Watkins, at that time conservator at the Institute of Archaeology, University of Oxford, flew to Guernsey to advise on how best to deal with the excavation and conservation of the grave goods. In the event the individual items were recorded *in situ* by Jenny Grant and lifted by Sarah Watkins in blocks with areas of the associated soil still adhering. The blocks were then transported back to Oxford so that the final excavation, study and conservation of the items could take place under laboratory conditions. Since details of this work have already been published (Watkins and Cameron 1987) there is no need to detail here the procedures adopted. However reference will be made to scientific studies leading to the identification of a range of organic residues representing materials buried with the original interment. These studies have greatly enhanced our understanding of Iron Age weapons. The careful drawings which illustrate this report were prepared by Christina Unwin in consultation with Esther Cameron at the Institute of Archaeology, Oxford. In the descriptions below the analysis of the organic remains is contributed by Esther Cameron. The wood species were identified by Jacqui Watson of the Historic Buildings and Monuments Commission, London.

1. Iron sword, its scabbard and the scabbard attachments (Figs. 57 and 58)

   The *sword* measured *c*.0.8 m in length (excluding the tang) and for most of its length it was parallel sided, some 46 mm in width and 5 mm in thickness. Towards the tip the blade narrowed slightly to a width of 30 mm. The blade was everywhere covered by the heavily corroded scabbard but viewed from a break was seen to be lenticulate in section. The hilt tang was intact measuring *c*.0.135 m in length: it was roughly oval in cross section and narrowed gradually towards the extremity which was flattened and slightly splayed. At the hilt end a campanulate hilt guard of iron was provided, while 40 mm from the terminal traces of an iron 'washer' could be discerned presumably once dividing the grip from the pommel. The entire tang was covered with mineralized organic remains which on analysis proved to be horn. The exact form of the hilt and pommel are now beyond recovery.

   The *scabbard* was formed from two thin sheets of iron, the front plate being wider than the back. This allowed the edges of the front plate to be beaten up and over the edges of the back plate creating lateral seams. The distal end was strengthened with a chape binding for a length of *c*.150 mm from the tip, and the upper part of the binding was held by a chape bridge in the form of a strip across the back plate which was wrapped around the edges and terminated, on the front plate, as two flattened chape clamps. At the hilt end some trace of a strengthening strip was noted following the campanulate terminal of the scabbard. The edges of the scabbard were also strengthened with binding running from here down to the level of the belt attachment loop. A sinuous bridging strip ran across the front plate joining the bridge strips and just lapped over the back plate.

   Details of the belt attachment system were well preserved. A simple bridge *c*.25 mm wide and fashioned from a thin strip of iron was joined to the back plate of the scabbard with semicircular attachment plates top and bottom. To the bridge two iron rings, one on either side, were bound with a leather thong which, for the most part, passed over and under the bridge but was twice wound around the scabbard above and below the bridge. The details of the arrangement are best appreciated by comparing the illustrations of the surviving remains with the reconstruction drawing (Figs. 57 and 58). In this system the rings would have been joined to the warrior's belt by looped straps. While it could be argued that the rings represent a later modification to the original strap bridge, the advantages of the rings, in providing a highly flexible mode of attachment, to a system comprising a single strap passing through the bridge are so great as to suggest that the system was designed in its more complex form from the beginning. The method described here conforms closely to that shown by Rapin (1985) to have been widespread in the La Tène period.

   The scabbard of the sword bore extensive traces of woven textiles preserved in its corrosion products. Two types were identified; both were of a plain tabby weave, Z-spun from bast fibres (Ryder and Gabra-Saunders 1987). The finer fabric which occurred near the hilt end had a thread count of 8/12 per cm. The coarser fabric which overlay it and covered most of the length of the sword had a count of approximately 5/5 per cm. The fabric remains are most evident on the back of the sword but traces were also found on the front. The arrangement of the two weaves might have arisen if the sword had rested upon a small fold of fine linen which in turn lay upon a coarser cloth which was more widely spread. The overlapping relationship between the two fabrics as well as the selective character of their preservation on the scabbard back and along one scabbard edge in particular suggests that the sword lay upon and close up against something, presumably the body, that was covered in cloth. Similarity between these and textiles found upon the iron fibula are marked not only by thread counts and fibre thicknesses, but also by the way in which the coarse weave overlies the fine, suggesting inner and outer garments.

2. Shield (Fig. 59)

   The shield was represented by the iron shield boss and staining in the soil adjacent to it which must represent the decay of the shield boards or their covering.

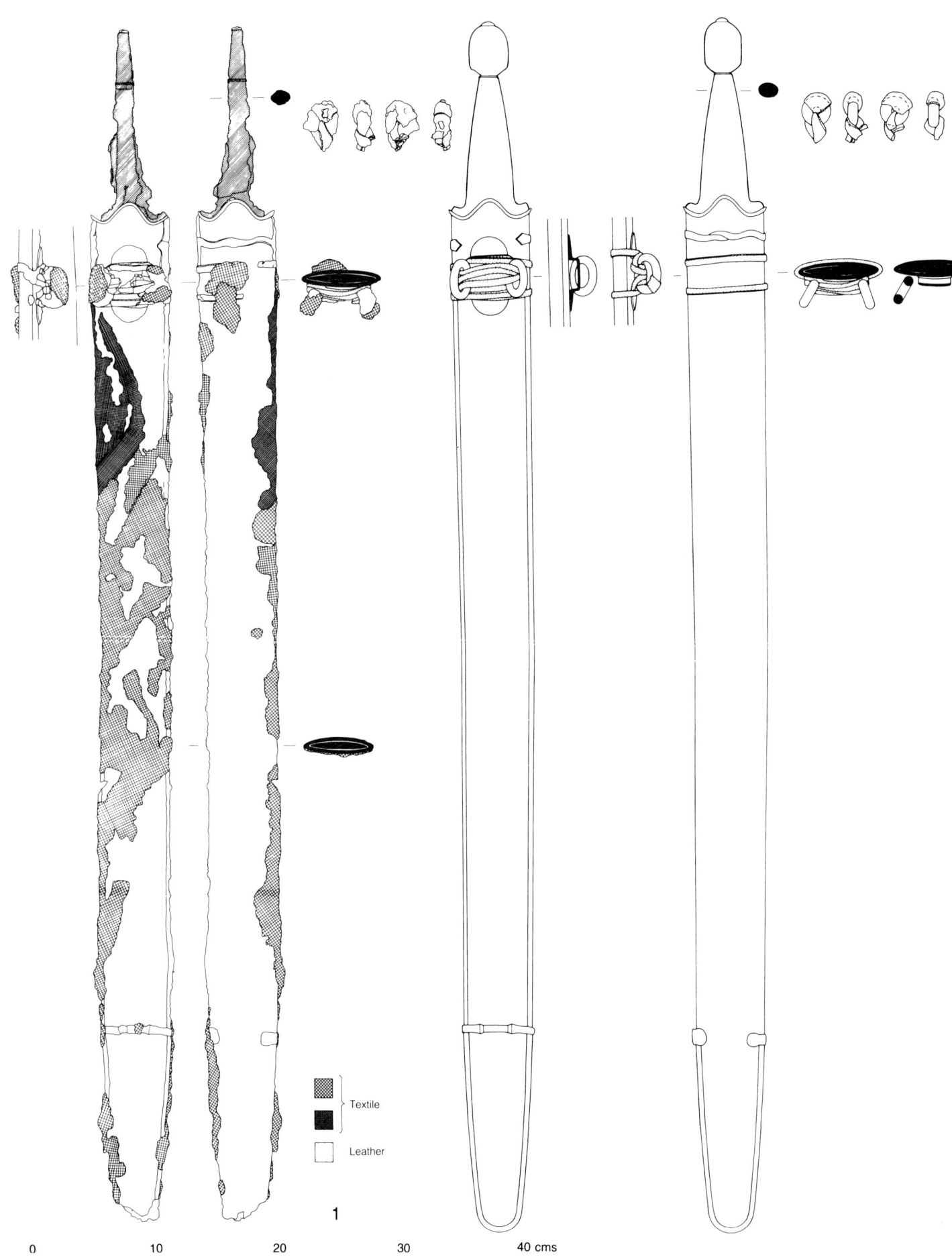

Figure 57 *Sword from the King's Road burial (actual and reconstruction)*.

Figure 58 *Sword from the King's Road burial.*

The boss was fashioned from a sheet of iron beaten up into an umbo in the centre. The umbo is slightly domed in a top-bottom section with the edges thickened to a triangular section and incised with four parallel lines. The attachment plates were both perforated by two rivet holes. Dome-headed rivets survived in all four, those closest to the boss having considerably larger heads than the outer rivets.

The preservation of organic material in the decay products beneath the attachment plates, and in particular around the rivets, allowed the structure of the shield itself to be reconstructed in some detail. The outer surface, i.e. the front, of the shield was covered by a layer of leather of unknown thickness grain side uppermost. Beneath this was a board of ash 8 mm thick into which had been set the hand grip composed of a strip of wood 23 mm wide and 5 mm thick where it is recessed into the shield board with a middle-lap joint. The joints were fastened with two iron rivets visible only on the X-ray. Fragments of leather found within the umbo may have been wrapped around the grip. The maximum diameter of the hand hole was 110 mm.

A leather-faced wooden shield of this kind would have combined lightness with resilience. The King's Road shield bears comparison with the shield recovered from Littleton Bog in the townland of Clonoura, Co. Tipperary. In this case the shield board is made from a single piece of alder wood. The grip is a strip of oak dovetailed into the board and both the outer and inner surfaces are covered with a sheet of leather, the whole being bound with a leather strip around the edge. The only significant difference is that the Irish example has a leather umbo.

3,4. Razor and shears (Fig. 60)
Against the outside of the sword close to the hilt was found a concreted mass of iron which after cleaning proved to be a razor and a pair of shears in a small leather pouch.

The shears measured 210 mm in length overall with blades up to 30 mm wide tapering to pointed ends.

The razor was roughly triangular in shape, 142 mm long and a maximum width 60 mm. Its single cutting edge was curved. The handle was recurved against the back and part of its extremity seems to have broken and been lost in antiquity.

The entire razor and the blades of the shears were covered with a mineralized organic residue identified as leather, probably sheep skin with traces of the fleece inside. The outer surface bears signs of having been decorated with parallel bands comprising pairs of tooled parallel lines. The spring/handle of the shears, which had a leather strap passed through it, projected beyond the pouch and had been wrapped in coarse woven textile, a Z-spun plain tabby weave comparable in thread count and yarn diameter to the coarse weave on the sword scabbard.

The combination of a razor and a pair of shears is interesting. The most likely explanation is that they comprised a 'barber's set' presumably the personal equipment of the deceased (Jacobi 1974, 87-90). Such sets are well known on the Continent and when buried with the dead are invariably found in male graves (Déchelette 1914, 1280-4). Several sets, some of them wrapped in fabric, were also found in the deposit at La Tène (Vouga 1925, pl. XXII and pp. 70-1). In closer geographical proximity to the King's Road burial we may quote the grave found in the Mount Batten cemetery near Plymouth, which produced shears and a 'knife' which from its description was evidently a razor (Bates 1871, 501; Cunliffe 1988a, 93-5). Shears were also found in the élite burial at Hertford Heath in SE England (Hüssen 1983, 17).

5. Iron spear (Fig. 60)
The iron spearhead lay in the north-east corner of the grave in a much corroded state. The blade was wider towards the base measuring a maximum of 43 mm across but rapidly narrowed to a parallel-sided form 22 mm across. The tip had broken off but the overall length of the blade would have been about 150 mm. The midrib was prominent for most of the length of the blade. The circular socket retained mineralized traces of the wooden shaft of ash.

The spear had been placed at the left hand side of the body: the shaft had completely rotted and the spear was without a ferrule.

6. Iron fibula (Fig. 61)
The much corroded iron fibula was simple in form and was made in one piece with a four-coil spring with external chord. The catch plate was fashioned by folding back the iron rod and wrapping it around the bow. It lay close to the hilt of the sword in such a position that it would probably have been on the right hand side of the chest of the deceased.

The corrosion products preserved traces of a fine weave and a coarse weave fabric suggesting that the fibula had been entirely wrapped first with the fine fabric and then with the coarse. Both textiles are Z-spun plain tabbies with thread counts and yarn diameters matching those on the scabbard.

7-8. Iron fittings (Fig. 61)
Two iron fittings were recovered from a small area close to the fibula. Both appear to have been clamps of approximately the same size, which had been driven into wooden boards of ash, possibly the shield, up to 40 mm in thickness. The points of one of the clamps had been clenched.

9-12. Iron nails (Fig. 61)
One large and three small iron nails were found within the grave fill. The large nail, no. 9, came

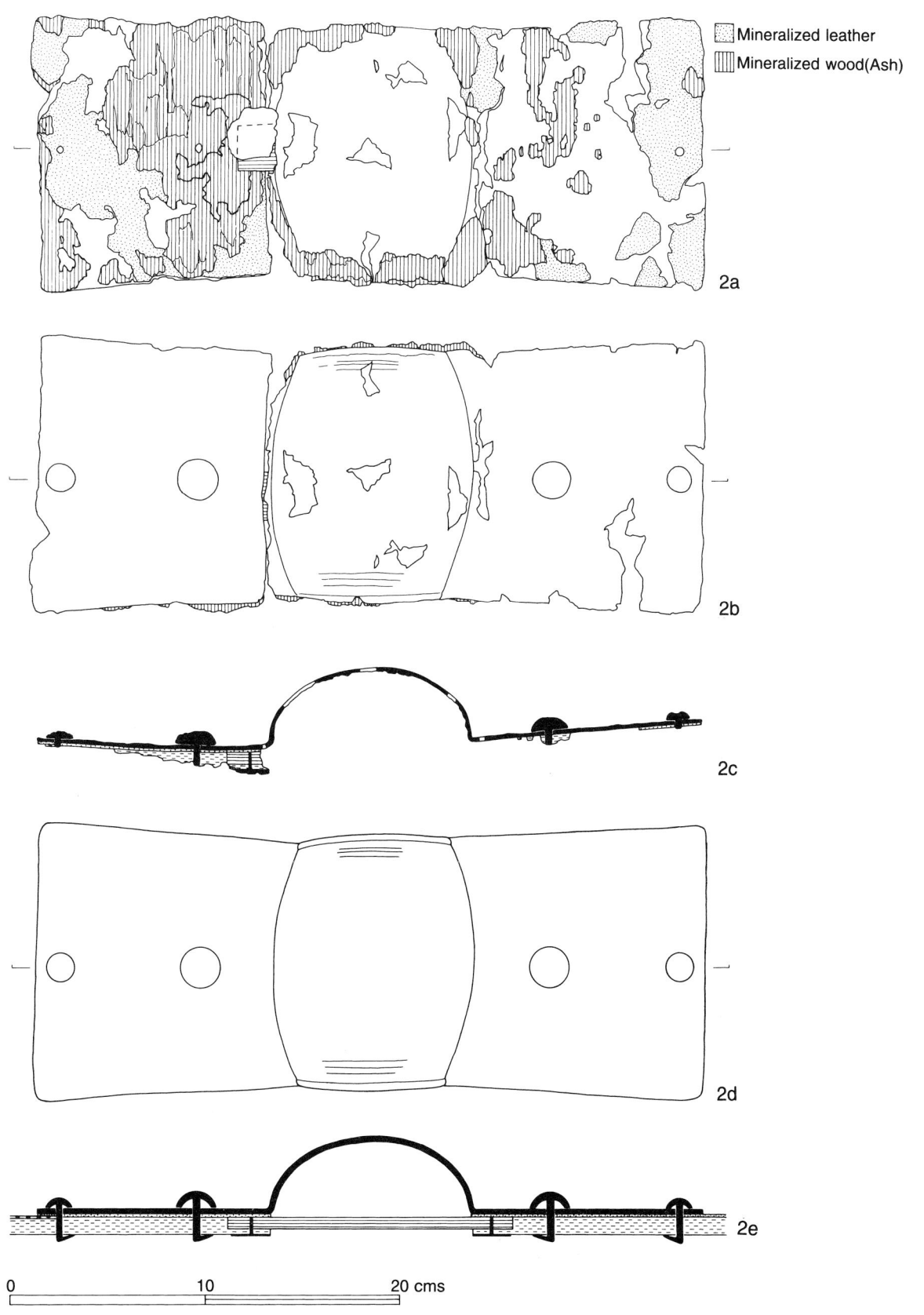

Figure 59 *Shield boss from the King's Road burial (actual and reconstruction).*

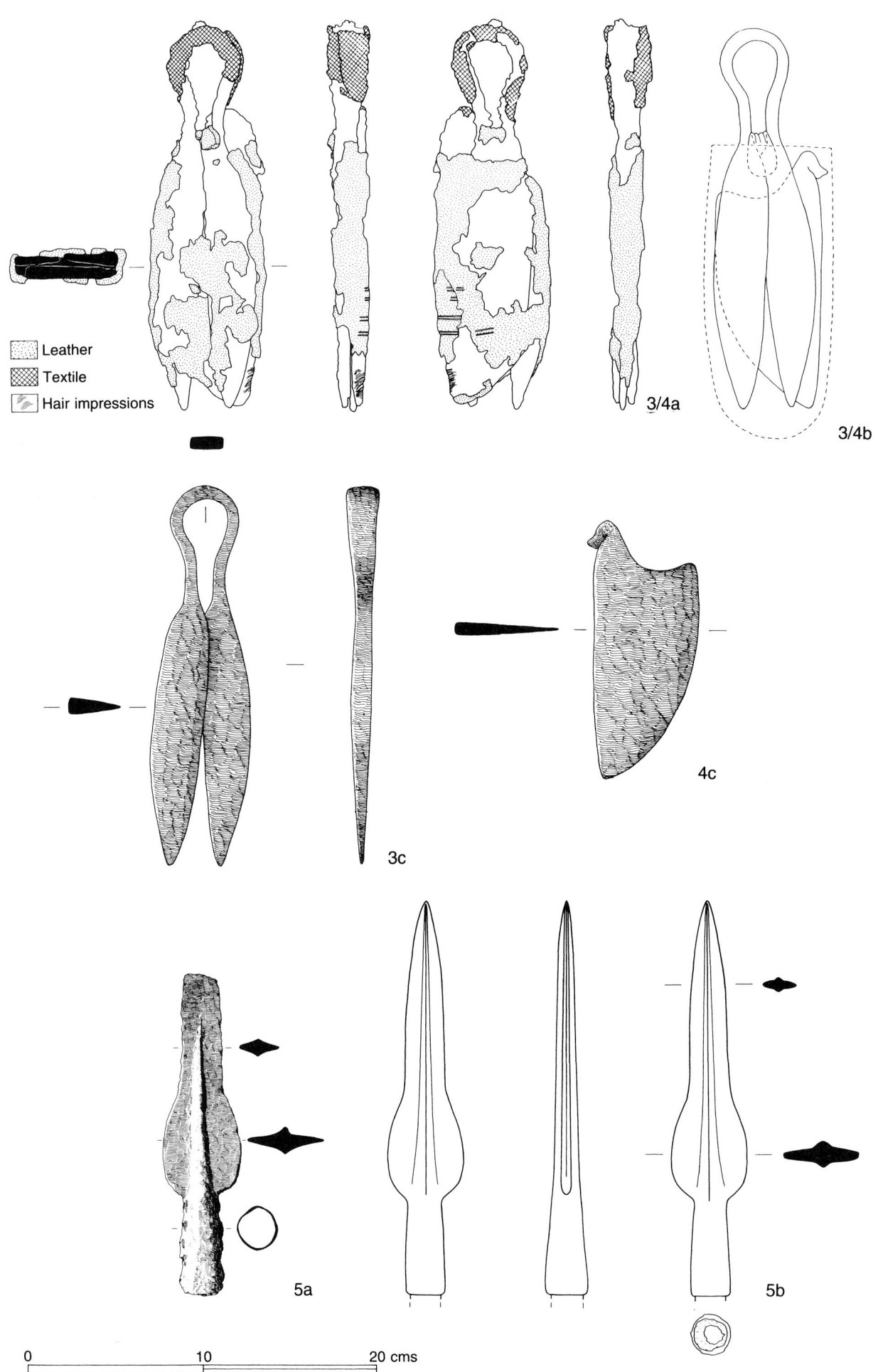

Figure 60 *Shears and spear from the King's Road burial (actual and reconstruction).*

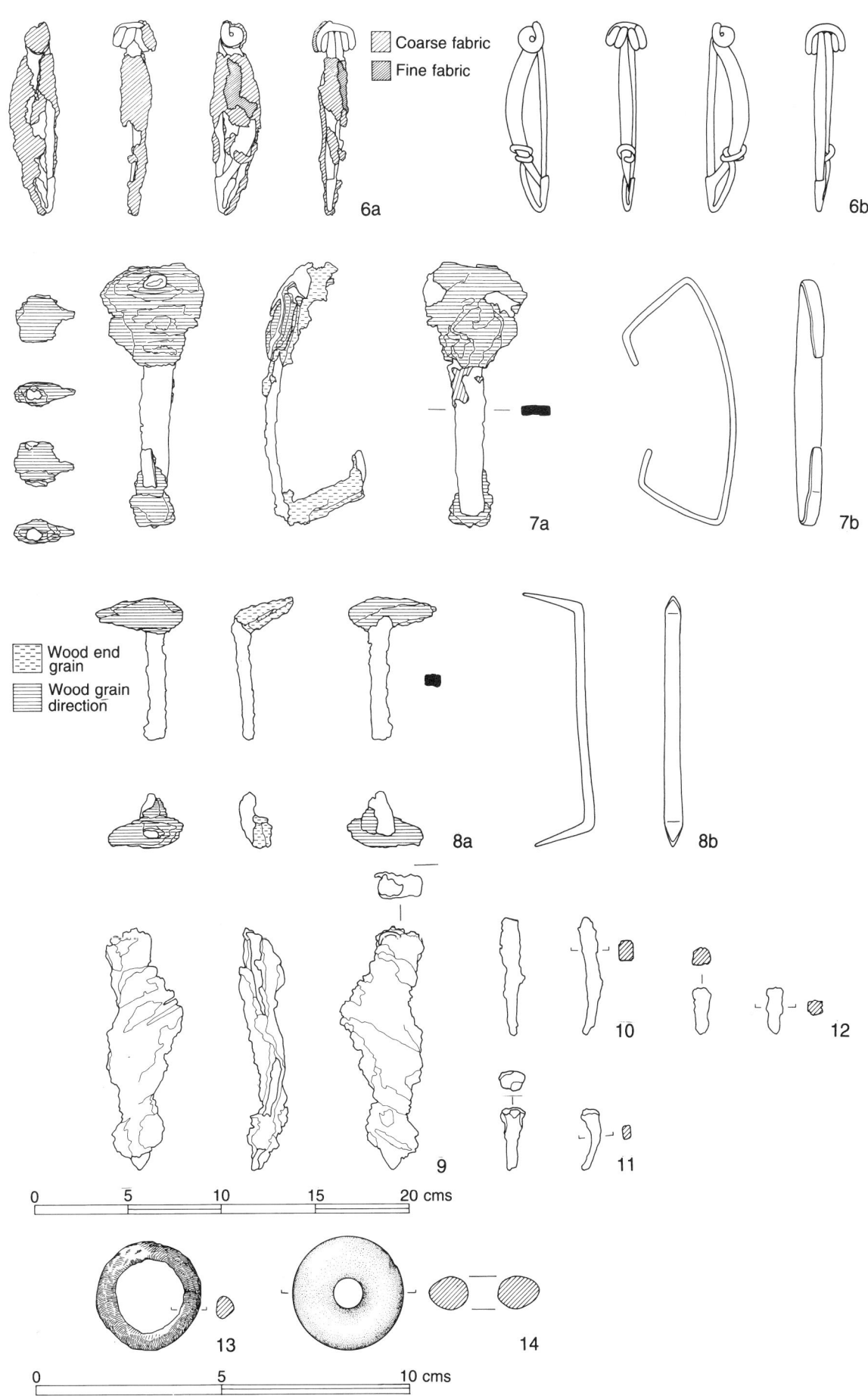

Figure 61 *Miscellaneous items from the King's Road burial*.

from post-hole 4, and may therefore have been part of the timber structure. It had been driven into a timber, identified as ash, traces of which were preserved in the corrosion products. The three smaller nails from the grave fill may also have derived from the timber structure but they could have been rubbish surviving from an earlier phase of the occupation.

13. Copper alloy ring (Fig. 61)
    Ring 27 mm in diameter externally with the central hole 18 mm across. D-shaped in section with the internal face straight: it is coarsely made and finished with a file or rasp. The ring was found beneath the shield board to the left hand side of the body in such a position that it could have been on a finger of the deceased.

14. Amber bead (Fig. 61)
    Bead 29 mm in diameter with a central perforation 7 mm across, well polished with little sign of wear. Found immediately adjacent to the sword at the hilt end suggesting that it may have been attached, perhaps by a leather thong, either to the sword hilt or to the attachment strap.

The cists at Le Catioroc, St. Saviour's

In 1845 three cists were found at Le Catioroc close to the megalithic tomb of Le Trépied. They appear to have been laid out parallel to each other sharing a common frontage. Each cist was built of small stones set on edge and capped with similar blocks: they averaged 2.1 m in length. In 1851 a fourth cist was found nearby, parallel to the other three. The roof was a rough construction comprised of granite blocks wedged together. It would appear that the side stones of the cist were erected after the deposition (whether artificial or natural is not recorded) of a layer of white sand. The cists were examined and described by Lukis (1848 and 1853) from which is derived the mention by de Guérin (1918, 136). Kendrick (1928, 190-3) adds little more but includes sketches of some of the finds.

Three of the four cists contained grave goods which are listed by Lukis.

Cist 1 a) 'several spearheads and fragments of knives'
b) 'a long sword within a steel scabbard'
c) 'a ring of brass'
d) 'part of an armlet also of steel'
e) 'some small ornaments'
f) 'a clay bead'
g) 'a fine shaped vase seven inches high'

Lukis adds that no trace of human remains were found but 'several fused masses like clinkers were strewed about the interior'.

Cist 2 a) 'some portions of steel armour'
b) 'a spearhead'.

Cist 3 was empty.

Cist 4 a) 'a falcated iron instrument' riveted and with a wooden handle found near the mouth of the cist with 'several traces of iron' nearby
b) 'a coarse earthen vessel much broken' was found at the far end of the cist, its base sunk some inches into the floor
c) 'several pieces of corroded iron were strewed about'.

From Lukis' descriptions and from the sketches with which he accompanied his text, it is possible to identify many of the grave goods from among the collection from Le Catioroc preserved in the museum, and to re-establish the groups, at least in part. Thus:

Cist 1
Probably the two swords (nos. 1 and 2), one of the spearheads (no. 6 or 7), the iron knife (no. 8), the iron ring (no. 14), the copper alloy bracelet (no. 19) and the complete pot (Fig. 67, no. 1). The 'clay bead' is missing and 'some small ornaments' are difficult to identify but may include some of the smaller items of iron (nos. 10-17).

Cist 2
Since Lukis specifically mentions a spearhead it is likely that one of the two surviving spears (no. 6 or 7) comes from this cist. The 'portions of steel armour' evidently include the shield boss (no. 4) and possibly also the second shield boss (no. 5). It is also possible that the sword (no. 3) came from this burial.

Cist 4
This context produced the sickle (no. 9) from near the mouth of the cist. The 'several pieces of corroded iron' presumably included some at least of the smaller iron objects (nos. 10-17). The two potsherds (Fig. 67, nos. 2 and 3) probably also came from this cist.

Finds from the cists at Le Catioroc (Figs. 62-6)

1. Fragments of an iron sword in an iron scabbard: very heavily corroded.
   The sword blade was originally c.45 mm wide: the length can no longer be estimated. The tang survives intact measuring some 120 mm long and bears evidence of the original horn hilt and pommel preserved in the corrosion products. The hilt terminated on a campanulate-shape hilt guard of iron. Radiography of the blade showed a striated structure (below, pp. 112-13).
   Fragments of the iron scabbard still adhere to the blade. It was made from two sheets of iron with front over back overlaps. No evidence survives of a chape or of additional bindings around the chape end. The hilt end was strengthened by an iron binding moulded to the shape of the hilt guard at the back but with a more elaborate moulding at the front. The strengthening continued down one side of the chape as a binding for 45 mm. Traces of a similar binding on the other side are apparent. Of the strap loop only the lower attachment with a single rivet survives.

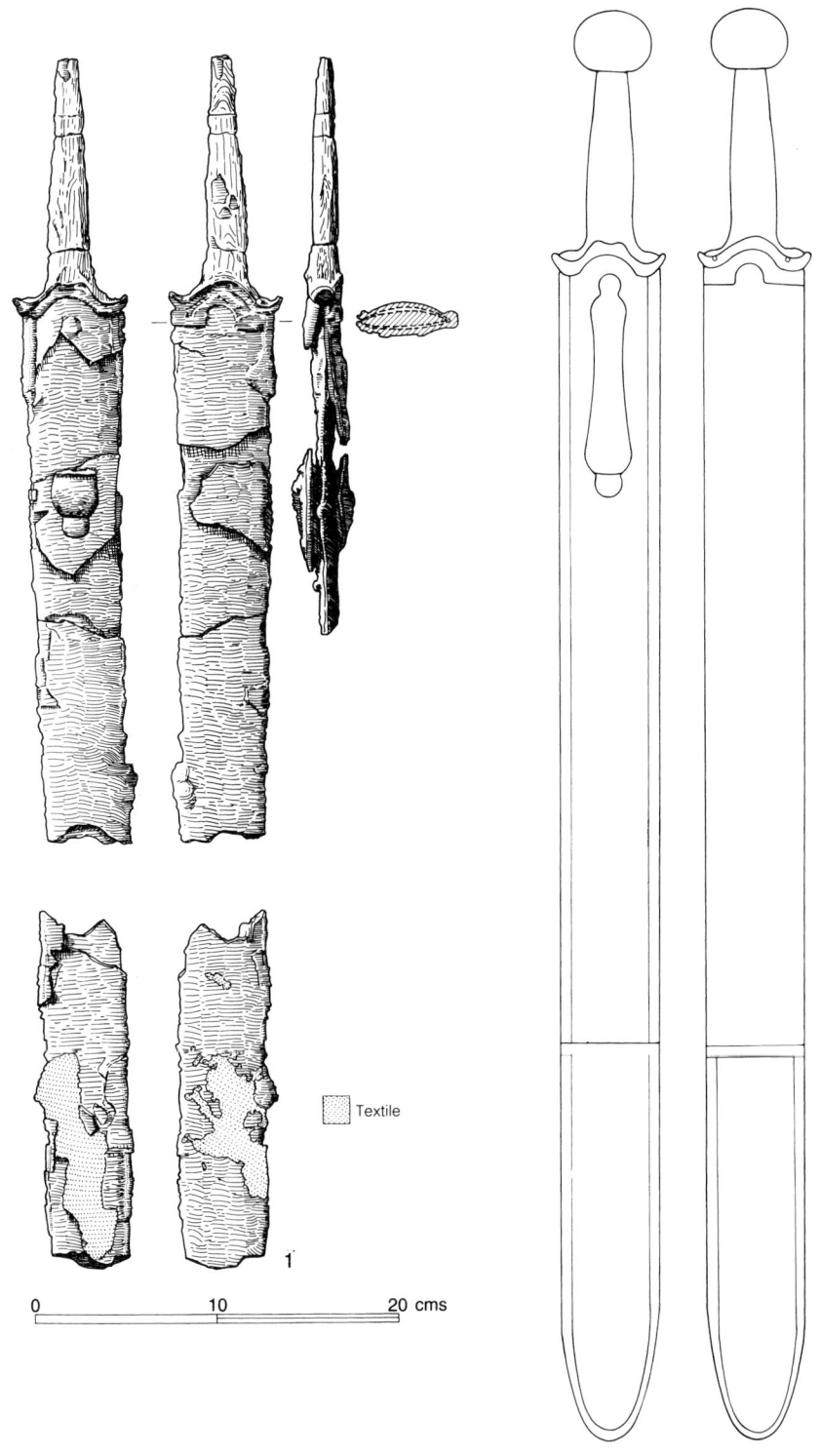

Figure 62 *Sword from Le Catioroc, Cist 1 (actual and reconstruction).*

On the front of the scabbard traces of yarn indicative of a woven fabric are preserved in the corrosion products.

(GMAG 3147). From Cist 1.

2. Iron sword and scabbard, corroded together, now broken into six joining fragments.

The sword is complete except for the tang. From tip to hilt it measured 620 mm. The blade is of even width throughout measuring 46 mm but narrows at the point. The thickness in the centre is about 6 mm but is distorted by corrosion. No evidence of the treatment of the hilt survives.

The scabbard is composed of two thin sheets of iron. The front plate is wider than the back and its edges are folded over to overlap the edges of the back plate. The overlap extends at least as far as the chape. The scabbard mouth is campanulate in shape and is thickened on the front with an edging strip which was continued for 40 mm down along the edges of the chape to give extra strength to the mouth of the scabbard. These side bindings were joined across the front of the sword with a strip composed of two joined iron strands. The lower end of the scabbard was strengthened with a chape consisting of a ground strip of iron binding the scabbard plates together in place of an overlap. The upper ends of the binding were attached to a chape bridge at the back with two circular chape clamps at the front. Four additional circular chape clamps, two on each side, were provided where the scabbard began to narrow to a point some 150 mm below the chape bridge. The suspension loop survives intact attached to the back of the scabbard allowing for a leather strap 20 mm wide. The attachment plates are triangular with slightly bound sides; no evidence of riveting was noted.

On the front of the sword at the hilt end traces of a woven fabric, preserved in the corrosion products, were from a loose tabby, 4/4 p.cm^2, woven from Z-spun yarn.

(GMAG 3144). Find-spot uncertain but probably Cist 1.

3. Two fragments of an iron sword blade of maximum width 34 mm and thickness 3 mm. The beginning of the tang can be seen at one end. Radiography of the blade showed a striated structure (below, pp. 112-13).

(GMAG 3150). Find-spot uncertain but probably Cist 1.

4. Iron shield boss.

The umbo is fashioned from a rectangular sheet of iron 2.5 mm thick. It is steeply curved in the horizontal plane and less steeply domed vertically. Its edges have been beaten into thickened ridges of triangular section. The attachment plates to the shield boards are not quite complete but appear to have been roughly square. Of the two plates only one is still attached to the umbo.

The other differs slightly and may not belong to the boss. Two domed rivets were provided for attachment through the original plate and apparently only one through the other. Traces of wood and leather, preserved by corrosion products, survive upon the inside edges of the umbo and on the underside of the attachment plate. The wood grain which originates from the shield board follows a single grain direction and was spanned at right-angles by the umbo. Wood grain around the innermost rivet is at a 90° angle to the rest and indicates the attachment of a wooden grip. Leather, which survives between the iron and the wood, was used to cover the board.

(GMAG 3145). Probably from Cist 2 ('portion of steel armour').

5. Iron shield boss.

The boss is substantially complete but fragmentary. It is fashioned from a rectangular sheet of iron with a high arched umbo thickened to a triangular-sectioned profile at the edges. No rivet holes were noted in the attachment plates but given their highly fragmentary nature this is not surprising.

(Unnumbered). Probably from Cist 2 ('portion of steel armour') but may have come from Cist 1.

6. Iron spearhead largely intact but with tip broken, originally measuring 240 mm long. The blade is wide (39 mm) with a prominent midrib. Traces of the wooden shaft survive in the hollow socket which was pierced by an iron rivet.

(GMAG 3146a). From Cist 1.

7. Iron spearhead broken across the middle of the blade. A tip possibly belonging to the same weapon survives. The blade is wide, measuring up to 65 mm and the midrib is prominent. Traces of the wooden shaft survive in the hollow socket pierced by an iron rivet.

(GMAG 3146b). From Cist 1 or 2.

8. Iron knife with partial socket formed to receive the horn handle, traces of which remain. The handle was secured by a small rivet. The blade is wide and square backed and originally tapered to a point which may have recurved slightly.

(GMAG 3146c). Probably from Cist 1.

9. Iron sickle with partial socket formed to clasp the wooden handle, some traces of which survive in the corrosion products. The handle was secured by a large rivet which passed through both sides of the socket. The blade was steeply curved and formed from two reworked saw-blades. The small fragment illustrated detached from it may not have been part of the original implement.

(GMAG 3149a). From Cist 4.

10. Tanged iron arrowhead with hollow socket containing wood remains and a rivet. The tip is missing.

(GMAG 3146d). Possibly Cist 4.

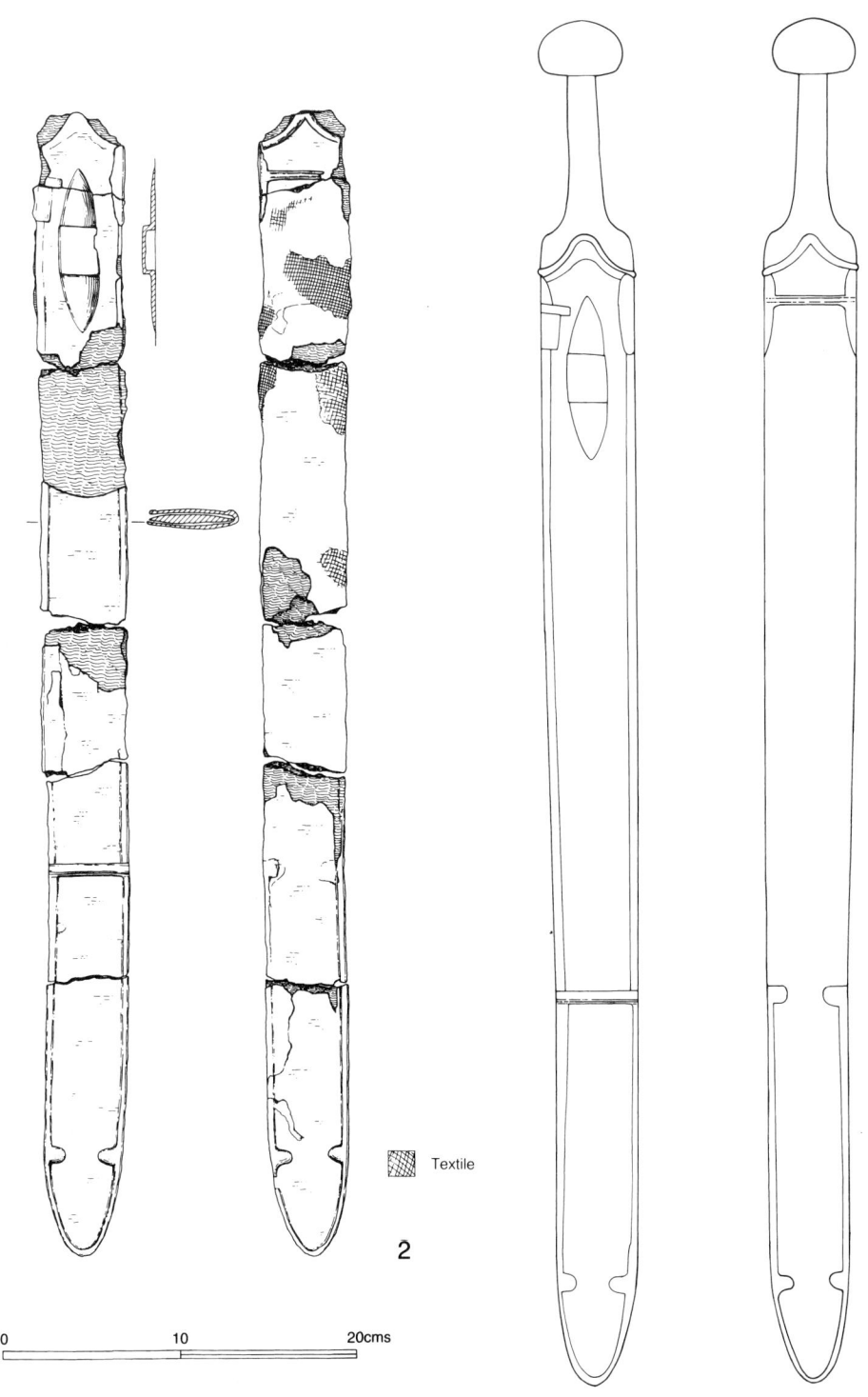

Figure 63 *Sword from Le Catioroc, Cist 1(?) (actual and reconstruction).*

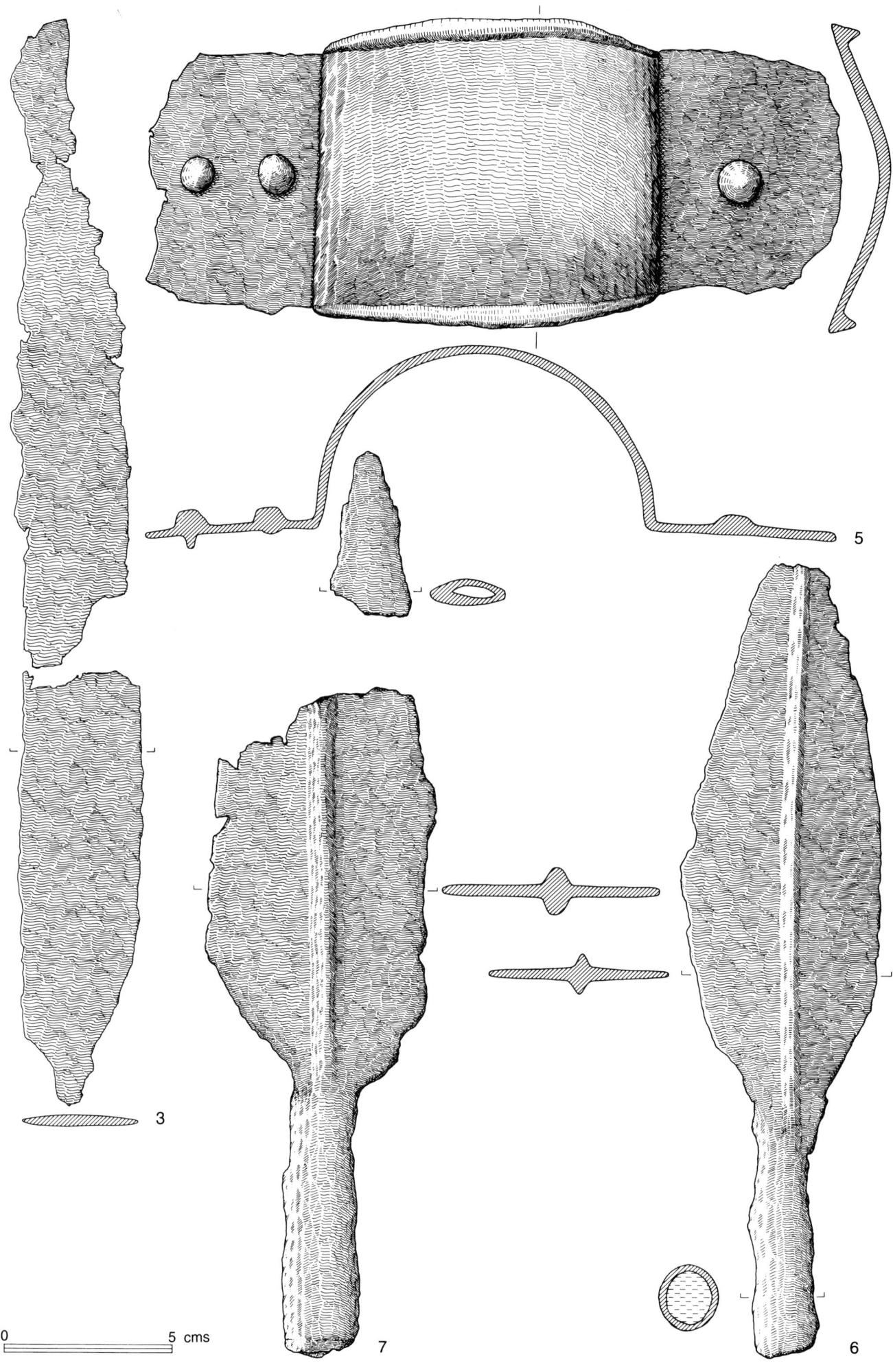

Figure 64 *Sword, spears and shield boss from Le Catioroc.*

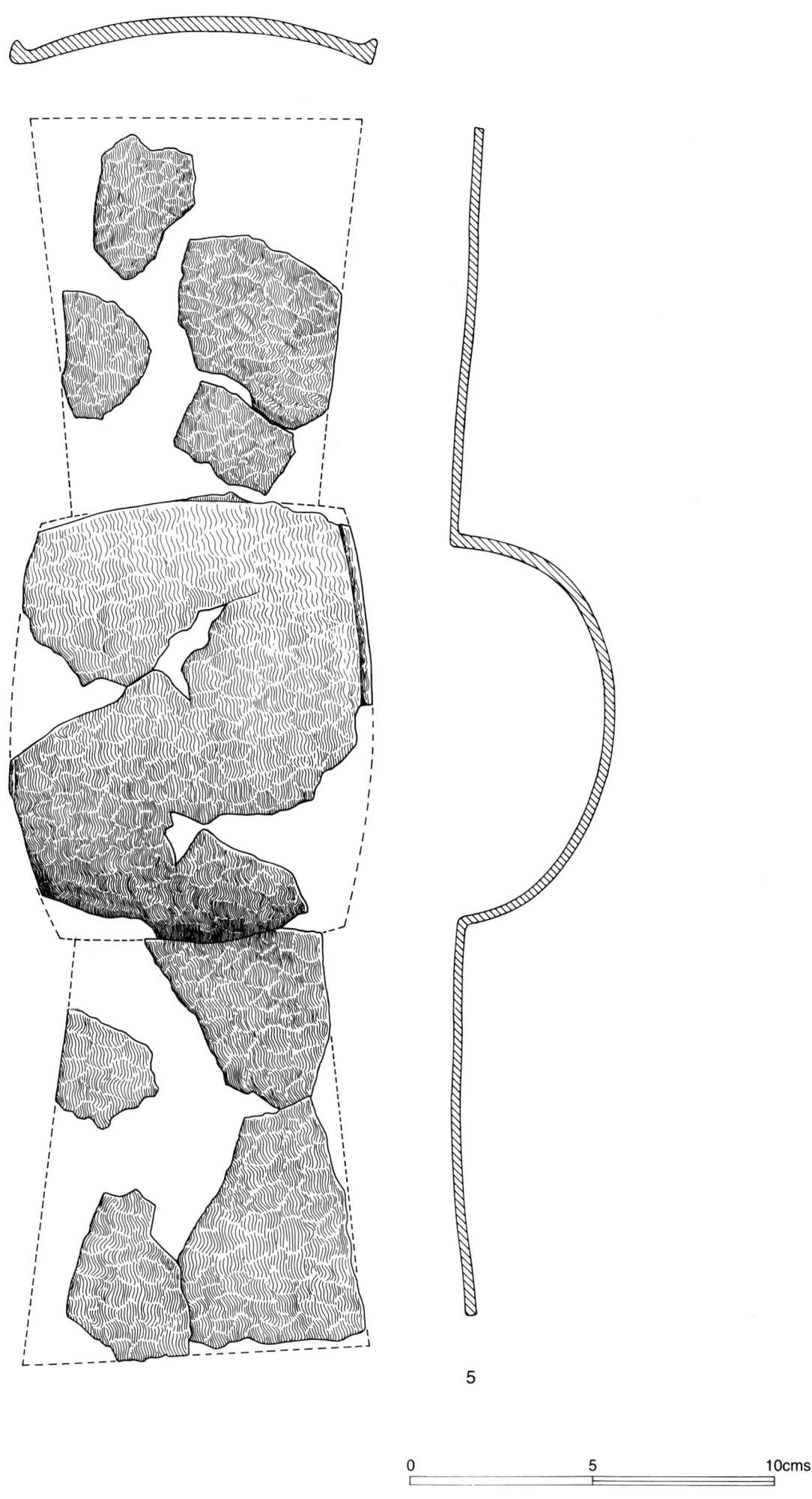

Figure 65 *Shield boss from Le Catioroc.*

Figure 66 *Miscellaneous items of iron and copper alloy from Le Catioroc.*

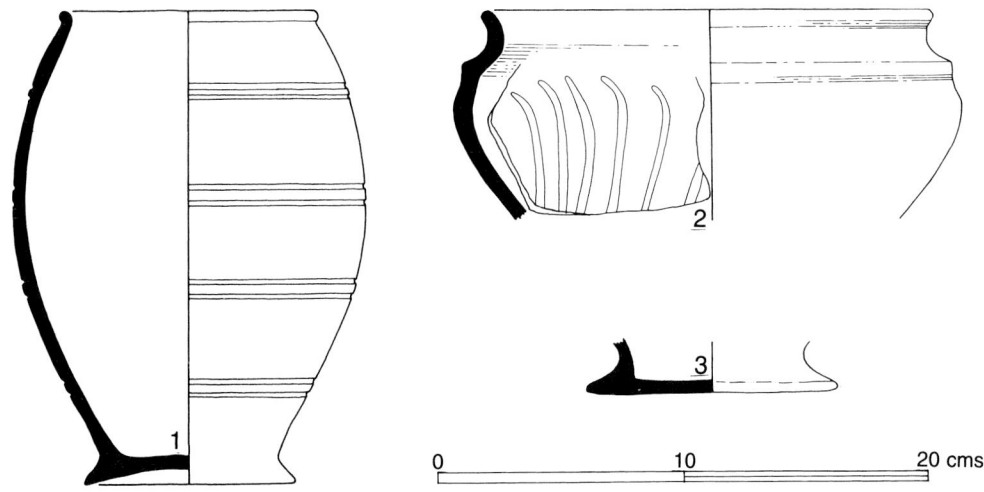

Figure 67 *Pottery from Le Catioroc.*

11. Iron fibula spring and part of the bow of a fibula. The spring has six coils with a cord across. The bow is of oval cross section.
    (GMAG 3146e). Possibly Cist 4.

12. Iron hook attachment. Ring with small hook attached. From a belt or strap attachment.
    (GMAG 3146e). Possibly Cist 4.

13. Small iron hook possibly broken from a larger item.
    (GMAG 3146e). Possibly Cist 4.

14. Iron ring. Three fragments of an oval (bent?) ring of diamond-shaped section.
    (GMAG 3146e). Possibly Cist 1.

15. Iron fitting. Iron strip/rod circular in section at one end, flattened at the other and semi-knotted in the centre.
    (GMAG 3146e). Possibly Cist 4.

16. Iron curved blade, broken. Possibly from a small 'reaping hook'.
    (GMAG 3146e). Possibly Cist 4.

17. Iron bar of rectangular cross-section bent with a double right angle. Broken at both ends.
    (GMAG 3146e). Possibly Cist 4.

18. Copper alloy ring.
    Plain ring 38 mm in external diameter. Oval section. Possibly for attachment of the sword to the belt. Very similar to the example from La Hougue au Comte.
    (GMAG 3748a). Possibly Cist 1.

19. Copper alloy bracelet.
    Decorated bracelet 64 mm in external diameter. Of flattish rectangular cross section with a simple hooked join. Decorated on the outer flat face with incised lines, three parallel to the edges crossed by others at right angles.
    (GMAG 3748b). Cist 1.

Pottery from Le Catioroc (Fig. 67)

1. Complete vessel. Grey brown sandy fabric: vesicular with small white inclusions. A fine black burnished surface. Wheel-turned.
   (GMAG 3148: Kendrick G 135). From Cist 1.

2. Part of a shouldered jar with neck cordon. Smooth grey, slightly vesicular ware with small white grits. The outer surface retains a reddish wash denser on the rim. Vertical burnished lines inside. Wheel-turned.
   (GMAG 3749). Probably from Cist 4.

3. Quoit-shaped base. Smooth reddish-grey vesicular ware. Wheel-turned.
   (GMAG 3750). Probably from Cist 4.

The cist at La Hougue au Comte, Castel

In 1885 quarrying operations on the property of Mr. N.P. Duquemin at La Hougue au Comte, Bas Séjour, Castel, brought to light evidence of Iron Age burials. The details of the find are obscure but a brief description was given by Derrick (1906) (whence de Guérin 1918, 137 and Kendrick 1928, 196-8) and the finds are now housed in the Guernsey Museum.

Structural remains consisted of a cist measuring 1.83 m long, 0.51 m wide and 0.46 m high constructed of 'rough unhewn stones'. It was built on a layer of gravel, aligned N-S, and was buried by about 0.9 m of soil. No trace of a body survived but a number of grave goods were found within the cist. About 0.9 m away, three complete pots were later recovered, the mouth of one of which was 'closed with pieces of iron built up across it' (Derrick 1906, 229). Associated with the complete pots was the base of another together with some sherds. In an undated manuscript note preserved in the Lukis papers in the Museum, Lukis records 'From account given by Mr. Duquemin junior who found these vessels he said that they seemed to stand on old iron – which I take to be portions of a wooden box lined with iron and hooped with ye same metal.'

The finds from the cist, listed in the original account, included:

a) portions of two or three swords
b) an iron spearhead
c) a bronze and an iron loop, found with the swords
d) 'two perfect bronze rings; one is 2 inches in diameter and flat-sided, the other is penannular, about the same diameter, but circular in section'
e) some fragments of rings, one of which is hollow
f) glass rings – in all five are mentioned
g) a half ring of a red material which may not be glass.

De Guérin's account (1918, 137-8) adds nothing more to the finds list but Kendrick (1928, 196-8) presents a fuller description of the objects together with illustrations of the principal items.

A photograph and some sketches of the finds in the Lukis archive in the Museum help to identify individual items. The only discrepancy which is evident concerns the spears. Kendrick notes only one, which he illustrates with a sketch. The Museum possesses two, neither of which conform to Kendrick's drawing. One however is closely similar to that sketched by Lukis in the archive note and the other bears some similarity to an indistinct item on the contemporary photograph. For that reason the museum record is taken to be correct.

Finds from La Hougue au Comte (Figs. 68-70)

1. Iron sword in an iron scabbard. In five fragments which join to make two parts. The overall length of the sword is difficult to judge but the surviving fragments add up to 730 mm (excluding the tang) and the original must therefore have been longer. The blade was parallel-sided, 35 mm wide and up to 6 mm thick in the centre. Radiography of the blade showed it to have a striated structure (below, pp. 112-13). A substantial part of the tang survives with a sub-rectangular hilt guard attached to the hilt with eight small iron nails. The hilt was of horn, the mineralized remains of which survive. In the horn, on either side of the hilt guard, are two holes which once contained copper alloy rivets.

    The scabbard was composed of two thin plates of iron, the edges of the front one being folded over the edges of the back. The end was strengthened with a chape binding joined on the back by a chape bridge below which, back and front, are pairs of pointed chape clamps. On the front plate of the scabbard, at the hilt end, the plate has an edge thickening conforming in shape to the campanulate hilt guard. To either side of this U-shaped bindings reinforced the scabbard edges from the mouth to the suspension loop. Between them are two applied strips of iron representing a curvilinear design which was probably once bilaterally similar. Corrosion is such that it is difficult to make out the form of the design. Behind this, rivetted to the back plate, the two attachments for the suspension loop survive though the loop itself has disappeared. The attachments are both 8-shaped. Remains of the mineralized leather strap running beneath the loop can be made out.

    Further down another strip of leather lies diagonally across the centre of the scabbard front. Traces of a linen fabric were also found scattered over the larger part of the scabbard front. They belonged to a plain tabby weave, thread count 5/5 p.cm^2, woven from Z-spun bast fibre with a yarn diameter of 1.5 mm.
    (GMAG 3271).

2. Iron sword and scabbard. Very heavily corroded and in two fragments which do not necessarily join and may not be part of the same object. The sword blade was c.30 mm wide. One fragment has an area of mineralized wood or horn attached to it.
    (GMAG 3272).

3. Iron spearhead: complete. The blade is 145 mm long by 30 mm wide at its widest and with a prominent midrib. The hollow socket contains mineralized remains of the wooden shaft.
    (GMAG 3266).

4. Iron spearhead: tip broken. The blade would originally have been c.100 mm long and was 30 mm wide at its widest. The midrib is prominent. A long tubular socket took the wooden shaft traces of which remain.
    (GMAG 3267).

5. Iron ring of circular cross section. 32 mm in diameter overall.
    (GMAG 3270a).

6. Iron ring. Two fragments with roughly rectangular cross section. Diameter estimated as 75 mm.
    (GMAG 3270b).

7. Copper alloy ring.
    Simple plain ring, 37 mm in external diameter. Probably from attachment of a sword to a belt. Very similar to the ring from Le Catioroc.
    (GMAG 3262).

8. Copper alloy bracelet.
    Much corroded fragment of a wire bracelet of circular cross section. Distorted so that original diameter is uncertain. Possibly same object as no. 9.
    (GMAG 3261a).

9. Copper alloy bracelet.
    Corroded and incomplete wire bracelet of circular cross section approximately 56 mm in

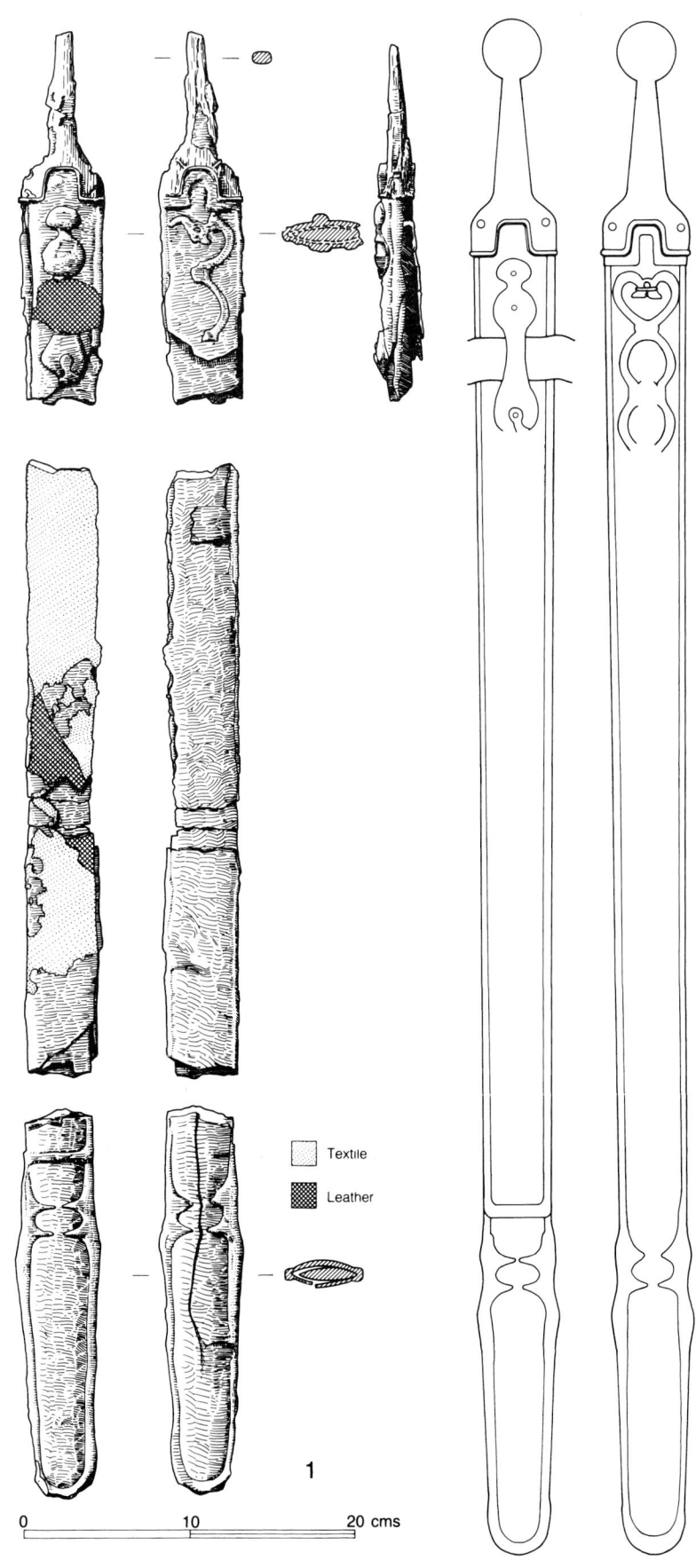

Figure 68 *Sword from La Hougue au Comte (actual and reconstruction).*

external diameter. Possibly same object as no. 8.
(GMAG 3261f).

10. Copper alloy bracelet.
Bracelet c.64 mm in external diameter. Oval cross section. Decorated with parallel incised grooves demarking lines of small pellets. Very worn in places.
(GMAG 3261e).

11. Copper alloy bracelet.
Bracelet c.58 mm in external diameter. Flattened oval cross section. Decorated with a central line of pellets bounded by incised lines with ribs at right angles on either side.
(GMAG 3261c).

12. Copper alloy bracelet.
Bracelet c.62 mm in external diameter. Flattened rectangular cross section. Undecorated.
(GMAG 3261b).

13. Copper alloy bracelet.
Bracelet, 67 mm in external diameter. Oval cross section flattened internally. Undecorated.
(GMAG 3261d).

14. Copper alloy bracelet.
Bracelet fragments: very corroded. Diameter uncertain. Hollow and of roughly circular cross section.
(GMAG 3268).

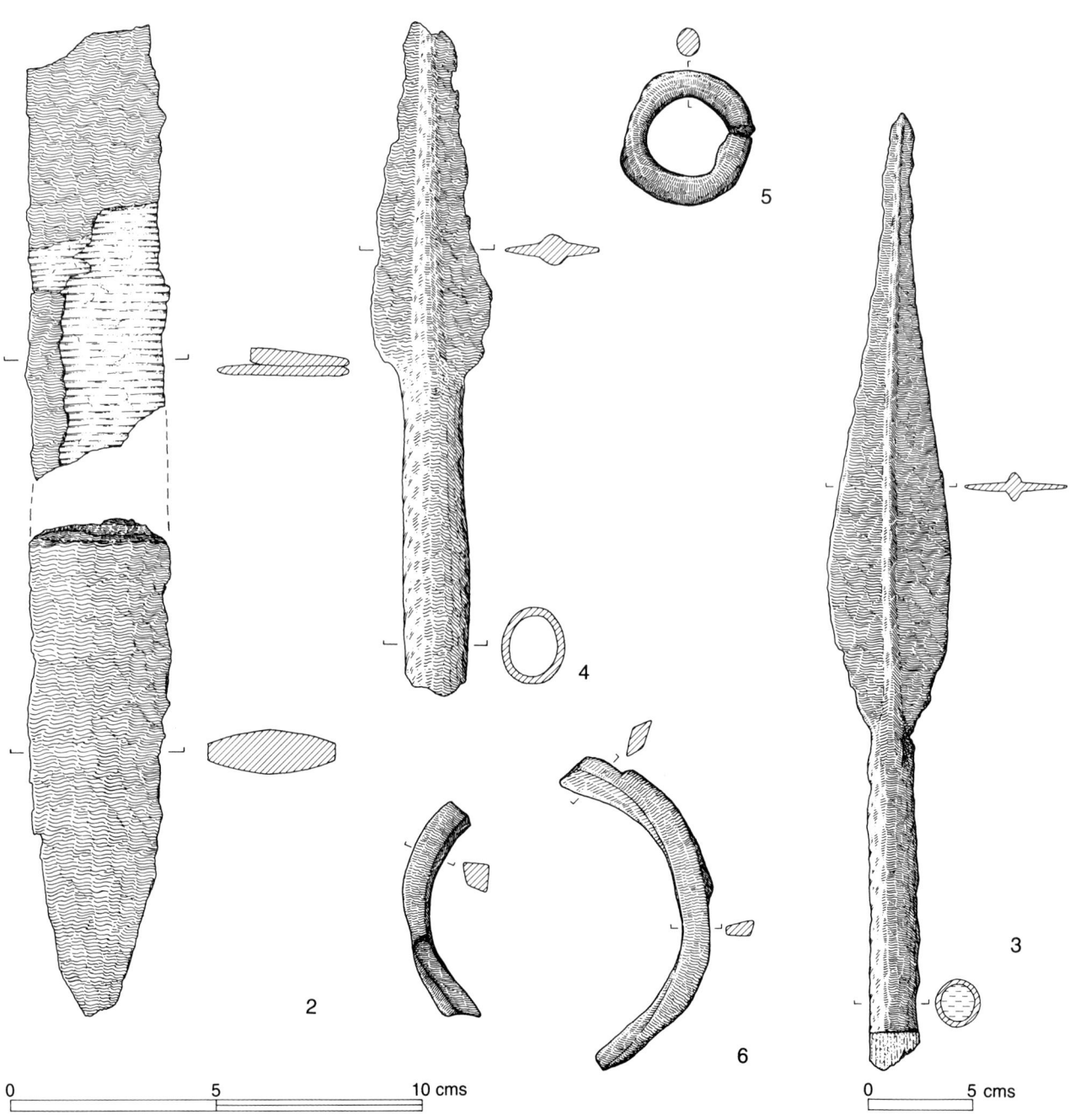

Figure 69 *Miscellaneous iron items from La Hougue au Comte.*

15. Copper alloy vessel fragment.
    Cannot now be located.
    (GMAG 3265).

16. Glass bead.
    Deep blue-brown glass.
    (GMAG 3264a).

17. Glass bead.
    Clear yellow-green glass.
    (GMAG 3264b).

18. Glass bead.
    Translucent greenish-yellow. The central hole has been enlarged by filing.
    (GMAG 3751a).

19. Glass bead.
    Greenish-blue with yellow spots.
    (GMAG 3751b).

For the composition of the beads see p.113.

20. Glass fragment.
    Purple glass.
    (GMAG 3264c).

21. Bead of jet.
    (GMAG 3751c).

22. Bead of amber.
    (GMAG 3263).

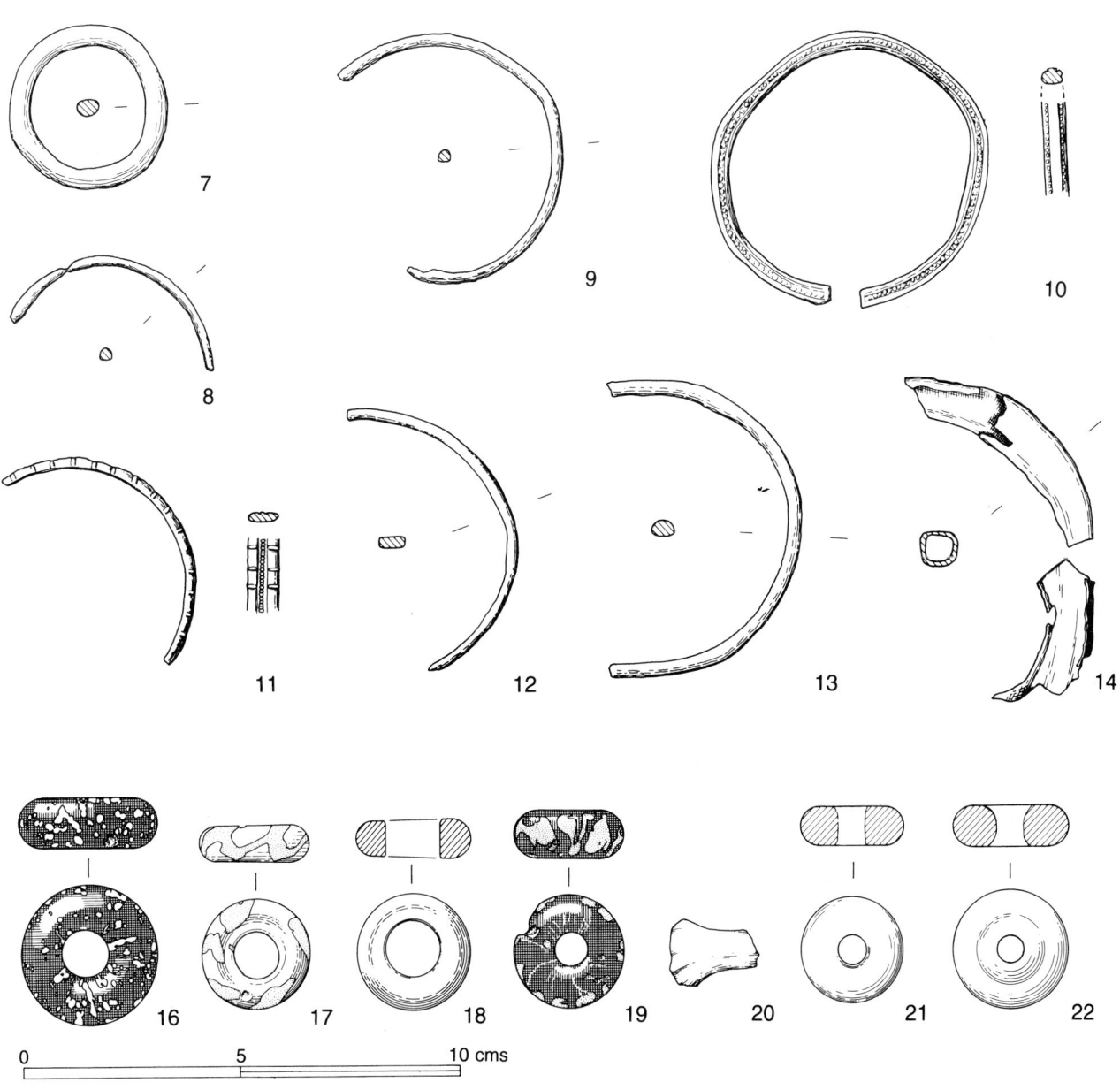

Figure 70 *Miscellaneous items of copper alloy, glass, amber and jet from La Hougue au Comte.*

Pottery from La Hougue au Comte (Fig. 71)

1. Shouldered jar. Light brown vesicular fabric with small white inclusions. Fired grey. Burnished on the shoulder to just below the lower cordon. Wheel-turned.
   (GMAG 3260: Kendrick G 134).

2. Shouldered jar. Light brown sandy fabric with some mica. Fired grey. Burnished lattice on shoulder. Upper part of vessel covered in graphite which extends in a band down the body and over the foot ring.
   (GMAG 3259: Kendrick G 131).

3. Shouldered jar. Light brown fabric with white grits. Fired black. Burnished upper part of body. Wheel-turned.
   (GMAG 3258: Kendrick G 132).

4. Jar. Smooth grey-brown vesicular fabric. Fired grey. Burnished surface.
   (GMAG 3257: Kendrick G 130).

5. Pottery fragment. Cannot now be located.
   (GMAG 3269).

The cist at Les Issues, St. Saviour's

In 1818 a cist was discovered two feet down on land belonging to Mr. T. Lainé at Les Issues. It was orientated E-W and measured 2 m in length. No human remains were discovered but grave goods survived including 'a sword and spearhead, and other portions of steel weapons; these articles were chiefly on the north side of the cist' (Lukis 1848, 306). Some days later a complete pot was found some 30 yards away, 0.38 m down. A handwritten note retained with the pot records, 'A stone grave was found near this spot a few days previously formed of flat stones on end in parallel lines and was six feet nine inches in length. No bones were found but a sabre and scabbard, a brass ornament and the remains of a pick or lance.'

The original discovery was described by Du Frocq (in Jacob 1830) where Jacob adds the observation that some of the stones were inscribed. Lukis only mentions the find in passing. De Guérin (1918, 136) repeats the original description listing the finds as 'a long sword in its scabbard, an iron spearhead, fragments of knives and of an iron chain, part of the umbo or boss of a shield and the fragment of a bronze ornament'.

The pot passed to the Lukis Museum while the rest of the finds were taken to Canada by the Lainé family. For this reason they were not available to Kendrick (1928, 195-6). The collection was eventually returned to Guernsey by Mrs. Mary Ann Lainé in 1934 and is now united with the pot in Guernsey Museum.

The finds as they survive include:
1. Iron sword and scabbard (GMAG 3153)
2. Iron shield boss (GMAG 3154c)
3. Iron spearhead (GMAG 3154a)
4. Iron ferrule
5. Wood fragments stained with bronze salts (GMAG 3154b)
6. Pottery vessel (GMAG 3152).

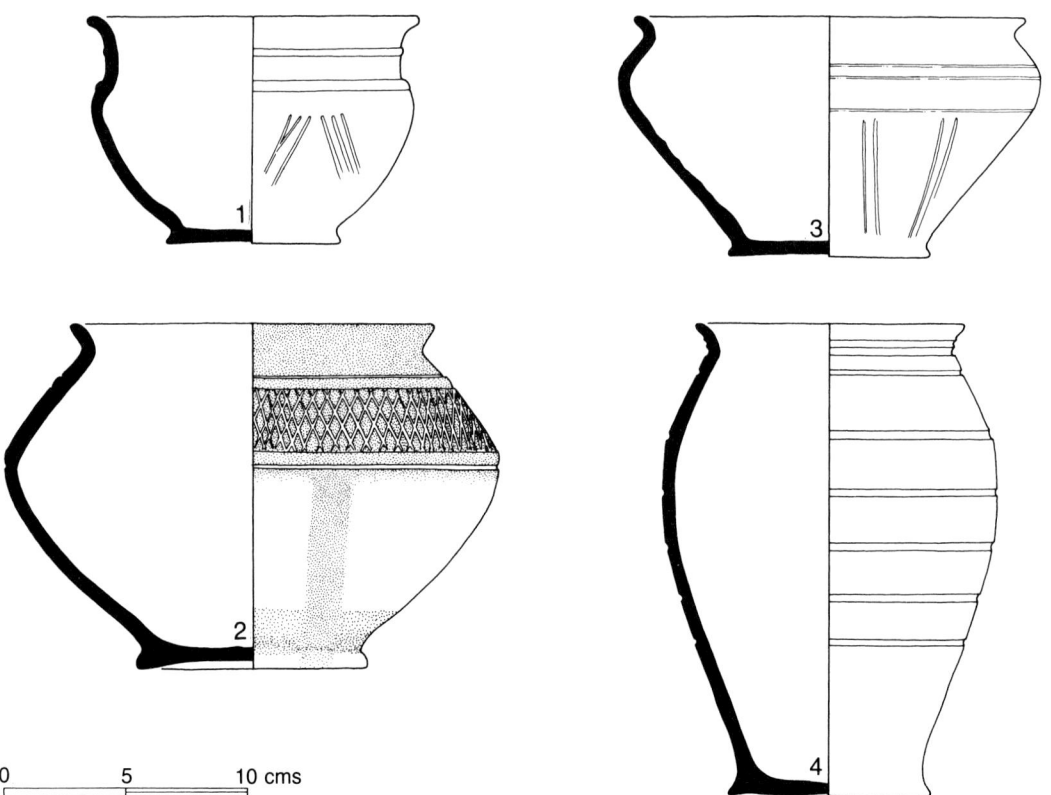

Figure 71 *Pottery from La Hougue au Comte.*

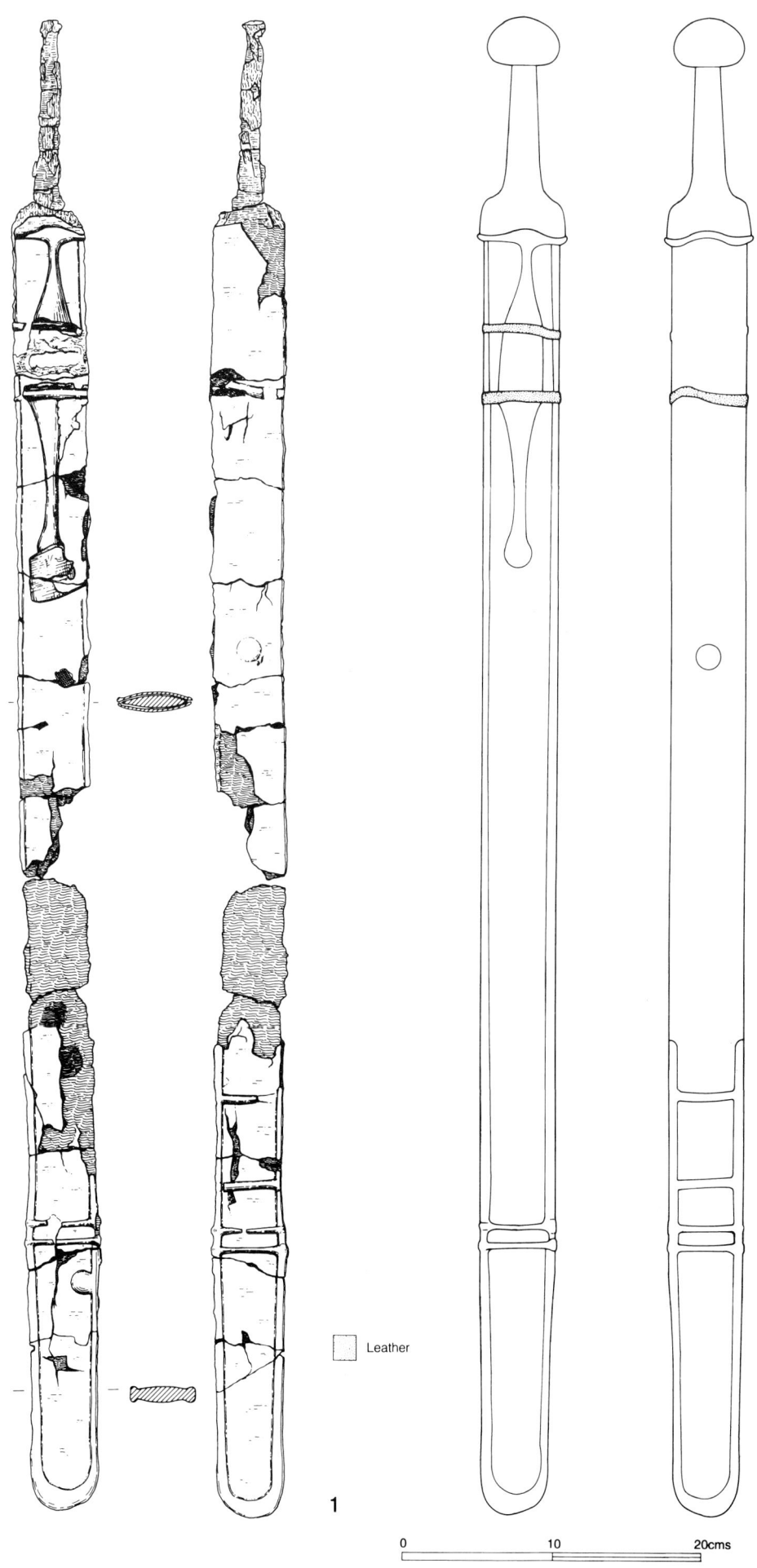

Figure 72 *Sword from Les Issues (actual and reconstruction).*

There is no trace of the 'bronze ornament', 'the iron chain' or 'the fragments of knives' but the collection returned from Canada includes a polished stone axe, 12 potsherds, six pieces of slag, two pig's teeth and a fragment of human skull. Whether or not they were associated with the burial is unrecorded.

Finds from Les Issues (Figs. 72 and 73)

1. Iron sword and scabbard.
   The iron sword is parallel-sided with a rounded tip measuring some 40 mm in width and $c.5$ mm thick in the centre. The length of the blade would originally have been in excess of 824 mm but an unknown portion of the middle section is missing. The tang is complete, measuring 117 mm in length. It is flattened in section but has a slightly expanded pommel. Traces of the mineralized wood or horn of the hilt survive along the entire length.

   The scabbard was composed of two thin sheets of iron. The front plate was wider than the back and its edges were folded over to overlap the edges of the back plate. The overlap extends the full length of the scabbard. The lower end of the scabbard was strengthened by a chape consisting of a ground strip of iron holding both plates together. The strip thickens considerably to give added strength to the extremity. A pair of iron strips bind the chape and the scabbard plates together while two further strips of iron bridge the edge bindings across the back of the scabbard. Below the paired bindings a single chape clamp can be made out on the front of the scabbard. No trace of the opposing clamp survives.

   At the hilt end the elongated attachment plates of the suspension loop survive though the wide bridge of the loop itself has disappeared. The end of the upper attachment plate expands to form a horizontal bar strengthening the top of the scabbard. The end of the lower attachment plate expands into a disc. Within the loop the mineralized remains of a leather strap survive. Two narrow strips of mineralized organic material, presumably leather thongs, lie across the attachment plates of the suspension loop immediately above and immediately below the bridge. The lower seems to have been bound right around the sword but the upper is visible only on the back. Further down the scabbard, partly obscuring the terminal of the lower attachment plate, is another piece of mineralized material, probably also leather. It appears to be the end of a strap 29 mm wide cut diagonally, possibly part of the dress of the dead man. A small patch of woven fabric less than 10 mm across is preserved in the corrosion products just below the strap.
   (GMAG 3153).

2. Shield boss fashioned from a plate of iron 3-4 mm thick. The umbo is steeply curved in a horizontal plane and slightly curved in a vertical plane with the edges thickened into a triangular cross section. The attachment plates are very fragmentary and no trace of rivet holes can be made out.
   (GMAG 3154c).

3. Iron spearhead with tip broken. The blade is 60 mm wide at the widest and would originally have been $c.150$ mm in length with a prominent midrib. Most of the socket survives containing mineralized traces of the wooden haft.
   (GMAG 3154a).

   The fragments of wood stained with bronze salts may have been part of the spear shaft preserved where mineralized.
   (GMAG 3154b).

4. Iron ferrule.
   Short ferrule containing traces of mineralized wood.

Pot from Les Issues (Fig. 73)

1. Jar. Dull red brown fabric. Fired to grey brown. Wheel-turned. A narrow iron strip has been wound around the lower part of the vessel just above the foot ring.
   (GMAG 3152: Kendrick G 136).

The Iron Age cist burials at Richmond, St. Saviour's

Between 1900 and 1905 five cists were found 'on a hill near Richmond and Perelle Bay'. The first cist, found in November 1900 by men working in a quarry, was largely destroyed before it could be adequately recorded, but contemporary accounts suggest that it was 2.1 m in length, 0.5 m broad and lay at 0.15-0.20 m below the surface. It was composed of small stone blocks set upright with their smooth surfaces facing inwards. The workmen claimed that the cist was empty when found (Anon. 1901, 59). In 1903 three cists were uncovered at Richmond, one of which is recorded to have produced a sword and an urn. Two years later in 1905 another, empty, cist was found nearby 'in quarrying in the lane south of Richmond Barracks' (*T.S.G.* V, 1905-8, 10).

Details of what would appear to be a small cemetery are sparse and its precise location ill-defined. No plans were published nor were the finds illustrated with the exception of a small sketch by Kendrick (1928, 192, fig. 88) which gives some impression of the 'sword'. The 'sword' was preserved in the Guille-Allès Museum but the urn cannot now be traced.

The Richmond grave goods

The Richmond 'sword', heavily corroded, had been covered with varnish, presumably soon after its discovery, and attached with some kind of cement to a wooden base. In this condition it was entrusted to the author in May 1979 and was taken to the laboratory at

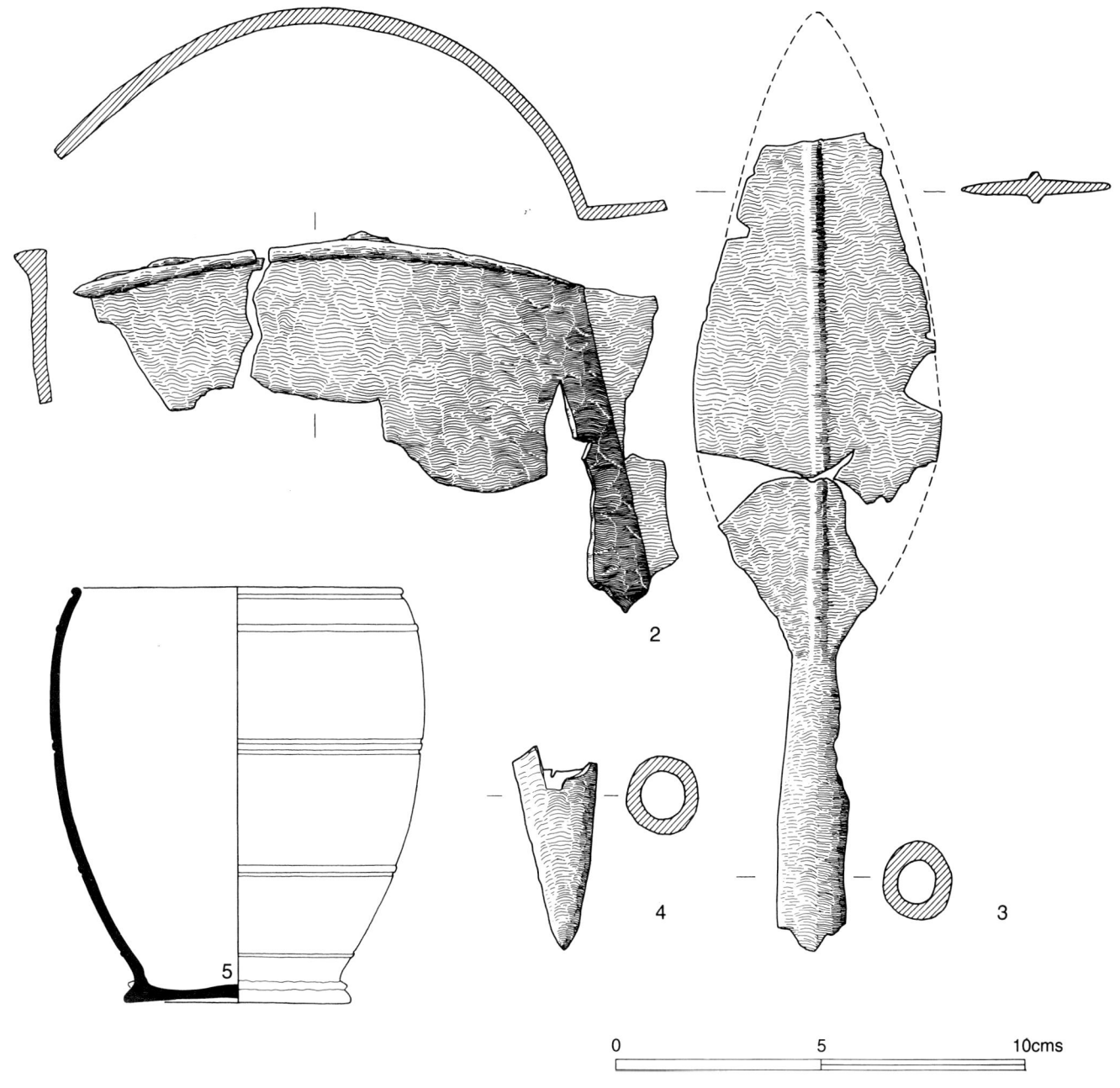

Figure 73 *Iron weapons and pottery vessel from Les Issues. (The pot is reproduced at half the scale.)*

the Institute of Archaeology, Oxford, for conservation and study.

Preliminary examination showed that the object was composed of two, possibly three, separate items. The main body of the specimen was indeed a sword but its 'hilt' was the socket of an iron spearhead, while its 'point' was the blade and tip of a spear. The two spear fragments do not fit each other but could well be part of the same object. It is impossible to be sure that the sword and spear were found together but in all probability they were. The combination of sword and spear in a single grave is, of course, well known in other Iron Age burials on the island.

1. The iron sword and its scabbard (Figs. 74 and 75)
    The iron sword and its scabbard have corroded together: no attempt has been made to separate them. The combined object is now in six joining sections which make up an overall length of 0.81 m.

The *sword* is complete with the exception of its tang and point but the overall length of the blade from hilt to point would have been between 0.9 and 1.0 m. The blade is of even width throughout averaging 55 mm. Its thickness is difficult to estimate through the corrosion but is in the order of 5 mm in the centre. The hilt end shows details of some interest. Mineralized wood or horn from the hilt is still attached to the tang and shoulders of the sword and it would appear that the facing of the hilt which abutted the top of the scabbard had been strengthened with small iron nails, 1.5 mm in diameter and up to 10 mm in length, which had been driven into the hilt at right angles. Traces of five can be made out on one side, none can be seen on the other: the

107

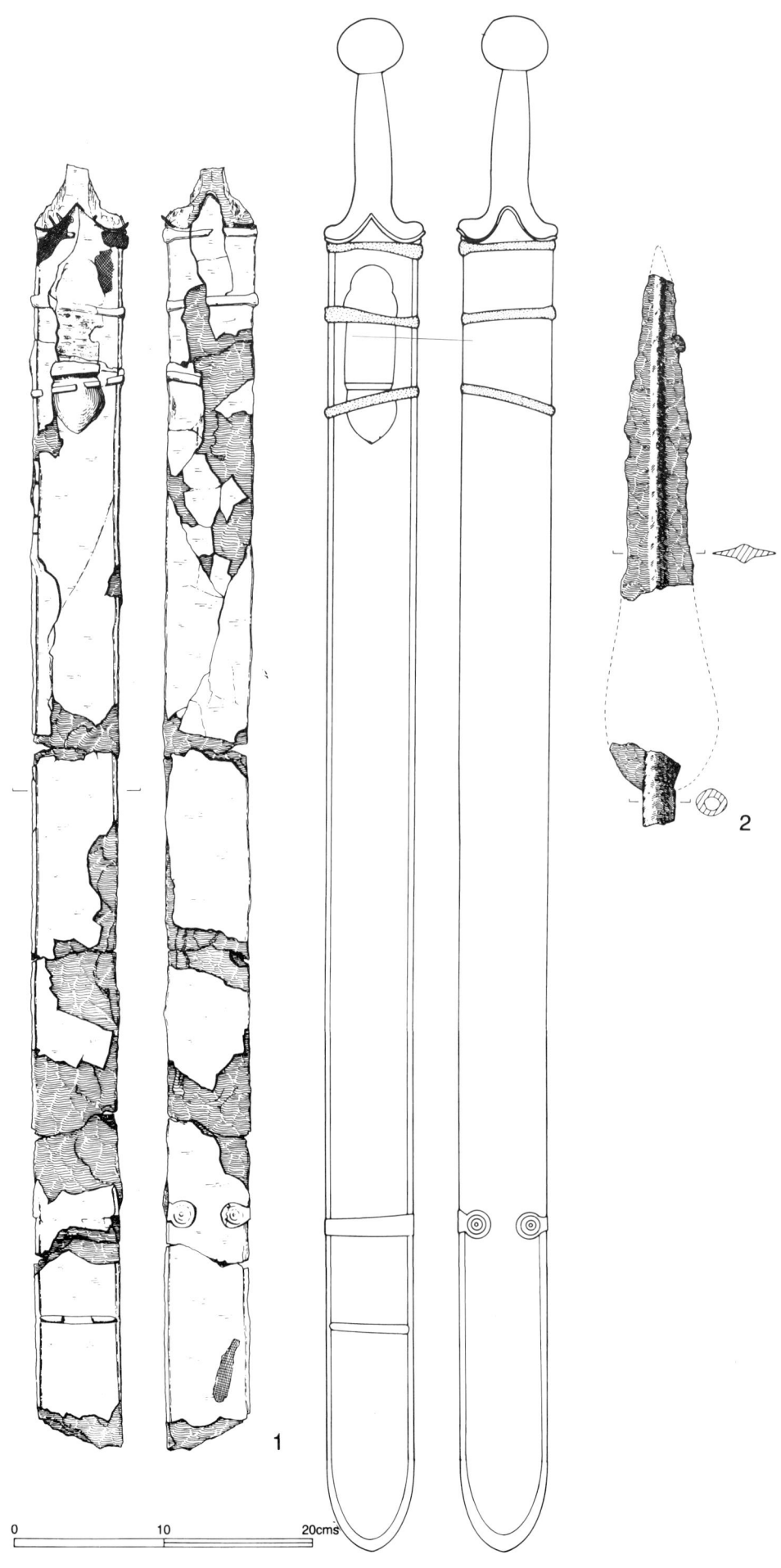

Figure 74 *Sword and spear from Richmond (actual sword and reconstruction).*

closest spacing between two adjacent nails is 3 mm. The nail heads are attached to a thin strip of metal which follows the shape of the scabbard end but is at right angles to the scabbard plates. There are two possible explanations for this arrangement: either the metal strip was attached by the nails to the hilt plate, or it represents a mouth guard attached to the scabbard top, the nail heads of the hilt plates merely being corroded to it. Unfortunately the corrosion was such that even detailed X-ray photographs failed to demonstrate the precise relationship between the nail heads and the strip. Although mouth guards are not uncommon they are usually more substantial than the strip on the present example: for this reason therefore it seems more likely that the strip was nailed to the hilt.

The *scabbard* was composed of two thin plates of iron cambered apart. The front plate was wider than the back and its edges were folded so as to overlap the edges of the back plate. This overlap extended from the hilt down to the chape. It is now generally believed that these overlapping seams were constructed with the sword in position. The mouth of the scabbard was of campanulate form and, as we have seen, probably had no separate guard, but to prevent the scabbard from being ripped apart when the sword was unsheathed or returned, the upper part of the scabbard was strengthened with three ferrules – rods of iron bound around the scabbard with their ends probably welded together. The upper ferrule was wrapped around the scabbard just below its mouth, the middle ferrule passed beneath the upper part of the suspension loop while the lower ferrule was placed just below the suspension loop, over the top of the lower attachment of the loop. The three ferrules were spaced at about 45 mm apart but were somewhat irregularly attached and were not parallel to each other.

The lower end of the scabbard was strengthened with a chape of which the upper part survives. Chape bindings consisting of grooved strips of iron run down the sides of the scabbard to keep the two plates together, functionally replacing the overlaps, and giving greater strength. The upper ends of the bindings are attached to a chape bridge at the back and to two circular chape clamps in front both decorated with concentric grooves. A second chape bridge was provided 65 mm below the top bridge. The lower part of the scabbard and the chape end are missing.

At the top of the scabbard part of the suspension loop survives. Originally the feature consisted of two round and domed loop plates attached to the back plate of the scabbard, with an integral metal strip between raised sufficiently from the scabbard to allow a thick leather strap to pass beneath it. Only the lower plate and part of the loop survives but the place of attachment of the upper plate can be traced. Since there is no evidence of a rivet we must assume that the plates were welded or stuck to the scabbard. The loop would have allowed for a strap some 35 mm wide and 5 mm thick. Organic traces of the leather are preserved in the corrosion product.

The highly corroded nature of the sword and scabbard makes illustration difficult. Fig. 74 presents a simplified but accurately measured view of the entire object without showing details of textures caused by the corrosion products: the shaded portion represents the sword blade, while the largely unshaded areas are the scabbard plates and bindings. Details of the distinctive features of the sword are shown in the plates (Fig. 75).

The corrosion products derived from the iron have preserved certain organic traces through mineralization. We have already noted the wood of the haft plates and the leather of the suspension strap; a third element represents patches of textile. Dr. John-Peter Wild of Manchester University kindly examined photographs of these traces and reports as follows:

'The remains consist of four small patches of replaced plain-weave textile: three lie near the hilt ($c.7$ cm^2), the fourth adheres to the opposite side nearer the tip ($c.3$ cm^2).

> System (1), weak S-spun, $c.11$ threads per cm, maximum length of largest piece near hilt 1.3 cm.
>
> System (2), weak S-spun, $c.13$ threads per cm, maximum length on piece near tip $c.4$ cm.

The yarns have a uniform character, but System (1) has more spin and may perhaps be the warp. The fibre has the visual appearance of flax; under very high magnification it might be possible to identify it positively.

The S-spin direction of the yarns in both systems can be readily paralleled among the known European Iron Age textiles. Plain weave, especially for linen fabrics, is common.

The fragments appear to adhere loosely to a film of corrosion products; but the oblique angle at which the yarns of System (1) (?warp) run across the face of the blade is worth noting. A Hallstatt sword from Bastheim (Ldkr. Mellrichstadt) was found to have been wrapped carefully before burial in a long strip of plain-weave linen, perhaps originally waxed. It might be suggested that the sword from Richmond had received the same treatment.'

2. The iron spearhead (Fig. 74)

Two heavily corroded fragments of a spearhead survive. While there is no reason why they must belong to the same weapon they are sufficiently similar to suggest that they may have done. The spearhead is socketed and with a heavy midrib. The blade is wide at the base but it probably

Figure 75a *Details of the sword from Richmond (See also Fig. 74, page 108).*

Figure 75b *Details of the sword from Richmond.*

narrowed rapidly to a long nearly parallel-sided blade gradually tapering to a point.

The drawing (Fig. 74, 2) gives some idea of what its original shape may have been like.

The cist burial found at Les Adams, St. Peter-in-the-Wood

In 1845 Lukis excavated a cist buried 1.5 m down. At the eastern end he found fragments of a human skull, while 'on the south side was an arm bone accompanied by part of a sword and knife, near which, a dagger and its haft cross were as if it had lain on the breast of the body' (Lukis 1848, 307). Potsherds were found in the soil above the cist. The find is mentioned by de Guérin (1918, 137) and by Kendrick (1928, 186) the latter recording that the finds had been dispersed.

Note on the technology of the swords based on a radiographic study
by Brian Gilmour

The three Guernsey swords (GMAG 3147 from Le Catioroc, 3150 from Le Catioroc and 3271 from La Hougue au Comte) were poorly preserved and appeared to be mostly mineralized. They were complete although very fragile and generally in a fragmentary condition, and were studied using x-radiography to look for technological details as well as other hidden features such as inlays or makers' marks.

Radiographs did not reveal any such additional features, although some detail relating to the original smithing of the swords was found, most notably in the radiographs of one of the swords from Le Catioroc (GMAG 3147), in which an early form of pattern-welding was visible (Fig. 76). This was not the more familiar twisted form of pattern-welding seen on many swords from third century AD and later contexts, but a form which gives a 'straight-grained' and banded form of pattern on a radiograph.

It is difficult to be sure of the exact form of this pattern-welded structure from the radiographs, but a series of perhaps five or six parallel bands, each approximately 5 mm wide running down the centre of the blade with a wider band on either side would seem probable. The clarity with which the straight-grained effect could be seen in the radiographs of the central part of the blade would suggest a simple, banded composite structure in which each band occupies the full thickness of the blade, as is suggested on the reconstruction diagram (Fig. 76).

This form of blade construction is similar to that reported for one (no. 4) of a group of five Late Iron Age swords from Llyn Cerrig Bach, Anglesey (McGrath 1968, 420, figs. 3 and 4).

In terms of its development, this simple banded form of pattern-welding would appear to come between that which occurs in one of the Late Iron Age swords which was recovered with its decorated (Late La Tène) bronze scabbard from the old bed of the River Nene at Orton Longueville in Cambridgeshire (site ref. OLB R22, now in Peterborough Museum), and the more familiar sword blades with pattern-welded central parts and separate cutting edges, the earliest (so far) dated example of which was found at the Roman fort at South Shields and dated stratigraphically to c.AD 200 (Tylecote 1986, 171; Richmond nd, 13). The Orton Longueville sword shows a very early or prototype-form of pattern-welding and is particularly important as the original heavily etched surface is almost perfectly preserved in places, showing that as a technique it was developed to be seen.

In the Orton Longueville sword the pattern shows up as a fibrous-looking effect on x-ray examination (Gilmour 1991, vol. 2, fig. 73), less regular than that seen on the Guernsey sword. On the x-ray of the Orton Longueville sword this fibrous effect continued to the edges of the sword. This fibrous pattern is still clearly visible along the central part of both sides of the sword, which had been heavily etched, although a margin (approx. 10 mm wide) along the edges on both sides showed a smooth surface where this part of the blade was resist protected, probably using some kind of wax or grease, to prevent the etching reagent attacking this part of the blade (Gilmour 1991, vol. 2, figs. 71 and 72). The particular form of pattern-welding seen on the Orton Longueville blade is a good example of a proto-type form of this technique – a form which would appear to be a forerunner to those blades using a composite banded construction – as well as providing proof as to how it was used as a decorative technique. It would seem that the Le Catioroc sword blade (GMAG 3147) shows a more developed form of pattern-welding and possibly one with separately welded-on cutting edges.

This interpretation of the structure of this particular Guernsey sword is only tentative at this stage as it could only be confirmed by metallographic study which has not so far been possible. There was no obvious sign of pattern-welding on either of the other two Guernsey swords although the radiograph of the sword from La Hougue au Comte (GMAG 3271) did show some signs of a fairly coarse fibrous effect on the upper part of the blade near the hilt. This may be the result of corrosion along fairly numerous slag filaments running parallel to and fairly evenly through the blade.

One possible interpretation for this blade is of a simple layered structure with some slag filaments trapped along the welds, although equally well, nearly all the slag in the blade may have resulted from the original smelting of the iron. A simple prototype form of pattern-welding, similar to that seen in the Orton Longueville sword, may however be more likely and the fibrous effect on the radiograph is quite similar to that seen on radiographs of the Orton Longueville sword.

The restriction of this fibrous effect to the upper part of the blade suggests that this is the only part of the blade that has any metallic iron surviving. Without a metallographic study of this part of the blade it is not possible to say much more about the structure.

The fragmentary second sword from Le Catioroc

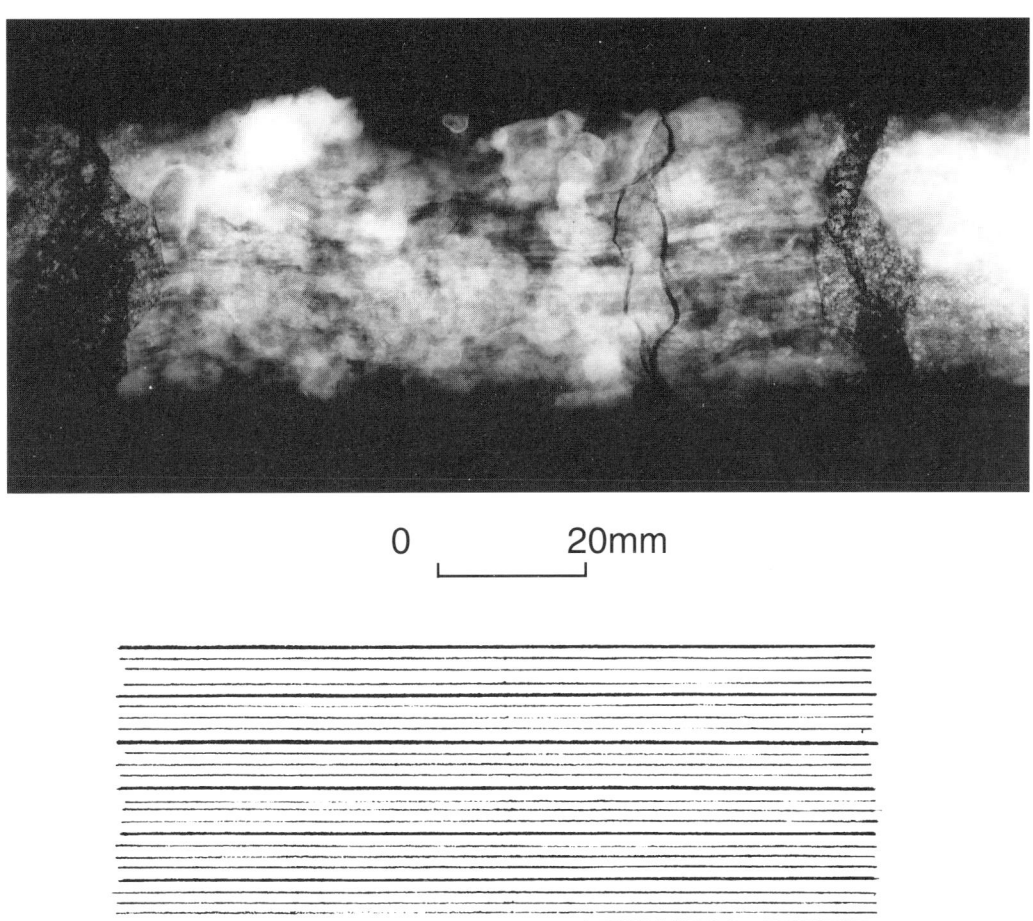

Figure 76 *Radiograph of the sword (GMAG 3147) from Le Catioroc with diagrammatic reconstruction.*

(GMAG 3150) also showed a fibrous effect on x-ray suggesting that there may be some metallic iron remaining, at least in the two main pieces. In this blade the fibrous effect seemed to be much finer and more diffuse in appearance than that seen on the other two blades suggesting a more even distribution of fine slag filaments throughout the metal. This would tend to suggest that a plain non pattern-welded, but possibly layered, structure is most likely for this sword blade. Again metallographic analysis would be necessary to sort out this structure, as well as to find out which iron alloys (mainly relating to the presence of carbon and phosphorus), and such details as the quality of the metal, smithing details and heat treatments which might have been used.

Acknowledgements

I would like to thank Esther Cameron of Oxford University, Institute of Archaeology for supplying me with the radiographs of the Guernsey swords which I used as a basis for this report, and also Jeremy Hall of the Royal Armouries for producing the photographs shown in Fig. 76. Jeremy Hall also produced the photographs of the Orton Longueville sword, including photographs of a radiograph (done by me at the Royal Armouries in 1989) which appear in my thesis (figs. 71-3).

Note on the technology of the glass beads by J. Henderson

The beads are all typical products of the 2nd-1st centuries BC and they are liable to have originated in the oppida zone, though direct evidence for their production, as opposed to evidence for generalised glass-working, has not been found. The beads were produced by spinning on a metal mandril. The decoration of no. 16 was applied around the hole through the bead when fluid and thrown outwards across the surface of the bead to form the final decoration. Further evidence for spun glass is that in no. 17 lines of impurities in the glass radiate from the face of the hole. No. 19 was initially formed as a smaller spun ring bead and an additional layer of glass was added to increase its thickness; the latter characteristic is rare, but found in other Continental examples.

Microsamples were removed from nos. 16, 17 and 19 for electron-probe microanalysis (Henderson 1988). All the translucent glass samples were found to have a typical Soda-lime-silicate composition consistent with their period of production with soda levels of $c.16$-18%, silica levels of $c.65$-70% and calcium oxide of 6-8%. The brown colour in no. 16 is due to iron in a reduced state, the green colour in no. 17 is due to iron in an oxidised state, and the blue colour of no. 19 due to cobalt oxide. The opacifier used in all three decorated beads was tin-based: SnO_2 in no. 16, $Pb_2Sn_2O_7$ in nos. 17 and 19. The use of tin is an example of Late Iron Age technological innovation, and the first recorded example of its use in the world (Henderson 1989, 51-52).

The beads from Catioroc are very important in that very few ring beads have been found in secure archaeological contexts in or near England (Guido 1978, Class 7). The reason for this is that the beads from Catioroc, like the others from the well-dated contexts at Hengistbury Head (Henderson 1987) lie on the periphery of their production zone.

Discussion

Burial rite

The burial rite involved interring each body individually in a stone-built cist. The bodies were probably laid in an extended position and were sometimes accompanied by grave goods. Little can be said of cemetery size because of the casual circumstances of discovery. It may be that the single cists found at La Hougue au Comte, Les Issues and Les Adams were indeed isolated burials but larger groupings are known: 2(?) at St. Saviour's Church, 4 at Le Catioroc, 4 at King's Road and 5 at Richmond, showing that some, at least, were arranged in cemeteries which may have served family or village communities.

The range of grave goods is summarized below.

With so small a sample, so ill-recorded, it is unwise to indulge in a detailed analysis, but several general comments may be offered. Seven of the eight burials produced at least one item of equipment appropriate to a warrior: swords, spears, shields and metal rings by which the sword strap was attached to the belt. Of these, four contained both swords and spears and if we allow the possibility that one of the swords assigned to Le Catioroc 1 in fact came from Le Catioroc 2 then the number is increased to five. That four of the burials produced shield bosses does not mean that only four shields were present. Shields were normally made of organic material such as wood or hide and their bosses were often fashioned from these materials: in such a case no remains would survive. Only three graves yielded belt rings but it is possible that the so-called 'iron chain' at Les Issues was in fact several belt rings corroded together. Fine rings of bronze or iron would in any case rapidly disintegrate in acid conditions.

Of the other burials Le Catioroc 4 is evidently an exception in having only arrowheads from among the possible array of warrior gear and in producing fibulae and a sickle. La Hougue au Comte is also exceptional in its rich array of grave goods including beads, bracelets and a bronze vessel more appropriate to female burials. The possibility must be allowed that the cist contained a warrior buried with a female companion.

Location

The location of the cist graves deserves comment since with the exception of the King's Road group they cluster in the western part of the island in such numbers that the distribution is hardly likely to result from accident of survival or discovery. Two possible explanations suggest themselves: either the burials reflect the territory occupied by a discrete cultural group or the region in which they were found was set aside for burial purposes. The problem is of some interest but cannot yet be resolved.

Cultural implications

Sufficient will have been said in the descriptive accounts above to show that the material culture associated with the cist burials is of La Tène III type and can be paralleled widely in western Europe. More specifically, the pottery vessels from Le Catioroc, Les Issues and La Hougue au Comte are similar to types made in Brittany and distributed widely, reaching as

	Swords	Spears	Shields	Belt rings	Knives	Bracelets	Fibulae	Beads	Pots	Other objects
Les Adams	1	–	–	–	1	–	–	–	–	'dagger'
Les Issues	1	1	1	–	?	–	–	–	1	bronze, knives? + iron chain
Richmond 1	1	1	–	–	–	–	–	–	1	–
La Hougue au Comte	2	2	–	2	–	6 or 7	–	7	[3+]	N.B. Pots outside the grave. Bronze vessel + large iron ring
Le Catioroc 1	2?	1?	1?	1	1	1	–	–	1	'some small ornaments', 'a clay bead'
Le Catioroc 2	–	1	1	–	–	–	–	–	–	–
Le Catioroc 4	–	–	–	–	–	–	2+	–	1+	arrowhead, sickle
King's Road 1	1	1	1	2	1	–	1	1	–	also shears with the knife

far north as the south coasts of Britain. However, only the graphite-coated vessel, no. 2 from La Hougue au Comte, was definitely made in Brittany, the rest being local island copies. In the first century BC therefore the Guernsey community can be said to have shared the material culture of Continental Europe and of Britain. Two aspects however demand further consideration: the rite of inhumation in cist graves and the rite of burying a warrior with his fighting equipment.

There is nothing particularly novel about the construction of a stone cist, especially in an area like Guernsey with its long tradition of stone sepulchral architecture. It could well be argued that the Iron Age cists were merely a modification of indigenous traditions to the demand imposed by the rite of single burial, but before assumptions of this kind are made it is necessary to examine the broader context. Cist burials of Iron Age date are known in the south west of Britain and in Brittany. In southern Britain two geographically distinct groupings can be recognized: the cists of the Cornish peninsula and those scattered along the southern coasts of Dorset. Both groups share certain characteristics in common: the graves are frequently arranged in distinct cemeteries, the bodies were usually inhumed in a flexed or crouched position and grave goods were often provided. Without going into a detailed presentation of the evidence it can be said that the cist burial rite was prevalent in the period from the first century BC into the second century AD. When precisely it began is a matter of some uncertainty but on present evidence there is nothing to suggest that any of the south Dorset group pre-date the mid first century BC and it remains a possibility that the known examples could all be fitted into the first two centuries of the first millennium AD.[2] The Cornish group however appears to have begun earlier, in the fourth or third century BC if the La Tène II fibula from Trevone and the Iberian-style brooches from Harlyn Bay and Mount Batten were buried soon after manufacture rather than being saved as heirlooms.[3] The principal difference between the Guernsey and British cist burials is that whereas the British cists were designed to take contracted inhumations, and were therefore squarer in plan, the Guernsey cists were longer so that the body could be laid in an extended position. While it is all too easy to over-emphasize the relevance of differences of this kind the significant point is that the Cornish and Dorset cist burials share in the indigenous British tradition of contracted inhumation. We are unlikely therefore to be dealing with an intrusive burial rite although the concept of cist building, the grouping of graves into cemeteries and the provision of grave goods may well have developed in the maritime areas of western Britain as the result of persistent contact with other communities.

The late La Tène cemeteries of north-western France are less well known but several relevant generalizations can be made. The surveys of Bertin (1975) and Duval (1975) clearly demonstrate that Normandy was, at this time, primarily a region of cremation burial. In Brittany, however, inhumation cemeteries, often incorporating cist burials, prevailed. Giot (1960, 185) has plotted the distribution of 14 cemeteries, many concentrating on the Quiberon and Penmarc'h peninsulas. Although more recently he has shown that some of these cemeteries should be dated to the sub-Roman period it should not obscure the undoubted late La Tène date of others such as the important sites at Tronoën (St.-Jean-Trolimon, Finistère) and Kerné (Quiberon, Morbihan).[4] The characteristics of these Breton sites – the arrangement of graves in specially designated cemeteries, extended inhumation often accompanied by grave goods and burial in cists – have much in common with the Guernsey burials. Thus, although the evidence is still too sparse for definite assertions to be made, it seems reasonable to distinguish between the burial traditions of Brittany and the Channel Islands on the one hand and south-west Britain on the other.

The second characteristic of the Guernsey burials which deserves consideration is the fact that a significant

	Sword	Spear	Shield	Belt rings and belt hook	Fibulae	Pot	
Whitcombe	1	1	–	2	1	–	hammer, iron tool, bronze fragment, perforated chalk
Owslebury	1	1	1	2+h	–	–	–
St. Lawrence	1	–	1	3	–	–	iron disc
Sutton Courtenay	?	–	1	?	5	1	–
Grimthorpe	1	1	1	–	–	–	bronze disc, bronze studs and nails, coral bead, iron edged with bronze, 16 bone points
North Grimston	2	–	1	2+h	–	–	amber and jet rings
Brigthorpe	1	–	–	–	–	–	2 bronze discs decorated with enamel beads, 2 bronze studs
Eastburn	1	–	–	–	–	–	–
Gelliniog Wen	1	–	–	1	–	–	–
Lambay Island				not recorded in their associations			

number of them are warrior burials. The burial of weapons with the dead is a long established and widespread tradition in Europe in the first millennium BC. It becomes particularly common in the third and second centuries BC and continues, in some regions, into the first century. In Britain a number of first century sword burials are known but show a surprisingly geographical scatter spreading indiscriminately across regions of totally different burial traditions.[5] The characteristics of these burials are briefly summarized on p. 115.

Comparison of the tables on p. 114 and p. 115 shows the similarities and differences between the Guernsey and mainland British warrior burial associations. Leaving aside the ill-recorded and dubious Sutton Courtenay burial, the British graves are notable for their lack of pottery vessels and for the paucity of personal ornaments such as fibulae, bracelets and beads, but with such a small sample apparent differences of this kind may not be significant. Of more interest is the observation that four of the burials (Sutton Courtenay, St. Lawrence, Grimthorpe and Whitcomb) were all crouched in the traditional British burial posture but the interments at Owslebury, Gelliniog Wen and North Grimston were extended. Add to this the fact that the majority of the grave goods accompanying the burials were of local British manufacture and the differences between the two traditions become clearer.

Late La Tène sword burials are comparatively rare in north-western France. In Normandy five or six cremation cemeteries have produced swords[6] but no inhumations with swords are recorded. In Brittany La Tène swords are even rarer and apart from river finds in the Loire near Nantes, only two find-spots are recorded: at Questembert (Morbihan) where a fragment of a sword was found and at the cemetery at Tronoën, St.-Jean-Trolimon (Finistère) where one inhumation was accompanied by a sword, spears, pottery vessels and several Celtic coins (Giot 1979, 260). The Tronoën find is of considerable interest since, as we have seen above, the cemetery shares other characteristics with the Guernsey sites.

No firm conclusions can be offered on such sparse evidence but sufficient will have been said to show that the cultural characteristics of the Guernsey cist burials – extended inhumation, weapons included as grave goods, the use of cists and the arrangement of the individual graves in cemeteries – are shared in different combinations with the maritime communities of southern Britain stretching from Cornwall to Hampshire, and with the inhabitants of Brittany. On present showing the closest parallels would seem to be with the cemeteries of the Finistère and Morbihan coasts. The tribes of Normandy appear to belong to an altogether different, cremating, tradition by the later part of the pre-Roman Iron Age.

Historical context

It is all too easy to allow one's imagination to range wide in problems of this kind but two generalizations of an historical nature can be offered with some degree of assurance. Firstly Armorica, the Channel Islands and south-west Britain were bound together by ties of reciprocal exchange, involving elements of long distance trade. These processes were in operation in the seventh century and had intensified by the first half of the first century BC. This much is implicit in the archaeological evidence and is made explicit by several classical writers.[7] Secondly the Roman conquest of Gaul between 58 and 52 BC caused widespread disruptions, not least Caesar's savage campaigns against the Armorican tribes in 56 BC. These events are likely to have created a flood of refugees and to have dislocated the traditional links between Armorica and Britain. Beyond these two bare statements lie a multitude of uncertainties and possibilities. It would be perfectly legitimate to suggest, as others have done, that Gallic refugees fled to the Channel Islands, some to Jersey where the great coin hoards reflect the uncertain times, others to Guernsey where the sword burials are those of the first generation immigrants (Kendrick 1928, 91-2). It would even be possible to go further and suggest that some of the refugees reached Britain and were dispersed among the native population acquiring native equipment but still retaining their style of inhumed burial accompanied by their weapons (though some were buried crouched in native style). Such hypotheses are not unreasonable but given that we are dealing with a long period of widespread contact, resulting from socio-economic forces, intensified by a major war, people, artefacts and ideas are likely to have been transported widely and not always rationally. Even if some elements of these patterns are reflected in the surviving archaeological data their meaning may have to remain obscure.

Endnotes

1. There is some confusion over the exact number. De Guérin makes the total 34 but regards the Le Catioroc and Les Adams cists as additional to the 20 noted by Lukis whereas Lukis implies that his figure of 20 was inclusive. Moreover Kendrick (1928, 195) says that two cists were found at St. Saviour's Church, not one.
2. The most relevant examples are from Bridport, Corfe Castle, Langton Matravers, Gallows Gore, at various sites on the Island of Portland, and in the environs of Weymouth. Detailed references and descriptions will be found in R.C.H.M. *Dorset South East* vol. III (1970).
3. The principal sites are Trevone, Trelan Bahow (St. Keverne), Mount Batten, Harlyn Bay and various locations on the Scilly Isles. For a brief discussion with references see Cunliffe 1991, 505 and for the Scilly Isles see Ashbee 1974, 120–47. A recent consideration of the important site of Harlyn Bay is given in Whimster 1978 and the Mount Batten cemetery is considered in Cunliffe 1988a, 87–99.
4. For a more recent survey of Iron Age and Roman burial tradition in Brittany see Galliou 1989.
5. Four in Yorkshire (North Grimston, Eastburn, Grimthorpe and Brigthorpe), one in Ireland (Lambay Island), one in Wales (Gelliniog Wen) and four in central southern England (Sutton Courtenay(?), Whitcombe, Owslebury and St. Lawrence). A number of other discoveries of swords may also originally have come from burials but details are lacking. These burials have been discussed several times recently (Collis 1973; Whimster 1981, 322–3; Cunliffe 1991, 498–506) with full bibliographies.
6. Le Manoir and Notre-Dame du Vaudreuil in Eure; Eslettes, Moulineaux and St. Wandrille in Seine-et-Marne and possibly Bernières-sur-Mer in Calvados. All listed in Bertin 1975.
7. This is not the place to restate the evidence. I have summarized it in Cunliffe 1991 (passim) with full references.

Gazetteer of Iron Age Sites and Finds in Guernsey, Herm and Sark

by R.B. Burns, Barry Cunliffe, Philip de Jersey and Mike G. Hill

To complete this report we offer a brief gazetteer of all Iron Age sites and finds known to us on the islands of Guernsey and Herm. For ease of reference the record is organized into the following categories:

- A Cliffside earthworks
- B Settlements
- C Cist burials
- D Other discoveries

The individual sites are located on Fig. 2.

A. Cliffside earthworks (MGH and RBB)

The major bank and ditch system which lies across the promontory at Jerbourg in St. Martin's parish has long been known. It is discussed briefly in the Lukis MSS and documentary references to the medieval defences there have been published in local learned journals. The inner bank of the rampart was excavated between 1978 and 1981 and the results of the excavations published (Burns 1988). The interest generated by those excavations stimulated an intensive campaign of fieldwork into the cliffside sites, which was carried out by Mike Hill between 1981 and 1989. As a result of his investigations, the presence of several hitherto undiscovered prehistoric earthworks was revealed. His work is recorded in an unpublished series of MSS and photographs kept at Guernsey Museum. The work, which includes cliffside fortifications of all periods, is summarized in a paper due to be published in the near future.

The details relating to the prehistoric earthworks listed below have, with the exception of the Jerbourg Main Rampart, been extracted from Hill's unpublished work.

A1 **Jerbourg Main Rampart, St. Martin's** (Fig. 77)
The excavations carried out on the inner bank revealed that a complex series of enlargements and replacements of the defences took place here from the late Neolithic to the Second World War. The earliest defences were commenced during the early part of the Bronze Age and successive enlargements and modifications were made to the original works during the later part of the Bronze Age. The pottery and flintwork, including petit tranchet and barbed and tanged arrowheads, were all of recognizable Bronze Age types. The Iron Age appeared, at least from that part of the rampart excavated, to have played little part in the earthwork's history, the only pottery of Iron Age type being discovered on the level ground at the rear of the inner bank. There are however two further banks, as yet unexcavated, which might have been constructed at a later period. The small earthworks at Jerbourg Point (see below) might be a contraction of the boundaries of the main rampart or could represent an earlier site; only further excavation will provide the answers.

References: Derrick 1904, 209; Kendrick 1928, 177-9; Burns 1988.

A2 **Jerbourg Point (Peastacks), St. Martin's** (Fig. 77)
A bank and ditch system across the narrow landbridge which joins this tiny promontory to the cliffside forms the main defensive work. The substantial main rampart runs up the east side of the promontory to the central rocky ridge. The central part of this rampart was built up with a stone face, the western corner was also stone-faced, but other stretches make use of the natural rocky outcrops. The entrance through the earthworks has not been positively identified but was most probably just to the east of the central rocky ridge. The banks and ditches on the western side of the promontory are less well-defined and it is possible that use was made of the steeply sloping nature of the cliffside as a natural defence. Two areas of occupation have been located on the eastern side at the rear of the earthworks and it is probable that the larger western slope was also occupied, although no artefactual evidence has been discovered. No excavation has been carried out on this site; the pottery discovered on the eastern side was revealed as a result of erosion.

Fig. 78

1. Jar with everted rim and angled shoulder. Reddish-brown fabric tempered with various sized grits. The surfaces of both inside and out are well burnished.
2. Jar with everted rim similar in form to no. 1. Fine reddish-brown sandy fabric with sparse fine grits. Heavily burnished inside and out.
3. Jar with everted rim probably similar in form to nos. 1 and 2. Grey-brown sandy ware with copious rounded grits. External surface is sealed.
4. Bowl? with projecting flange. Grey-brown sandy ware heavily tempered with varying sized flint grits. The external surface is well sealed.
5. Jar with 'pie-crusted' rim. The two sherds are probably of the same vessel. Reddish-brown sandy fabric with copious angular grits.
6. Jar? Grey sandy ware with sparse grits.

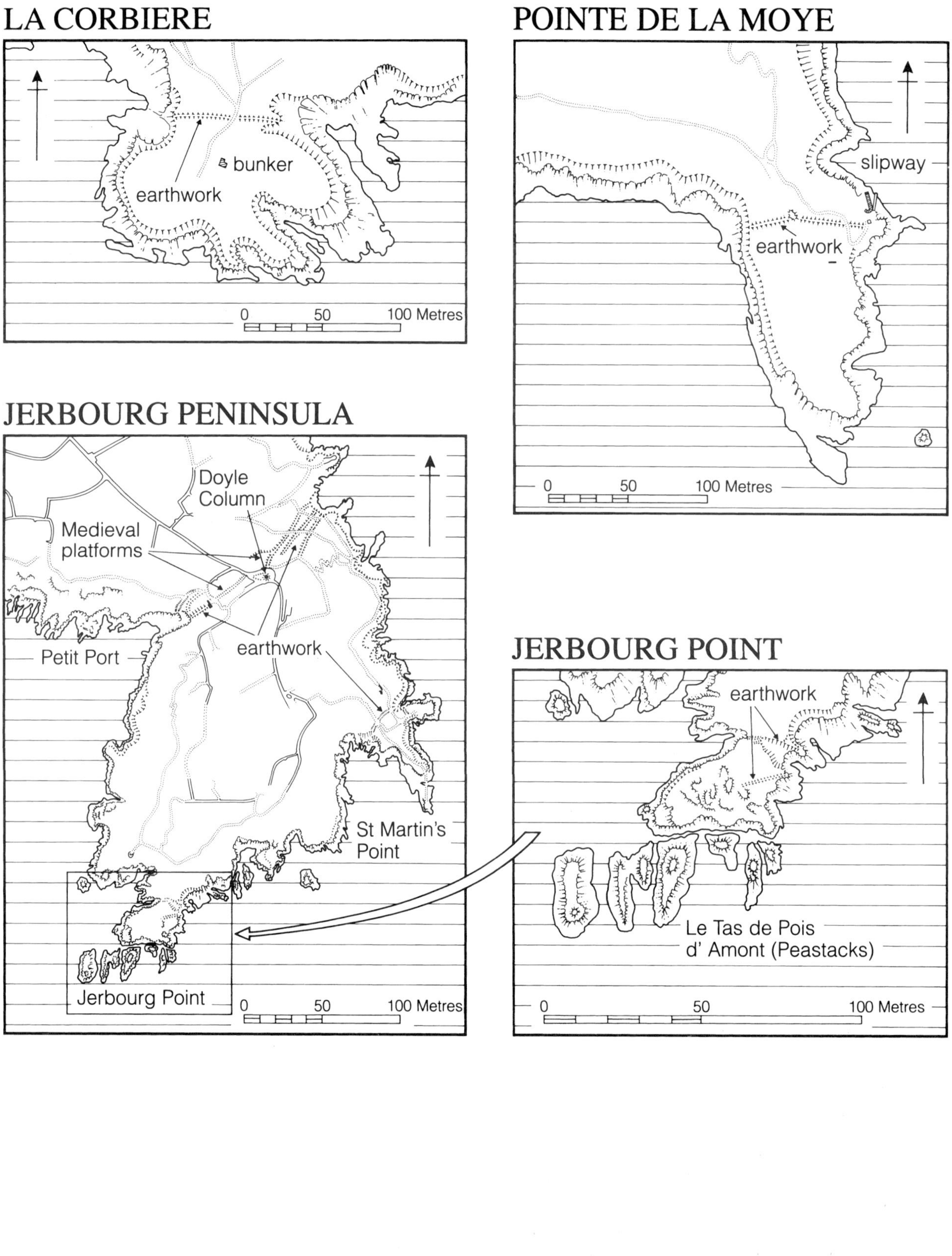

Figure 77 *Cliffside earthworks.*

7. Jar? Grey sandy ware with sparse grits. Could be same vessel as no. 6.

8. Sherd from a base(?) with two circular perforations made before firing. Dark grey-brown sandy ware with occasional large rounded grits.

9. Base. Reddish-brown sandy ware with copious varying sized angular grits. Outer surface was roughly burnished but has partially eroded.

10. Base. Blackish-brown sandy ware with copious varying sized angular grits. The surfaces are eroded.

The collection would appear to be of about the same date which, judging from the finely made tripartite jars and the 'pie-crusted' rim, should be placed in the Late Bronze or Early Iron Age, say 800-500 BC. The flanged vessel, no. 4, is a notable and unusual form.

A3 **Pointe de la Moye, Forest** (Fig. 77)
This major promontory is defended by a substantial main rampart with further smaller banks and ditches across its narrowest point. These banks, coupled with the sheer sea-cliffs on either side, combine to form an effective defence-work. The main rampart is of massive proportions and the entrance through it is situated approximately a third of the way up from its eastern end. The smaller, landward, bank and ditch system is more complex and really needs further study; the east and west sides probably differ. A large open area is situated behind the rampart and entrance, which has possible traces of inturned defensive works. There are indications further south, on the eastern side of the promontory, of levelled areas scarped into the slope. No excavation has been carried out and only a single sherd of undiagnostic pottery has been discovered here.

A4 **Corbière Promontory (Corbière Castle), Forest** (Fig. 77)
The banks and ditches thrown across the neck of this promontory have not been satisfactorily dated. The Legge Report illustrates a stone-built castle on the site (Legge 1680) and documentary references in the archives of the Royal Court make specific references to stone-robbing of the structures being carried out as early as 1603. It is possible therefore that the earthworks are of medieval or late medieval date. Recent cliffside earth falls have revealed the presence of a well-built stone wall in the core of the inner bank. No excavation has yet taken place and no artefactual evidence gathered.

B. **Settlements**

B1 **The Tranquesous, St. Saviour's** (Figs. 79-80)
(RBB)
Aerial photography revealed this site during the very dry summer of 1976. Subsequent excavation revealed a series of circular post-built houses, enclosed by palisaded ditches. The pottery was, in general, of later form to that discovered at King's Road, although there were a few examples of shallow bowls produced in the vesicular Fabric 3,

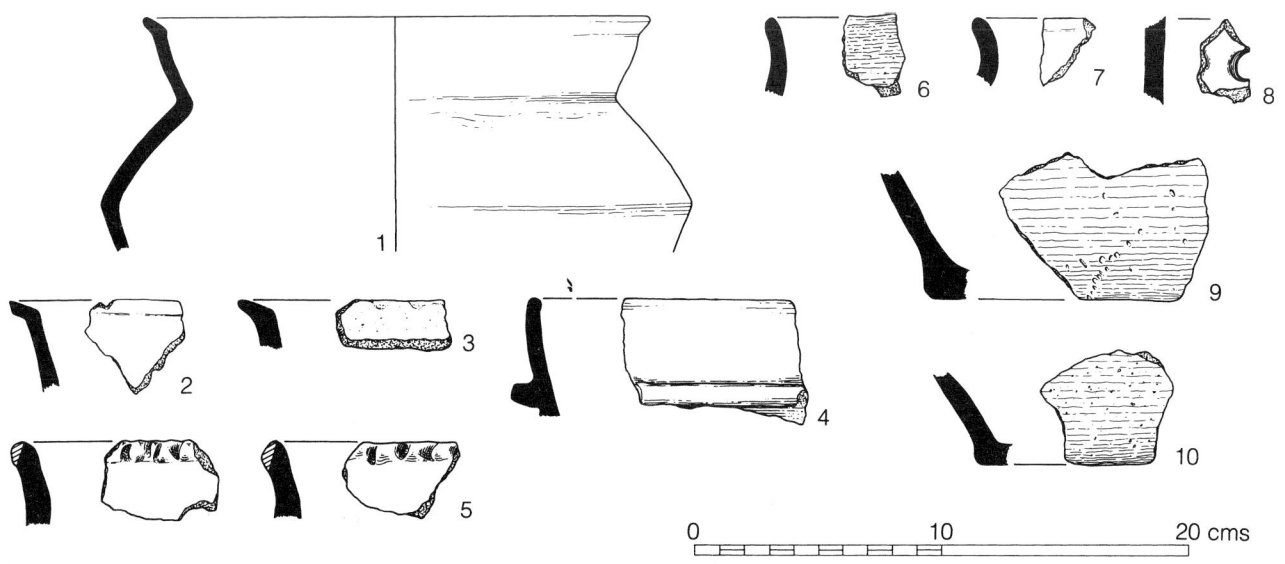

Figure 78 *Pottery from Jerbourg Point.*

Figure 79 *Cropmarks at the Iron Age site at the Tranquesous, St. Saviour's.*

indicating an earlier phase at the site. The main period of occupation of the site was from *c*.50 BC-AD 80. The site lies on undeveloped agricultural land and has only been partially sampled. The aerial photographs show clearly that it extends over a considerable area and that further excavation in the future would be of benefit.

Reference: Burns 1977.

B2 **The Vale Castle, St. Sampson's** (RBB)
Excavations at this late medieval fortification, situated in the north of the island close to St. Sampson's Harbour, showed that the hill upon which it sits had earlier been the site of a banked and ditched earthwork. The pottery recovered from the Iron Age layers contained few diagnostic sherds but the general appearance of the wares suggests a date earlier in the Iron Age, possibly of the sixth or fifth century BC.

Reference: Barton 1984.

B3 **King's Road, St. Peter Port** (BC)
Iron Age settlement occupied from the Early Iron Age to the Gallo-Roman period though not necessarily continuous. Examined in rescue and research excavations 1980-3. The Early Iron Age site, represented by a ditch, lay to the south of the Late Iron Age nucleus where ditches, pits and timber structures were revealed. The pottery from the Late Iron Age settlement included imports from Armorica and Roman amphorae suggesting that the major phase of use lay in the first half of the first century BC. A cemetery (see below) developed beyond the settlement to the south. The site was occupied in the second century AD.

Reference: This volume, pp. 3-82.

B4 **Richmond, St. Saviour's** (BC)
Briquetage from salt-working found eroding on cliff edge. Two coins found also (see D4).

Reference: Burns 1986, 91.

B5 **Le Catioroc, St. Saviour's** (BC)
Briquetage from salt-working found. (See coin D3 below.)

Reference: Jee 1958; Burns 1986, 91.

B6 **Fort Grey, St. Peter-in-the-Wood** (RBB)
Briquetage from the northern side of the causeway leading to this fortified islet. When the fortification was constructed shortly before 1804 (Kendrick 1928, 188), a number of urns were found (the present whereabouts of these pots is unknown).

B7 **Herm** (RBB and HS)
Briquetage situated on the small cliff below Fisherman's Cottage. Associated finds include Gallo-Roman wares of the second and third centuries AD (Kendrick 1928, 216).

C. Cist burials (BC)

The cist burials from Guernsey are fully discussed in this volume (pp. 83-116) to which reference should be made for detail. The list to follow is provided for ease of reference.

C1 **King's Road, St. Peter Port**
Four stone-lined graves discovered in the course of systematic excavations in 1982-3. Grave 1 contained the burial of a warrior with weapons. Graves 2-4 produced little except for three strips of iron in Grave 3.
References: This volume, pp. 83-92.

C2 **Le Catioroc, St. Saviour's**
Three cists were found in 1845 and a fourth in 1851. Three contained grave goods and one was 'empty'.
References: Lukis 1848; 1853; de Guérin 1918, 136; Kendrick 1928, 190-3; this volume, pp. 92-9.

C3 **La Hougue au Comte, Castel**
A cist was found during quarrying operations in 1885. It contained a range of grave goods.
References: Derrick 1906; de Guérin 1918, 137; Kendrick 1928, 196-8; this volume, pp. 99-104.

C4 **Les Issues, St. Saviour's**
A cist was discovered in 1818 containing a range of grave goods. A pot was found, possibly in another burial, nearby.
References: Jacob 1830; Lukis 1848, 306; de Guérin 1918, 136; Kendrick 1928, 195-6; this volume, pp. 104-6.

C5 **Richmond, St. Saviour's**
Five cists were found between 1900 and 1905: only one appears to have contained grave goods.
References: Anon. 1901, 59; Kendrick 1928, 192; this volume, pp. 106-12.

C6 **Les Adams, St. Peter-in-the-Wood**
A single cist was found in 1845 accompanied by grave goods.
References: Lukis 1848, 307; de Guérin 1918, 137; Kendrick 1928, 186; this volume, p. 112.

D. Miscellaneous finds

D1 **The Doyle, L'Ancresse Common** (RBB)
In 1994 a group of bronzes was found by workers excavating for a main drain. Although limited

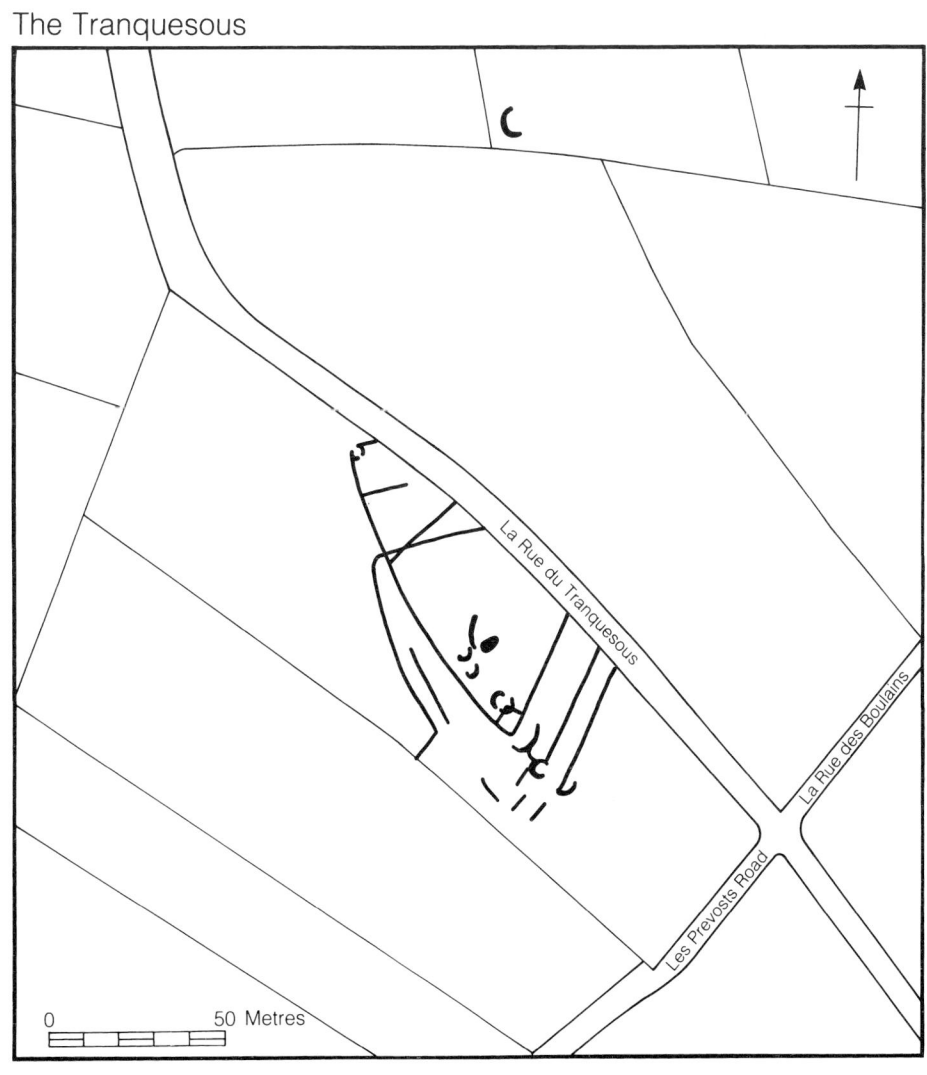

Figure 80 *The Tranquesous: plan of features.*

excavations were undertaken to locate the exact findspot, its location remains unknown. A single human tooth stained with copper deposits was found with the group indicating that it possibly formed part of a burial deposit. Parallels for the bronzes are unknown in the Channel Islands and southern England but a bracelet similar to no. 1 was found at Nalliers in the Vendée, and is now in the collections of the museum at Fontenay-le-Comte (Pautreau 1985, fig. 3). Another bracelet of similar form, discovered at Caen, is in the collections of the Musée de Normandie (Verney 1993, fig. 2, no. 3). In the same paper Verney illustrates a bracelet similar to nos. 3 and 4, also found at Caen (*ibid*. fig. 2, no. 9). I would like to thank Val Rigby, British Museum for bringing the Vendée example to my attention.

Fig. 81

1. Bracelet with hollow knobbed terminals, four grooves close to each terminal.

2. Bracelet with solid terminals, five grooves close to each terminal.

3. Bracelet with solid flattened terminals.

4. Bracelet with solid flattened terminals.

5. Twisted neck-ring with hooked terminals.

D2 **St. Peter Port Harbour** (RBB)
Rough-out of a Kimmeridge shale armlet, hand-cut. Found by a diver in St. Peter Port Harbour.

D3 **Le Catioroc, St. Saviour's** (PdeJ)
Bronze core of a gold-plated stater discovered during the excavation of a briquetage site in 1958 (Site B5 above). Identified by D.F. Allen as a coin of the Aulerci Cenomani. Present whereabouts unknown.
References: Jee 1958; Burns 1986, 91; de Jersey (forthcoming).

D4 **Richmond, St. Saviour's** (PdeJ)
Two billon staters of the Coriosolitae (class II) discovered by a metal-detector user *c*.1980, apparently near the briquetage site (B4). On display in Guernsey Museum.
References: Burns 1986, 91; de Jersey (forthcoming).

D5 **Herm** (RBB)
Pottery present in the Lukis collection includes a group of Late La Tène wares from this small island, situated some three miles to the east of Guernsey. There are considerable numbers of small cists and also a passage grave scattered around the slopes of two hills in the north of the island. These were investigated by Lukis in the middle of the nineteenth century and the finds from them are kept at the Guernsey Museum. It is difficult to establish exactly which groups of finds were found at specific sites, but in the main they are late Neolithic or Early Bronze Age in date. It has not proved possible to isolate which of the sites produced the group published here. Lukis did however illustrate the finds in his works (Lukis, *Coll. Ant*. III, 69).

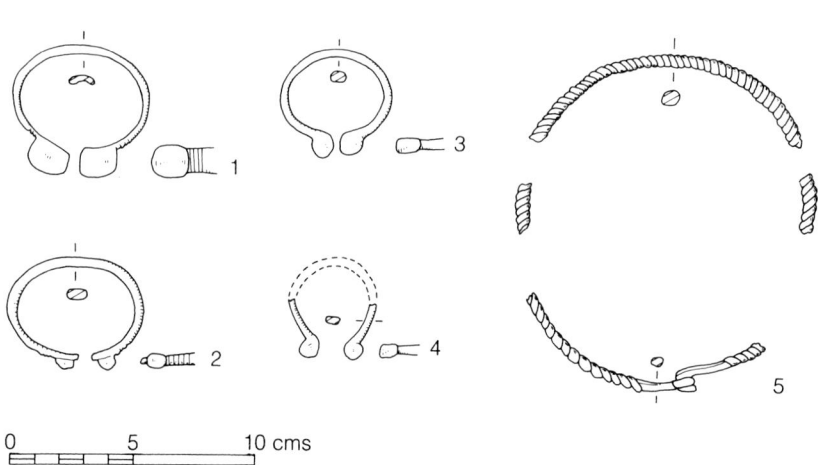

Figure 81 *Copper alloy objects from the Doyle.*

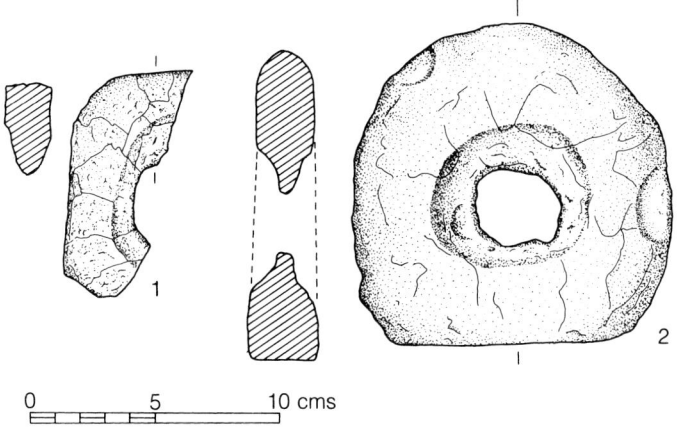

Figure 82 *Kimmeridge shale roughouts from St. Peter Port Harbour and Herm.*

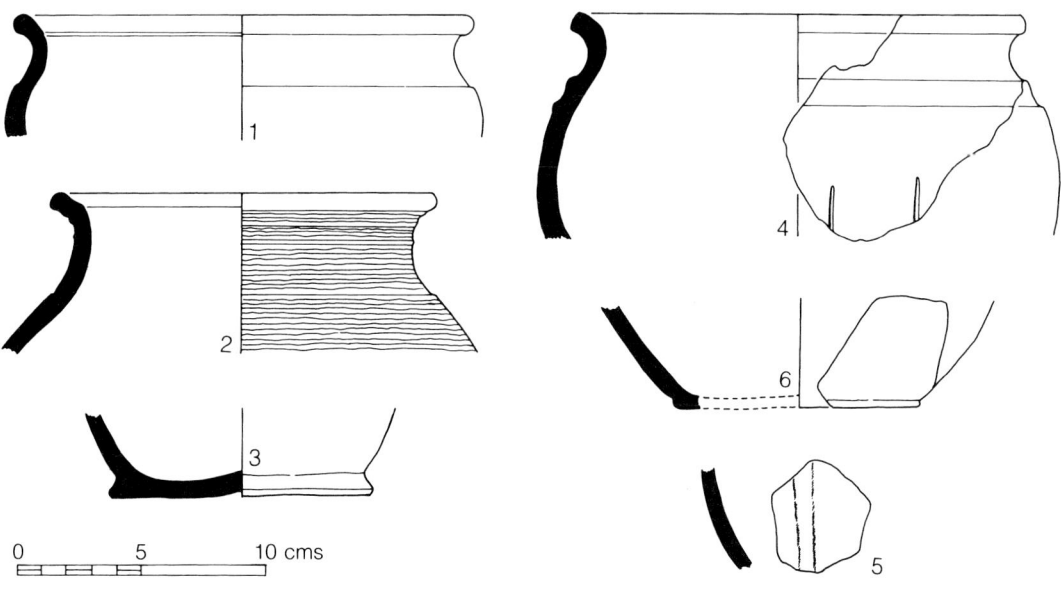

Figure 83 *Pottery from Herm.*

Fig. 83

1. Rim. Grey-black exterior, black to reddish-brown fracture, reddish-brown inside. Fabric finely sorted with no large inclusions. Small mica flecks.

2. Rim. Fabric as for no. 1. Finely burnished with a small blunt tool giving striations on the outside.

3. Base. Fabric as for nos. 1 and 2.

4. Rim. Mid-brown exterior, brick red fracture, reddish-brown inside. Vertical burnished lines on exterior.

5. Bodysherd. Black exterior, grey fracture, grey interior. Hard sandy fabric. Shallow burnished lines on exterior.

6. Base. Mid-brown exterior, brown fracture, brown interior. Vesicular fabric as King's Road type 3.

The collection also contained part of a rough-out Kimmeridge shale bracelet, hand-cut (Fig. 82).

D6 **Sark** (BC)
Hoard found in 1739 and subsequently lost. A pottery vessel, bound with a band of iron, contained 18 Celtic and Roman Republican coins. With the vessel there were 13 items of decorated metalwork, mostly gilded silver discs or phalerae, in Thracian style. The coins would indicate a date *c*.30-20 BC and the metalwork may well have been collected as military loot. Fully described in Allen 1971.

Guernsey and the Channel Islands in the First Millennium BC

by Barry Cunliffe

Having assembled the archaeological evidence for the occupation of Guernsey during the Iron Age it remains to offer a brief discussion of the context within which the disparate fragments should be considered. To do this we must begin by putting Guernsey into its local context, as one component in a complex of islands and peninsulas, and to consider this region against the broader development of the Atlantic system as a whole.

A necessary starting point is the stark contrast between the known archaeological record of Guernsey and that of Jersey during the first millennium. Given the amount of archaeological attention which both islands have enjoyed over the last two centuries it is reasonable to assume that the differences fairly reflect the differing social and economic developments of the two islands. This divergence first became evident by the beginning of the Late Bronze Age (c.1300 BC) and, on present evidence, still appears to have been a significant factor throughout the Roman period until the early fifth century AD. The reasons must surely lie in the different potential of the islands in relation to maritime interaction: Guernsey, by virtue of its more distant location, clear of reefs and shoals, was more attractive to those engaged in journeys between Armorica and Britain: it was a better landfall and more centrally located on the north-south route. This generalization is valid but in detail the situation is likely to have been more complex.

Central to any consideration must be a better understanding of changes in sea-level. Evidence from the surrounding mainland at Hengistbury Head (Dorset), Nacqueville (Manche) and St. Servan in the estuary of the Rance (Côtes d'Armor), shows that significant changes occurred in the Iron Age and Roman period. At Hengistbury it was possible to demonstrate a general lowering of sea-level during the later part of the first millennium BC with a rise again in the Roman period. That the sea-level was lower in the Iron Age than at present is again evident at Nacqueville and St. Servan while at the latter a significant sea-level rise in the late Roman period has been amply demonstrated. If these isolated observations are relevant to the entire region then it seems likely that the ridges of the Minquiers and Ecrehous, which, pincer-like, threaten Jersey, could have been significant land masses in the period of low sea-level c.500 BC-AD 200, and it may have been only with the rise in sea-level in the late Roman period that rapid maritime erosion began to reduce them to the reefs and scattered islets which they are today. This important issue is currently being investigated by Dr. Warwick Rodwell to whom I am grateful for discussing it with me.

In a period of low sea-level Jersey would have been a difficult and dangerous place to approach by sea. Against this background, imperfect though at present it is, we may better understand the differences in the archaeology of the two islands.

In the Late Bronze Age there is very little evidence to indicate that Guernsey played a significant part in the exchange of bronze along the Atlantic sea-ways. This is in marked contrast with Jersey where a number of hoards have been found spanning the Late Bronze Age (Cunliffe 1994), and Alderney where the Longy Common hoard of Carp's Tongue bronzes indicates contacts in the seventh century BC. If the absence of Late Bronze Age hoards from Guernsey reflects a reality, rather than an accident of survival, then it would seem that the island lay outside the main flow of activity in this period. Excavations on the rampart of Jerbourg (Burns 1988) did, however, indicate occupation some time during this period.

The Early Iron Age (roughly 700-400 BC) is comparatively well represented in the archaeological record of Guernsey. At Vale Castle there is evidence of occupation associated with a possible small hilltop defence, occupying a promontory overlooking St. Sampson's harbour (Barton 1984). The pottery is not particularly diagnostic but suggests a date in the sixth to fifth centuries BC. Just 2 km to the north, at the Doyle, L'Ancresse Common, four copper alloy bracelets with knobbed terminals and a twisted copper alloy neck ring were discovered in 1994 (this vol., pp. 121-2). The presence of a single human tooth discoloured by copper salts suggests that the bronzes may have accompanied an inhumation burial. Similar items from Lower Normandy, and in particular the region of Caen (Verney 1993), are currently dated to the late sixth or early fifth century.

The King's Road excavation also produced evidence of Early Iron Age occupation in the form of a ditch (on Site 2). Little of this early settlement was examined but pottery from the ditch again indicates a date in the sixth or fifth century. Among the more distinctive forms is a large cylinder-necked jar which can be paralleled among Breton assemblages of the Early Iron Age. Another sherd, a small bipartite bowl decorated with an iron-rich slip, is highly reminiscent of southern British types currently dated to the seventh or sixth century. An unstratified group of sherds from Jerbourg Point (this vol., pp. 117-19) is of approximately the same date though necked jars with internally bevelled rims, which are characteristic of the assemblage, are similar to Breton vessels considered to belong to the fifth century.

Together, these four discoveries provide a fascinating insight into the Early Iron Age of the island. They indicate a community in contact with Armorica, Normandy and southern Britain at a time when evidence from the harbour site of Hengistbury Head shows there to have been an upsurge in activity associated with a developing intensity of exchange linking central southern Britain to wider Atlantic networks (Cunliffe 1987, 336-8). What commodities were exchanged is difficult to discern but among them may have been iron from Hengistbury and Kimmeridge shale from Purbeck. In this context the two hand-cut rough-outs of Kimmeridge shale bracelets, found in St. Peter Port and on Herm, *may* be relevant but both are undated.

If, then, the Early Iron Age was a period of developing contact in the central Channel zone what of the other Channel Islands? The remarkable collection of pottery found in a hut at Les Huguettes on Alderney (Wilson 1983) suggests the presence of an active community commanding the principal harbour of Longy on the southern side of the island. The harbour would have been a welcome haven to anyone sailing north from Guernsey and wishing to round the Cap de la Hague to reach the northern coast of Lower Normandy. Those intending to sail from Guernsey to the Solent would probably have steered well clear of Alderney altogether. Jersey has produced little evidence of Early Iron Age occupation suggestive of it having played a significant part in exchange networks. It could be that sea-levels were such that its sea approaches were becoming uncongenial by this time.

The Middle Iron Age (*c*.400-120 BC) does not appear to have been a period of extensive contact between Britain and the Continent, a fact which may in some part have been due to the disruption caused by folk movement in Continental Europe. But this said, there is evidence of maritime links along the Atlantic sea-ways to south-western Britain (Cunliffe 1988a and 1990), and several classical texts speak of an active tin trade linking the tin-rich peninsulas of south-western Britain and Armorica to the Mediterranean markets (Cunliffe 1983). If the lack of recognizable material of this period from the Channel Islands fairly reflects the actual situation, then the simplest explanation is that the mid-Channel axis of contact, binding the Côtes-d'Armor, Cotentin and central southern Britain, was little used during the Middle Iron Age. The 'local' nature of the developments in central southern Britain at this time offers strong support for such a view.

This does not, of course, mean that the islands were depopulated (although this is a possibility) but simply that the cultural systems became insular. In such a situation local pottery types might be difficult to distinguish from earlier or later material. It is possible, for example, that the 'early' assemblage from King's Road (Figs. 47 and 48) includes material of Middle Iron Age date. The clearer definition of this period in Guernsey's history is a matter of high priority.

In the Late Iron Age (*c*.120-50 BC) the situation becomes much clearer and there is ample evidence, largely gleaned from the distribution of distinctive pottery, to show that the mid-Channel axis was reinvigorated as a broad corridor of trade and communication. The evidence has been extensively discussed in a number of publications (Cunliffe 1982; 1987; Galliou 1986) and does not need to be rehearsed in detail here. Suffice it to say that commodities from the Mediterranean, most notably wine in distinctive Dressel 1A type amphorae, but also lower bulk goods, including purple and yellow glass, metal tableware and figs, were introduced as trade goods into the Atlantic exchange systems and found their way into settlements throughout Armorica, Lower Normandy and in a more restricted zone in central southern Britain focused on Hengistbury Head. Along with these Mediterranean exotics local commodities were transported, those most evident in the archaeological record being Kimmeridge shale from Purbeck and whatever commodities were contained in an array of distinctive ceramics manufactured in Armorica. In addition to these archaeologically-recognizable goods were no doubt many others, such as cloth and the hides, metals, hunting dogs and slaves, mentioned by Strabo as among the exports of Britain.

The reasons for this apparent intensification of maritime trade in the Late Iron Age are complex but the catalyst must have been the expanding market economy of the Roman world which, after the 120s BC, began to make a significant impact on Gaul (Cunliffe 1988b, 80-105). What we are seeing in the mid-Channel zone is simply a revitalization of traditional patterns of exchange given a new impetus by still-distant Roman demands. The emphasis of the exchange system on the Solent shores, to the apparent exclusion of the metal-rich south-western peninsula of Britain, is interesting. It may, in part, reflect a change in the nature of the bulk commodities in demand. Metals may no longer have been at a premium and instead it may have been the products of Wessex – corn, wool and hides – that now had enhanced value. Another possibility that deserves consideration is that the Wessex élite system may have been undergoing a social transformation that demanded luxury products to sustain itself. In other words the socio-economic system of Wessex may have actively sought trade rather than passively accepted it. These issues are as complex as they are fascinating.

The axis of the revitalized trading system is clearly demonstrated by the distribution of Dressel 1A amphorae and Armorican-made pottery. Very large quantities of both have been found at Hengistbury Head, strongly suggesting that it served as the principal port-of-trade for southern Britain at the time, and as such may have supported a community of Armorican traders. If we are correct in supposing that the lower sea-level of this period rendered the approaches to Jersey dangerous, then the most likely port-of-call between the Solent and the harbours of northern Armorica would have been Guernsey, the ideal haven being St. Peter Port.

The Late Iron Age pottery found at King's Road provides ample evidence of maritime contacts. Amphorae of Dressel 1 type have been recovered together with a range of imported Armorican vessels including black cordoned wares, rilled wares and graphite-coated wares. What is of even more significance is the influence of these Armorican forms on local ceramic production, giving rise to a range of types, produced in distinctive local fabrics but copying Armorican forms (Figs. 43-5). These developments suggest sustained links over a period of time. The contrast to Jersey is considerable: here, although a few scraps of imported Armorican wares have been recorded (Cunliffe 1994), little distinctive pottery appears to have been produced locally.

The King's Road settlement and the earliest phase of the settlement at the Tranquesous belong to the Late Iron Age. Little can be said of the date of the cliffside fortifications, but the excavation at Vale Castle produced nothing to suggest occupation after the Early Iron Age, and the only pottery recovered from the Jerbourg peninsula is of similar early date. It is possible, therefore, that the island had no fortifications in the Late Iron Age. Two of the west coast sites producing briquetage, derived from salt production, have yielded Late Iron Age coins (p. 120) indicating the possibility of activity at this time.

The evidence of settlement is not particularly extensive but it is sufficient to suggest a thriving community benefiting from its position astride a major trade route. In addition to providing a safe haven and fresh water the islanders would have been able to contribute salt and no doubt a range of foodstuffs, to the pattern of commerce.

It is within this context that the rich burials may best be interpreted. The 6 known cemeteries have together produced 12 burials of which 8 were provided with grave goods comprising weapon sets, personal ornaments, tools and pottery. Chronologically all that can be safely said is that they all probably belong to the Late Iron Age. Some of the swords could be a little earlier, as indeed is the style of the brooch from King's Road, but these may be archaisms. The pottery is clearly of Late Iron Age type and one of the vessels from La Hougue au Comte (Fig. 71, no. 2) is an Armorican import.

There is nothing among the Late Iron Age assemblage that need suggest anything more than a local élite adopting selectively from the general cultural milieu those elements which it felt were the most appropriate symbols of status. It is quite possible that the beads, bracelets and weapon sets were items of commerce offered to the islanders in exchange for goods and services. Visions of invading warriors are unnecessary and inappropriate in such a context as this.

Once more, the contrast with Jersey is striking. The complete absence of burials, richly furnished or otherwise, must imply a totally different tradition, quite possibly one out of the mainstream of contemporary developments.

The Caesarian conquests in Gaul disrupted the long-established systems of contact and introduced new economic imperatives (Cunliffe 1988b, 125-44). The mid-Channel system remained but the intensity of activity seems to have decreased as more direct routes between Gaul and eastern Britain came into operation. In the 90 years or so between Caesar's conquest of Gaul and the Claudian invasion of Britain, trade between Armorica and the Solent continued though Hengistbury gave way to Poole Harbour as the principal port of contact. The settlements at the Tranquesous and King's Road continued in use and at both Gaulish pottery of Terra Nigra type, some of it made in the newly established kilns at Rennes, shows that cargoes continued to reach the island in ships plying the traditional mid-Channel routes. During the second and third centuries AD Guernsey's position in the Atlantic network is amply demonstrated by the evidence of shipwrecks and other debris littering the channel between the east coast of the island and Herm (Rule and Monaghan 1993, 1-5) and the traces of the harbourside settlement at La Plaiderie and more recently the Gallo-Roman deposits being excavated beneath the markets of St. Peter Port.

The discoveries of the last two decades have revolutionized our understanding of Guernsey in the Iron Age and Roman period and have enabled this contextual sketch to be written. The work of elucidating this crucial formative period in the island's history has begun: with energy, careful planning and some luck the next two decades could be equally productive.

Bibliography

ALLEN, D.F. 1971: The Sark Hoard. *Archaeologia* 103, 1-31.

ANON. 1901: Note of monthly meeting held November 20th, 1901. *Trans. Soc. Guernesiaise* IV (1901-4), 59.

ASHBEE, P. 1974: *Ancient Scilly* (Newton Abbot).

BARTON, K.J. 1984: Excavations at the Vale Castle, Guernsey, Channel Islands. *Trans. Soc. Guernesiaise* XXI (1981-85), 485-538.

BARTON, K.J. and BURNS, R.B. forthcoming: *Excavations at Castle Cornet, Guernsey*.

BATES, C.S. 1871: A British cemetery near Plymouth. *Archaeologia* 40, 500-10.

BAYARD, D. 1980: La commercialisation de la céramique commune à Amiens, du milieu IIe à la fin du IIIe siècle après J.-C. *Cahiers Archéologiques de Picardie* 7, 147-209.

BERTIN, D. 1975: Préliminaire à une étude de l'Age du Fer en Normandie. *Annales de Normandie* XXV (4), 227-40.

BRETT, C.E.B. 1975: *Buildings in the Town and Parish of St. Peter Port* (Belfast).

BURNS, R.B. 1977: The Late Iron Age Site at the Tranquesous, St. Saviour's, Guernsey. *Trans. Soc. Guernesiaise* XX (1976-80), 188-218.

BURNS, R.B. 1986: Recent work on the Iron Age and Gallo-Roman period in the Bailiwick of Guernsey. In Johnston, P. (ed.), *The Archaeology of the Channel Islands* (Chichester), 89-97.

BURNS, R.B. 1988: *Excavations at Jerbourg, Guernsey* (Guernsey Museum Monog. no. 1: Guernsey).

BURNS, R.B. 1993: Warrior Burials in Guernsey. In *Les Celtes en Normandie*. *Rev. archéol. Ouest* Suppl. 6, 165-71.

BURNS, R.B. and BURNS, A.G. 1985: Gallo-Roman finds from Guernsey and Herm. *Trans. Soc. Guernesiaise* XXI (1981-85), 652-66.

CASE, H., BAYNE, N., STEELE, S., AVERY, G. and SUTER-MEISTER, H. 1965: Excavations at City Farm, Hanborough, Oxon. *Oxoniensia* 29, 1-98.

COLLIS, J.R. 1973: Burials with weapons in Iron Age Britain. *Germania* 51, 121-33.

COTTON, M.A. and GATHERCOLE, P.W. 1958: *Excavations at Clausentum, Southampton, 1951-1954* (London).

CREW, P. 1987: Bryn y Castell Hillfort – a late prehistoric Iron Working settlement. In Scott, B.G. and Cleere, H.F., *The Crafts of the Blacksmith* (Belfast), 91-9.

CUNLIFFE, B.W. 1982: Britain, the Veneti and beyond. *Oxford Journ. Archaeol.* 1(1), 39-68.

CUNLIFFE, B. 1983: Ictis: is it here? *Oxford Journ. Archaeol.* 2(1), 123-6.

CUNLIFFE, B.W. 1987: *Hengistbury Head, Dorset. Vol. 1: The Prehistoric and Roman Settlement, 3500 BC-AD 500* (Oxford Univ. Comm. Archaeol. Monog. 13: Oxford).

CUNLIFFE, B. 1988a: *Mount Batten, Plymouth. A Prehistoric and Roman Port* (Oxford Univ. Comm. Archaeol. Monog. 26: Oxford).

CUNLIFFE, B. 1988b: *Greeks, Romans and Barbarians: spheres of interaction* (London).

CUNLIFFE, B. 1990: Social and economic contacts between western France and Britain in the early and middle La Tène period. *Rev. archéol. Ouest* Suppl. 2, 245-51.

CUNLIFFE, B. 1991: *Iron Age Communities in Britain* (3rd edition: London).

CUNLIFFE, B. 1994: *Jersey: a centre or a periphery* (St. Helier).

DAIRE, M.Y. 1992: *Les Céramiques Armoricaines de la Fin de L'Age de Fer* (Rennes).

DÉCHELETTE, J. 1914: *Manuel d'archéologie. Préhistorique, Celtique et Gallo-Romaine. Vol. II Archéologie Celtique ou Protohistorique Troisième Partie. Second Age du Fer ou Époque de la Tène* (Paris).

DE GUÉRIN, T.W.M. 1918: Evidence of man in Guernsey during the Bronze and early Iron Age. *Trans. Soc. Guernesiaise* VIII (1918-20), 127-41.

DE GUÉRIN, T.W.M. 1921: List of Dolmens, Menhirs and Sacred Rocks. *Trans. Soc. Guernesiaise* IX (1921-25), 30-64.

DE JERSEY, P.E. forthcoming: Celtic coins in Guernsey. In Sebire, H. (ed.), *Guernsey Connections: Papers in honour of Bob Burns*.

DERRICK, G.T. 1906: Archaeological remains in Guernsey. *Trans. Soc. Guernesiaise* V (1905-8), 229-30.

DUVAL, A. 1975: Quelques aspects nouveaux de la sépulture d'Inglemare. *Rev. Soc. Sav. Hte-Normandie* 77, 35-46.

DYSON, T. (ed.). 1986: *The Roman Quay at St. Magnus House, London: Excavations at New Fresh Wharf, Lower Thames St., London 1974-1978* (London and Middlesex Archaeol. Soc., Special Paper no. 8: London).

FITZPATRICK, A. 1985: The distribution of Dressel 1 amphorae in north-west Europe. *Oxford Journ. Archaeol.* 4(3), 305-40.

GALLIOU, P. 1984: Days of wine and roses? Early Armorica and the Atlantic wine trade. In Macready, S. and Thompson, F.H. (eds.), *Cross-Channel Trade between Gaul and Britain in the pre-Roman Iron-Age* (Soc. Ant. Occ. Pap. 4: London), 24-36.

GALLIOU, P. 1986: Wine and the Atlantic trade in the later Iron Age. In Johnston, P. (ed.), *The Archaeology of the Channel Islands* (Chichester), 75-88.

GALLIOU, P. 1989: *Les tombes romaines d'Armorique. Essai de sociologie et d'economie de la mort* (Doc. Archéol. Française no. 17: Paris).

GILMOUR, B.J.J. 1991: The Technology of Anglo-Saxon Edged Weapons (unpublished Ph.D. thesis, University College, London).

GIOT, P.-R. 1960: *Brittany* (London).

GIOT, P.-R. 1979: L'Age du Fer. In Giot, P.-R., Briard, J. and Pape, L., *Protohistoire de la Bretagne* (Rennes), 217-360.

GIOT, P.-R., BRIARD, J. and PAPE, L. 1979: *Protohistoire de la Bretagne* (Rennes).

GIOT, P.-R., DAIRE, M.Y. and QUERRE, G. 1986: *Un Habitat Protohistorique. Le Moulin de la Rive en Locquirec* (Rennes).

GREENE, K.T. 1979: *Report on the excavations at Usk 1965-1976: the Pre-Flavian fine wares* (Cardiff).

GUIDO, C.M. 1978: *The Glass Beads of the Prehistoric and Roman periods in Britain and Ireland* (Soc. Ant. Res. Rep. 35: London).

HAWKES, C.F.C. and HULL, M.R. 1947: *Camulodunum, First Report on the Excavations at Colchester 1930-1939* (Soc. Ant. Res. Rep. 14: London).

HENDERSON, J. 1987: Glass and glass-working. In Cunliffe, B.W. 1987, 160-3 and 180-6.

HENDERSON, J. 1988: Electron probe microanalyses of mixed-alkali glasses. *Archaeometry* 30, 1, 77-91.

HENDERSON, J. 1989: The scientific analysis of ancient glass and its archaeological interpretation. In Henderson, J. (ed.), *Scientific Analysis in Archaeology, and its interpretation* (Oxford Univ. Comm. Archaeol. Monog. 19 and UCLA Institute of Archaeology Research Tools 5), 30-59.

HILL, M.G. 1990: The excavation on La Hougue Catelain (Banque à Barque), L'Ancresse, Vale, 1982 and 1983. *Trans. Soc. Guernesiaise* XXII (1986-90), 827-70.

HOLWERDA, J.H. 1941: *De Belgische Waar in Nijmegen* (The Hague).

HÜSSEN, C.-M. 1983: *A rich Late La Tène Burial at Hertford Heath, Hertfordshire* (Brit. Mus. Occ. Pap. 44: London).

JACOB, J. 1830: *Annals of some of the British Norman Isles constituting the Bailiwick of Guernsey* (Paris).

JACOBI, G. 1974: *Werkzeng und Gerät aus dem Oppidum von Manching* (Die Ausgrabungen in Manching 5: Wiesbaden).

JEE, N. 1958: Archaeological report, 1958. *Trans. Soc. Guernesiaise* XVI (1955-59), 313.

KENDRICK, T.D. 1928: *The Archaeology of the Channel Islands. Vol. 1: The Bailiwick of Guernsey* (London).

KINNES, I.A. forthcoming: *Excavations at Les Fouaillages, Guernsey*.

LAMBOGLIA, N. 1955: Sulla cronologia delle anfore romane de eta republicana. *Rivisti Studi Liguri* 21, 252-60.

LANGOUET, L. 1978: Les Céramiques Gaulois d'Alet. *Les Dossiers de Centre Régional Archéologique d'Alet* 6, 57-104.

LANGOUET, L. 1989: *Un Village Coriosolite sur L'Isle des Ebihens* (St. Malo).

LAUBENHEIMER, F. 1986: *La Production des Amphores en Gaule Narbonnaise* (Paris).

LE BIHAN, J.P. 1984: *Villages Gaulois et Parcellaires Antiques* (Cahiers de Quimper Antique no. 1: Quimper).

LE BIHAN, J.P. 1986: *Aux Origines de Quimper* (Quimper).

LUKIS, F.C. 1848: Sepulchral caves in the Isle of Guernsey. *Journ. Brit. Archaeol. Ass.* 1, 305-9.

LUKIS, F.C. 1853: Sepulchral cave. *Journ. Brit. Archaeol. Ass.* VIII, 64-7.

LUKIS, F.C.: *Collectanea Antiqua* (A series of manuscript volumes detailing excavations and finds made by the Lukis family during the nineteenth century. Unpublished, held at Guernsey Museum).

McGRATH, J.N. 1968: A report on the metallographic examination of five fragmentary early Iron Age sword blades from Llyn Cerrig Bach, Anglesey. *Bulletin of the Board of Celtic Studies* 22, 418-25.

MENEZ, Y. 1985: *Les céramiques fumigées de l'ouest de la Gaule* (Cahiers de Quimper Antique no. 2: Quimper).

MERLANGE, A. 1979: Sépultures de La Tène dans la vallée de l'Yonne (sauvetages en sablières entre Joigny et Appoigny). *Les Sénons avant La conquête, à la lumière des dernières découvertes* (Soc. Archéol. Sens), 6-13.

MONAGHAN, J. 1990: Pottery from marine sites around Guernsey. In Perrin, R. (ed), *Journal of Roman Pottery Studies* 3, 63-9.

NICOURT, J. 1986: *Céramiques Médiévales Parisiennes* (Ermont).

PAUTREAU, J.P. 1985: Quelques aspects de la métallurgie du bronze sur l'habitat du Camp Allaric à Aslones (Vienne) dans son contexte poitevin au Premiere Age du Fer. *Revue Archéologique de L'Est et du Centre-Est* (Paris), 283-99.

PEACOCK, D.P.S. 1969: A contribution to the study of Glastonbury Ware from south-western Britain. *Antiq. Journ.* 49, 41-61.

PEACOCK, D.P.S. 1971: Roman amphorae in pre-Roman Britain. In Jesson, M. and Hill, D. (eds.), *The Iron Age and its Hill-Forts* (Southampton), 169-88.

PEACOCK, D.P.S. 1977: Recent discoveries of Roman amphorae kilns in Italy. *Antiq. Journ.* 57, 262-9.

PEACOCK, D.P.S. 1984: Amphorae in Iron-Age Britain, a re-assessment. In Macready, S. and Thompson, F.H. (eds.), *Cross-Channel Trade between Gaul and Britain in the pre-Roman Iron Age* (Soc. Ant. Occ. Pap. 4: London), 37-42.

PEACOCK, D.P.S. and WILLIAMS, D.F. 1986: *Amphorae and the Roman Economy* (London).

PLATT, C. and COLEMAN-SMITH, R. 1975: *Excavations in Medieval Southampton 1953-1969* (Leicester).

RAPIN, A. 1985: Le système de suspension des fourreaux d'épées Lateniens aux IIIe siècle av. J-C. Innovations techniques et reconstitution des élements perissables. In *Celti ed Etruschi nell'Italia centro-settentrionale da IV secolo a.C alla romanizzazione* (Bologna), 529-39.

RICHARDSON, B. 1986: Pottery. In Dyson, T. (ed) 1986, 96-138.

RICHARDSON, B. and TYERS, P.A. 1984: North Gaulish Pottery in Britain. *Britannia* 15, 133-41.

RICHMOND, I.A. nd: *The Roman Fort at South Shields*.

RULE, M. and MONAGHAN, J. 1993: *A Gallo-Roman Trading Vessel from Guernsey* (Guernsey Museum Monog. no. 5: Guernsey).

RYDER, M.L. and GABRA-SAUNDERS, T. 1987: A microscopic study of remains of textiles made from plant fibres. *Oxford Journ. Archaeol.* 6(1), 91-108.

SABIR, A. and LAUBENHEIMER, F. 1983: Production d'amphores vinaires republicaines en Gaul du Sud. *Documents d'Archéologie Meridionale* 6, 109-13.

SALTER, C.J. 1991: In Sharples, N.M., Maiden Castle: Excavations and field survey 1985-1986. *English Heritage Archaeological Report* 19, 165-70.

SANTROT, M.H. and SANTROT, J. 1979: *Céramiques communes Gallo-Romaines d'Aquitaine* (Paris).

SEALEY, P. 1985: *Amphorae from the 1970 Excavations at Colchester Sheepen* (Brit. Archaeol. Rep. 142: Oxford).

STOCKLI, W.E. 1979: *Die Gros-Und Importkeramik von Manching* (Die Ausgrabungen in Manching 8: Wiesbaden).

TCHERNIA, A. 1983: Italian wine in Gaul at the end of the Republic. In Garnsey, P., Hopkins, K. and Whittaker, C.R. (eds.), *Trade in the Ancient Economy* (London), 87-104.

TEICHERT, M. 1975: Osteometrische Untersuchungen zur Berechnung der Widerristhohe bei Schafen. In Clason, A.T. (ed.), *Archaeozoological Studies* (Elsevier), 51-69.

TUFFREAU-LIBRE, M. 1980: *La céramique commune Gallo-Romaine dans le Nord de la France (Nord, Pas-de Calais)* (Lille).

TYLECOTE, R.F. 1986: *The Prehistory of Metallurgy in the British Isles* (Institute of Metal: London).

VERNEY, A. 1993: Les Nécropoles de L'Age de Fer en Basse-Normandie. *Rev. archéol. Ouest* Suppl. 6, 95-113.

VILLES, A. 1983: Autour des tombes 20 et 26 de Pernant et 80 de Bucy-le-Long (Aisne). *Les Celtes dans Le Nord du Bassin Parisien* (Rev. Archéol. de Picardie 1).

VON DEN DRIESCH, A. 1976: *A guide to the measurement of animal bones from archaeological sites* (Peabody Museum Bulletin 1: Harvard University).

VOUGA, P. 1925: *La Tène* (Leipzig).

WATKINS, S. and CAMERON, E. 1987: An Iron Age warrior's grave from Guernsey: the excavation, conservation and interpretation of its contents. In Black, J., *Recent advances in the conservation and analysis of artefacts* (Jubilee Conservation Conference, Institute of Archaeology, University of London), 51-7.

WHEELER, R.E.M. and RICHARDSON, K.M. 1957: *Hillforts in Northern France* (Soc. Ant. Res. Rep. 19: London).

WHIMSTER, R. 1978: Harlyn Bay reconsidered: the excavations of 1900-1905 in the light of recent work. *Cornish Archaeol.* 16, 61-88.

WHIMSTER, R. 1981: *Burial practices in Iron Age Britain* (Brit. Archaeol. Rep. Brit. Ser. 90: Oxford).

WILSON, K. 1983: Excavation of an Iron Age 'A' site at Les Huguettes, Alderney. *Trans. Soc. Guernesiaise* XXI (1981-85), 393-427.

WOOD, M. 1990: Céramiques inédites de La Tène Finale et de L'Epoque Gallo-Romaine trouvées à Alderney et la découverte récente d'amphores à Jersey et Herm (Iles Anglo-Normandes). *Association Manche Atlantique pour la Recherche Archéologique dans les Iles* 3, 47-60.

WOOD, M. 1991: Ceramiques Romano-Britanniques trouvées à Alet jusqu'en 1986 et étude des relations commerciales d'Alet au Bas-Empire. *Les Dossiers du Centre Régional Archéologique d'Alet* 19, 35-53.

WOOD, M. forthcoming: La céramique du Bas-Empire dans Les Isles Anglo-Normandes et dans deux sites côtiers du golfe normano-breton. *Revue du Nord.*